P9-BJM-346

MEXICAN WORKERS IN THE UNITED STATES

Mexican Workers in the United States

Historical and Political Perspectives

edited by

George C. Kiser

and

Martha Woody Kiser

UNIVERSITY OF NEW MEXICO PRESS

Albuquerque

Library of Congress Cataloging in Publication Data
Main entry under title:

Mexican workers in the United States.

Bibliography: p. 285
Includes index.
1. Mexicans in the United States—Employment—Addresses, essays, lectures. 2. Alien labor—United States—Addresses, essays, lectures. 3. United States—Foreign population—Addresses, essays, lectures.
I. Kiser, George C., 1939– II. Kiser, Martha Woody, 1937–
HD8081.M6M39 331.6'2'72073 78-55710
ISBN 0-8263-0489-3

Manufactured in the United States of America
Library of Congress Catalog Card No. 78-55710
International Standard Book Number 0-8263-0489-3

DEDICATED TO OUR PARENTS:
Bertha Woody, Roy Woody,
Denver R. Kiser, and Patsy Carico

Acknowledgments

We wish to express our warm appreciation to the authors and publishers whose work appears in this anthology. It is a sobering thought to realize that without them there would be no book.

We also wish to thank Carl Mora of the University of New Mexico Press for encouraging this project and for his helpful advice along the way, particularly his suggestion for including some Mexican sources. In addition to giving moral support, Dr. Hibbert Roberts, chairperson of the Department of Political Science at Illinois State University, generously adjusted the senior editor's teaching schedule to allow more time for this book.

We also owe a debt of gratitude to Dr. Wilbur Nachtigall, Professor of Spanish at Illinois Wesleyan University, for his translation of the article from *Hispanoamericano*. We are grateful to the United States Embassy in Mexico City for the helpful information it provided.

A number of individuals have encouraged our research on Mexican labor over the years and they have all left their impact on this book. Among them are Howard J. Wiarda, Lewis Hanke, Gilbert Martinez, Dwain Ervin, David Silverman, Harvey Kline, George Sulzner, Wayne Rasmussen, Joe Navarro, and George Gordon. To all of them we are grateful.

Several libraries have been particularly cooperative and helpful in the research which culminated in this book. In addition to the National Archives in Washington, they are the Truman Library in Independence, Missouri, and the libraries of the University of Texas, the University of Colorado, and the University of Southern Colorado.

We are grateful to the anonymous reviewer who read the manuscript for the University of New Mexico Press. We also wish to thank Steven Cox, Mike Matthews, and Lois Matthews for their careful and critical review of portions of the manuscript.

We wish to warmly thank the University of Southern Colorado and the Harry S. Truman Library Institute for grants which aided our research in Independence, Missouri.

And finally we wish to thank Marcia Willets, Toni Call, Patricia Moncelle, Mike Christian, Kathy McClanahan, and Rhonda Johnson for their generous and able assistance with the typing.

Contents

Introduction

Ever since the early years of World War I, substantial numbers of Mexican nationals have been crossing into the United States and finding jobs here.* Viewed from any one of several different perspectives, this movement has proven most remarkable. For instance, considered in terms of sheer numbers alone, it has brought millions of workers to this country and, since 1917, has furnished the United States with its single largest supply of foreign labor. It is also likely that this migration represents the world's most massive flow of workers from any one country into another during this same period of time.

Equally remarkable has been this migratory stream's dogged persistence. It has continued from the World War I era right down to the present day, having been interrupted only briefly by events of the Great Depression. In fact, today it is apparently stronger than ever. Observers are almost unanimous in estimating that the number of Mexican workers in the United States now stands at an all-time high. As one looks back over the years, it becomes obvious that this movement has developed a large degree of immunity to events that might have been expected to drastically curtail it. For instance, its size has apparently been little affected by such developments as denunciations of it by the Mexican and American governments or serious deteriorations in overall relations between the two countries.

Still another remarkable feature of this movement has been the political fireworks it has generated. Time and again, presidents and others have declared the Mexican labor issue settled, only to have the controversy surrounding it flare up anew. No American president from Woodrow Wilson to Jimmy Carter has failed to find his administration entangled in the

*Nobody knows the exact numbers because so many have entered illegally. Estimates regarding the illegals should be regarded as "educated guesses" which are hopefully within shouting distance of the truth.

conflict between the supporters and opponents of Mexican labor usage. On the one hand, many employers have claimed an urgent need to recruit Mexican nationals for jobs which allegedly fail to attract sufficient numbers of qualified American applicants. On the other hand, many people have charged that rather than pay Americans a living wage, these employers prefer the more desperate and hence more docile Mexican worker.

Mexican labor in the United States has hardly inspired the impressive body of scholarly literature that might be expected from such a remarkable movement. Until recent years very few scholars have devoted any serious attention to it. Fortunately that situation is changing. The last fifteen years or so have brought as much scholarly attention to this movement as it received during its first half-century. However, many important aspects of Mexican labor in the United States remain unexplored.

A second problem with the literature is that much of it is not readily usable in the classroom. A disproportionate amount of it is found in such scattered sources as journals, graduate theses, out-of-print publications, and unpublished material in government archives. The difficulty of using the available literature is further complicated by the fact that Mexican sources are rarely available in English.

The purpose of this anthology is to make some of the more useful but less accessible literature readily available. Until now no book of readings has been devoted to this task.

A few words should be said about the criteria used in selecting readings for inclusion here. With one or two exceptions, the material has not been reprinted from books that are presently in print. The overriding concern has been with bringing less accessible sources to a broader audience. Readability of the materials has also been considered; it is believed that all of the articles will prove quite readable even for persons who have little or no knowledge of the subject area.

Although several of the selections represent a high level of scholarship, there has been no effort to make this book "scholarly" from cover to cover. For example, some highly opinionated materials have been included because they express views that need to be taken into account. It is important to remember that the Mexican labor issue has generated much bitterness and that some of the selections have been reprinted precisely because they convey some of this anger first-hand. However, the anthology itself does not represent an attempt to champion any set of ideological viewpoints in preference to others. The perspectives of both the champions of Mexican labor and its opponents come through.

As indicated earlier, one of the most glaring problems with the available literature is that readily available Mexican sources in English are almost nonexistent. Several of the selections included in this anthology were written by Mexican authors.

The readings are divided into five sections. Section One provides important historical background by focusing on the earliest years in which large numbers of Mexican nationals were employed in the United States. This period coincides roughly with the World War I era. Why Mexico became an exporter of labor at this time is only too apparent. It was going through one of the most violent revolutions of the twentieth century, much of its economy was devastated, and many of its people were utterly impoverished. Confronted with such horrors, it is not surprising that large numbers of Mexicans fled to the United States.

The pressures pushing Mexicans from their country tell, of course, only half of the story. By the second decade of the twentieth century, there was also a growing demand for Mexican labor in the United States. By then the American Southwest was coming into its own economically with the development of both industry and large commercial farms.

Conditions such as these stimulated an expanding movement of Mexican labor into the United States even before World War I. From all indications, most of these workers came in violation of American immigration laws. After all, to come as a legal immigrant, one faced such restrictions as literacy requirements and a head tax—exactly the kind of standards that could hardly be met by most homeless and impoverished people fleeing the horrors of revolution.

As the United States became involved in World War I, the number of Mexican workers entering this country increased. Growing numbers of employers led by southwestern farmers claimed that they were losing large numbers of employees to the military and war-related industries. Many of them urged the American government to temporarily relax its immigration standards at the southwestern border to permit the short-term entry of Mexican workers.

In response to these pressures, the United States government established in 1917 a special Mexican labor program which provided for the entry of temporary workers. They were not subject to the requirements governing the admission of regular immigrants. These workers could be admitted to the United States only after official certification of labor shortages claimed by individual employers, and they were restricted to the jobs and employers for which they had been certified. Under this program, employers were to give the workers written contracts containing a number of specific guarantees. The Mexicans were not to bring dependents to the United States, and upon completion of their contract obligations they were to be returned to Mexico.

A basic premise underlying this program was that it was strictly temporary, designed to cope with a special labor emergency, and that once the crisis had passed the program was to be terminated. As it turned out, this was to be the first of several Mexican labor programs based on these assumptions. They have all come to be known as "*bracero*" programs. In Spanish, the word "*braceros*" means "day-laborers," and in Mexico it is used to refer to workers much as we call them "hands."

The first bracero program remained in effect until 1921, having lasted some four years. Over seventy-thousand Mexican workers entered the United States under its provisions. The vast majority of them were certified for farm work, but some were approved for other jobs as well.

How the first bracero program was actually carried out differed markedly from its elaborate formal specifications. History indicates that officials tended to take employer claims of labor shortages at face value rather than to carefully investigate them. Many braceros apparently left the jobs for which they had been certified and worked at others. History indicates widespread employer violation of the contract guarantees. There is also evidence that many of the workers were not returned to Mexico upon expiration of their contracts.

The World War I era of Mexican labor in the United States has been particularly neglected in the scholarly literature. Until recently there was only a single published study of the first bracero program.* Yet this earlier period is important not only in its own right but also for understanding later Mexican labor developments in the United States. For instance, the really fundamental arguments for and against the use of Mexican labor have not changed significantly since 1917. Many pressure groups continue to take almost exactly the same position today as they did during that time.

Section Two is devoted to the repatriation of Mexican workers (and nonworkers) from the United States during the Great Depression of the 1930s. Until recently this whole era had been virtually ignored in the scholarly literature. However, several studies have been published in recent years.

Paradoxically, termination of the first bracero program marked the be-

*That was Otey M. Scruggs, "The First Mexican Farm Labor Program," *Arizona and the West* 2 (1960): 319–26.

ginning of an era in which American employers hired Mexican nationals in unprecedented numbers. During the 1920s very lax enforcement of United States immigration laws at the Mexican border enabled vast numbers to enter illegally.

With the onset of the Great Depression, traditional opposition to the use of Mexican labor grew much more vehement and widespread. The United States government came under massive attack for not repatriating Mexican workers as a means of opening up jobs for unemployed Americans. The exclusionist movement also used a host of other arguments, including openly racist assertions.

This grass-roots pressure eventually led to massive repatriation of Mexican nationals during the early 1930s. These were apparently the only years between 1917 and the present day that more Mexican workers left the United States than entered.

There has been some tendency to depict the Mexican exodus as nothing more than massive deportations conducted by the American government. Although some formal deportations were carried out, much more frequently repatriation involved Mexicans leaving "voluntarily" in response to pressures from various combinations of local and state governments, the national government, and private organizations.

It is quite possible that the Depression era exodus did more to embitter Mexicans toward the United States than anything else in this century. It was charged in Mexico that repatriation was carried out with little sensitivity for due process of law. For example, many children born in the United States to Mexican nationals were routinely repatriated despite the fact that their birth in this country made them American citizens. Much resentment also sprang from the fact that Mexico, herself suffering from the Depression, had to absorb large numbers of people with little advance notice. It was also pointed out that illegal Mexican workers in the United States were illegal in a very narrow sense; although they came here in violation of American immigration laws, they were encouraged to do so by the fact that the United States had never made any serious effort to enforce these laws at the Mexican border. Mexicans charged that the lax law enforcement had resulted from the political clout of rich employers who wanted an abundant supply of inexpensive and exploitable labor.

Section Three deals with the second bracero era which lasted from 1942 through 1964. There were actually several bracero programs during this period, each one reflecting adjustments resulting from renegotiations with Mexico. However, the movement of braceros into the United States was never interrupted for any substantial period of time during these twenty-two years, so all of these programs will be referred to collectively as "the second bracero program."

With American involvement in World War II, a great deal of history repeated itself. Once again the government was told by certain employers, particularly growers in the Southwest, that recruitment was becoming very difficult as men went off to war and workers moved from lower-paying jobs to more lucrative ones in defense industries. Once again they urged the government to relax its immigration requirements for temporary Mexican workers, and once again a bracero program was created.

Despite significant similarities of the conditions under which the first and second bracero programs were established, substantial differences also existed. For instance, the first one was almost exclusively a creation of the United States. During World War I, Mexico was too preoccupied with her own revolution to devote much attention to such matters as the flow of labor into the United States, and the United States did not bother to invite much input from Mexico's government.

A host of significant changes between the two wars laid the foundation for substantial Mexican input into the second bracero program. By 1941, the United States was more willing to listen to Mexico. By then President Roosevelt had proclaimed his "Good Neighbor Policy" toward Latin America, pledging mutual cooperation and respect rather than unilateral action. If the United States was more willing to listen, Mexico was more able to assert itself once the chaos of revolution had passed. Also, dissatisfaction with previous United States labor policies motivated Mexico to try to head off still further undesirable developments. In particular, Mexico was reacting against the first bracero program and the massive repatriation of the Depression years. There was a strong tendency in that country to perceive both of those events in terms of the helplessness of Mexico and the Mexican workers, manipulated by the government and wealthy employers of the United States.

There were other significant differences between the first bracero program and the second one. Far more workers entered under provisions of the latter, and regulations governing it tended to be better enforced. The first bracero program was terminated after five years while the later one lasted some twenty-two years.

The second bracero program was finally terminated by the United States due to growing political opposition to it. It fell victim to the Kennedy administration which ended it as a means of opening up more jobs for the unemployed.

Although the second bracero era ended over a decade ago, it would be short-sighted to conclude that it will prove to be the final one. Since 1964, members of Congress have occasionally proposed that the United States negotiate still another agreement with Mexico. It should be remembered, too, that during some twenty-two of the last thirty-six years, the United States has had a bracero program and that the absence of one has become the exception rather than the rule.

Section Four turns attention to illegal Mexican workers, popularly known as "wetbacks." Their apparent numbers suggest something of their significance. Over the years since 1917, they have comprised a very large segment of all Mexican labor in the United States. In fact, scholars generally agree that they have actually outnumbered legal Mexican workers. Moreover, it appears that in this same era they have comprised the majority of all illegal aliens employed in this country. Their numbers have apparently been growing since the second bracero era ended in 1964, and according to most estimates the number of illegal Mexican workers in the United States now stands at an all-time high. It is likely that they constitute the single largest national group of illegal workers in any country on earth.

At least some of the reasons for this massive flow of illegal Mexican labor into the United States are rather apparent. One of the world's wealthiest nations is located alongside a relatively poor, third-world country. Mexico is plagued with the usual problems of developing nations which severely limit economic opportunities for their people. Among these are high birth rates, high unemployment and underemployment, relatively low wages, and widespread poverty. In light of these chronic problems in Mexico, it is little wonder that many of its citizens have been attracted by the substantial demand for workers in the United States. Even persons with full-time jobs in Mexico have found that they could earn much higher wages in the United States. Add to these considerations the fact that much of the American Southwest was once part of Mexico and that much of its geography and culture do not differ all that much from what many Mexicans are accustomed to at home.

Such factors as these have combined to motivate far more Mexicans to seek work in the United States than could possibly be accommodated under the immigration laws or special bracero programs. Also, despite mountains of rhetoric to the contrary, neither country has ever made a serious and prolonged effort to bring an end to the illegal migration. For Mexico, it has provided jobs for too many unemployed people and remittances from their earnings have comprised an important source of income for that nation. In the United States, efforts at serious enforcement of the immigration laws at the Mexican border have almost invariably been blocked by powerful government officials sympathetic to the recipients of Mexican labor.

While the illegals are highly significant in their own right, they are also important for understanding legal Mexican workers. The literature indicates that changes in either segment of the Mexican labor force are likely to have repercussions in the other one. For instance, when Mexicans found that they could no longer enter the United States under the first bracero program, more and more took the illegal route to jobs in this country.

Section Five of this book turns attention to certain Mexicans who work for American employers while still residing in Mexico. "Commuters" literally commute from their homes to jobs in the United States. In order to do so, they obtain regular immigrant visas from the United States government. Although United States law requires "immigrants" to actually live in this country, immigration officials long ago carved out an exception for Mexican "commuters." In some areas along the border, these workers comprise a very significant proportion of the total labor force.

Section Six deals with a second program under which Mexicans work for American employers without residing even temporarily in the United States; they hold jobs in Mexico's Border Industrialization Program. Under the terms of this program, launched in 1966, American firms locate in certain designated zones inside Mexico. Strictly speaking, their Mexican employees do not fall within the subject area suggested by the title of this book. However, these workers have been included because they are important for understanding Mexican labor in the United States. From the perspective of American firms, the Border Industrialization Program serves as a substitute for bringing Mexican labor to the United States. The idea is to take the jobs to the workers instead of bringing the workers to the jobs.

I

The World War I Era

As the United States became involved in World War One, many commercial farmers in the Southwest complained of an alarming loss of farm labor to industry and the military. They claimed that they were helpless to cope with this problem because in a vigorous wartime economy, farm jobs naturally lost much of their attractiveness due to the inability of farmers to pay high wages or to offer year-round employment. The growers called for government assistance on the grounds that the uninterrupted production of food and fiber was essential to the nation's war effort.

These farmers did not leave it to the government to identify additional labor to fill the vacuum. From the beginning, most of them claimed that the ideal solution lay in expanding the flow of labor from revolution-ravaged Mexico.[1] From their perspective, they needed the Mexicans to plant and harvest the crops and the Mexicans desperately needed the work to keep from starving. They also argued that sundry other considerations supported a Mexican solution to their labor problems. Among these were the proximity of Mexico to the United States, the already established reliance of the American Southwest on Mexican labor, and the proven suitability of Mexican nationals for stoop labor in agriculture.

In response to these escalating pressures during the early months of 1917, the United States government instituted the first bracero program. Paradoxically, only three months earlier, Congress had enacted the most restrictive immigration act in American history. That act contained a host of provisions that would seem to have precluded the apparently large-scale Mexican labor program that southwestern growers were demanding.

For example, it levied a head tax of eight dollars on each immigrant and it barred persons over the age of sixteen who could not read—precisely the kind of barriers that were likely to make immigration from a poverty-ridden country such as Mexico extremely difficult. A third provision also seemed tailor-made to keep out Mexican workers: it barred the entry of persons immigrating in response to promises of work.[2]

In light of the restrictiveness of the Immigration Act of 1917, how was the Mexican labor program possible? Prior to passage of that act, various southwestern employers had feared that their traditional reliance on Mexican workers might fall victim to the growing public sentiment against immigration. Consequently, they had pressured Congress to make an exception for aliens entering this country for *temporary* employment. The concession they won was inserted as the Ninth Proviso to Section Three of the Immigration Act of 1917.[3] It read: "That the Commissioner General of Immigration with the approval of the Secretary of Labor shall issue rules and prescribe conditions . . . to control and regulate the admission and return of otherwise *inadmissible* [emphasis added] aliens applying for temporary admission." This crucial proviso became the legal foundation of the first bracero program.

On May 23, 1917, the Secretary of Labor issued an order exempting Mexicans entering for temporary farm work from the head tax, contract labor, and literacy clauses of the immigration act.[4] In later orders, Mexicans entering temporarily for a few non-farm jobs were also made exempt, but throughout its existence the bracero program remained primarily a supplier of *farm* labor.

When the Secretary of Labor announced establishment of the Mexican labor program, he promised that it would be carefully controlled by the government, and he supplied an elaborate set of rules and regulations under which it was to be administered. For instance, to qualify for Mexican workers, the employer would have to demonstrate his need for them, enter into specified contracts with them, and accept responsibility for eventually returning them to the Mexican border.[5]

The Labor Department rules also provided that the Mexican workers were to be photographed and given identification cards as they entered the United States. Each worker was required to verify his understanding that he was to work only in agriculture and workers violating the terms of their admission were to be arrested and returned to Mexico.[6]

These elaborate rules went largely unenforced.[7] Large numbers of workers deserted their employers and apparently engaged in non-farm work, there was no systematic mechanism for compelling employers to comply with contracts, and claims of labor shortages were not carefully investigated.

From the beginning, both southwestern growers and the United States government depicted the Mexican labor program as strictly temporary, necessitated by the war-induced labor shortage. However, it was not terminated until 1922, three years after the end of the war. As the war came to a close, growers continued to claim a desperate need for Mexican labor, arguing that farm workers who had gotten a taste of better jobs would simply not return to the lower paying, seasonal agricultural jobs.

Once the war ended, the government came under mounting pressure to terminate the bracero program since it could no longer be justified as a national defense measure. Also, organized labor had long feared that Mexican nationals would be used to undermine American workers, and once the war ended, its opposition intensified. Moreover, during the war years, public opinion had grown increasingly suspicious of foreigners in the United States. And at the close of the war, finding jobs for former servicemen became a national priority. Developments such as these finally brought an end to the first bracero program in 1922.

When the Secretary of Labor issued the regulations under which the program was to be administered, many employers attacked them as excessively restrictive. They were joined by a number of government officials, including Food Administrator Herber Hoover. The first selection consists of a letter Hoover wrote to the Labor Department urging it to ease the restrictions to facilitate the entry of urgently needed Mexican workers and to permit them to remain in the United States permanently. The regulations were never changed to his satisfaction.

During World War I, the United States government showed little eagerness to assess critically the claims of labor shortages, particularly in agriculture. Yet not everyone agreed that Mexican workers were really needed. Both in the United States and Mexico, there were charges that employers merely used the war as a convenient excuse to claim a labor shortage while their real purpose was to flood the labor market so they could keep working conditions and wages at the lowest possible levels. The selection from the Mexican newspaper *El Pueblo* indicates Mexico's vice consul at Globe, Arizona, shared that suspicious view of employers. According to the article, while employers in that area claimed that they were faced with desperate labor shortages, the vice consul saw large numbers of Mexican nationals who were unable to find jobs. The article notes his charges of widespread mistreatment of Mexican employees in the United States.

On a number of occasions while the World War I bracero program was in effect, Mexico formally protested the treatment of its workers in the United States. The third selection is a note from the Mexican Foreign Affairs Department charging widespread violation of work contracts and the failure of the American government to protect braceros from such exploitation.

The recent article by Lawrence Cardoso is perhaps the finest available study of the World War I era. Based on research in Mexican archives, it focuses on Mexican attitudes toward the first bracero program, an aspect that has been largely ignored by American scholars. Cardoso found evidence of a Mexico preoccupied with revolutionary upheaval while the United States unilaterally created a Mexican labor program on its own terms. He found that the posture of Mexican officials toward the program was marked by ambivalence and vacillation. Though reluctant to see compatriots leave for the United States, the Mexican government found that it was unable to stop the exodus. Consequently, it developed a reluctant acceptance of the program and sought to make the best of a bad situation by escalating protests against the ill treatment of Mexican workers in the United States.

NOTES

1. On the World War I era, see: Mark Reisler, *By the Sweat of Their Brow* (Westport, Connecticut: Greenwood Press, 1976), pp. 24–48; Otey M. Scruggs, "The First Mexican Labor Program," *Arizona and the West* 2 (1960); 319–26; John Martinez, *Mexican Emigration to the U.S., 1910–1930* (San Francisco: R and E Research Associates, 1971), pp. 17–33; and George C. Kiser, "Mexican American Labor Before World War II," *Journal of Mexican American History* 2 (1972): 126–31.
2. U.S., *Statutes at Large*, vol. 34, part 1, pp. 874–98.
3. Scruggs, "The First Mexican Labor Program," p. 320.
4. Kiser, "Mexican American Labor," p. 127.
5. Scruggs, "The First Mexican Labor Program," pp. 321–22; Reisler, *By the Sweat of Their Brow*, pp. 29–30; Kiser, "Mexican American Labor," p. 127.
6. Kiser, "Mexican American Labor," pp. 128–29.
7. Ibid., pp. 130–31.

1

"Mexican Labor Urgently Needed in United States"

Herbert Hoover

We have several times had the question of the Mexican labor situation up with the Department. The situation has come to our notice in connection with the production of food in the southern border states, and the presence of Mr. Peden, the Texas Food Administrator, in Washington these last few days has brought to a head some of the questions which the Food Administration would like to have disposed of in this connection. There are several restrictions in force which are handicapping the movement of Mexican labor north across the border.

The first of these is the restriction which permits this labor to come in for agricultural purposes only. It is hardly necessary to say that these men are needed for various other kinds of work in Texas and New Mexico, and this restriction first of all should be disposed of.

Next, there is a provision that twenty-five cents a day must be deposited (until fifty dollars is reached) as a guarantee that the laborer will return. This, too, is bad, as it is deducted from his wage and further, we do not want him to return.

There also exists a clause providing that he must return in six months and, although this period is possible of extension, the restriction should be waived so that there is no limit on his stay in the states.

A further objection is a provision to the effect that two photographs must be made of each immigrant. The Mexican has a primitive suspicion of the camera and besides has been given the idea that this proceeding is to net him into the Draft and this one feature, though apparently insignificant, has been a great deterrent to immigration.

Yet another provision is that the farmers must meet and contract with the laborer at the border. We hope to overcome this by having special representatives make these contracts at Brownsville, Eagle Pass, Laredo and El Paso.

Letter from Herbert Hoover (Food Administrator) to Felix Frankfurter (Assistant to the Secretary of Labor), June 4, 1918, National Archives, Record Group 85, File No. 54261/202.

All these restrictions should be removed if possible in the immediate future. We need every bit of this labor that we can get and we need it badly and Mr. Peden is authority for the statement that we will need it for years to come.

2

"Mexican Labor May Not Be Needed in United States"

El Pueblo

The Mexican Vice Consul at Globe, Arizona, United States of America, in an official communication dated March 13th last, informs this Department as follows:

With reference to the enclosed newspaper clippings from which you will see that the agriculturalists of the Salt River Valley (Arizona) region have requested from the Department of Labor of this country permission to bring in several thousand laborers from Mexico to work on the plantations and farms on the ground that there is a scarcity of laborers, I beg to make the following observations:

1. In this district of Globe and Miami there are at the present time several hundred Mexicans without work who have for months past been trying to have their passports returned by the various mining companies. These companies demand of the Mexicans in order to obtain employment that, among other things, they give up their Mexican nationality, and our Embassy at Washington has been making representations to relieve their situation.

2. In the district of Clifton-Morency and MacTaft (Arizona) also there are a great many Mexicans who are idle and trying to get work from the mining companies of those places.

Translated copy of article from *El Pueblo*, April 15, 1918, National Archives, Record Group 85, File No. 54261/202.

3. In other mining camps of this State the same conditions obtain with respect to the situation of our countrymen.

4. It may well be that in this importation of Mexicans the only object is to flood the State with laborers so that the various industries can reduce wages on the ground that there is an abundance of labor, because they have for some time been trying to make such a reduction.

5. There is a marked tendency in this section at the present time to naturalize our countrymen; in some cases naturalization is indispensable for employment.

6. This consulate as well as others have been struggling incessantly to snatch our people away from the various recruiting agencies, as many of them have already been recruited on the ground that they have violated the military laws of the country.

7. [To sum up], there is an abundance of labor here and what is lacking is a good wage and above all good treatment. . . .

3

"Mexico Protests Mistreatment of Workers"

E. Garza Pérez

. . . I have the honor to inform Your Excellency that the Department of Gobernación has stated to me that, according to reports which it has received from various sources, Mexican laborers receive very bad treatment from their employers and that frequently the contracts made with them, principally with respect to payment, are not fulfilled; that the regulations of the Commissioner General of Immigration of the United States of America do not offer any guarantee against these evils or against the lack of fulfillment of the respective contracts; that if the Government of the United States should be disposed to cooperate with ours to the end of doing away with these difficulties and annoyances to Mexican laborers, we would be glad to provide facilities for the emigration referred to. . . .

Translated copy of Despatch No. 1152, from E. Garza Pérez (Subsecretary of State for Foreign Affairs) to ambassador Fletcher, June 17, 1918, National Archives, Record Group 85, File No. 54261/202.

4

"Labor Emigration to the Southwest, 1916 to 1920: Mexican Attitudes and Policy"

Lawrence A. Cardoso

From 1916 to 1920 the government of Venustiano Carranza, first chief of the Constitutionalist Army and president of Mexico, attempted to slow down and regulate the exodus of Mexican laborers to the United States. This policy consisted of two major thrusts: advising would-be emigrants of the pitfalls which awaited them and protecting those workers already across the border. Despite their efforts, Mexican authorities could do little to keep their fellow citizens at home. Economic developments in both nations provided a continuous impetus to emigration. In the United States the expanding agricultural areas of the Southwest and the economic mobilization brought on by World War I necessitated the immediate importation of hundreds of thousands of unskilled workers. Mexico's revolution-wracked economy gave added cause for workers to flee their native land for the security of the United States. Carranza and other governmental officials sought to protect Mexicans in the United States once it became evident that administrative controls were not sufficient to keep nationals at home. This protective policy was severely restricted because of lack of funds and shortage of consular personnel, but did meet with some success, particularly in the areas of employer-employee disputes and difficulties with officials of the United States Selective Service system.

Emigration to the United States increased rapidly from 1916 to 1920. In Mexico, the revolution begun by Francisco I. Madero on November 29, 1910, initiated a decade of inflation, violence, and anarchy. The revolution uprooted and scattered hundreds of thousands of panic-stricken families. Few persons, peasant or landlord, could be assured of personal safety because of the destruction of age-old institutions and relationships. The near collapse of agricultural production resulted when the wholesale flight

---

Lawrence A. Cardoso, "Labor Emigration to the Southwest, 1916 to 1920: Mexican Attitudes and Policy," *Southwestern Historical Quarterly* 79 (1976): 400–16. Reprinted by permission of the author and the Texas State Historical Association.

of peons left a labor force insufficient in size to tend crops and herds. Few landowners were willing to make the heavy investments of time and money needed for agricultural production in the face of the threat of land and crop seizures by peasants, revolutionary groups, and federal forces. In many areas of heavy population concentration previously productive lands lay entirely abandoned. Although statistics for the period are inadequate, they do show a sharp decline in food supplies. One source suggests that the production of corn and beans, the basic staples for the majority of the populace, fell precipitously from 1910 to 1918. In the latter year corn supplies dropped to 1,930,000 metric tons compared to 1,975,000 tons available in 1910; the bean crop in 1918 was only 107,000 tons compared to the 1910 figure of 160,000 tons.[1]

The peasantry also suffered disproportionately from rampant inflation. Wages remained what they had been before 1910, but prices rose rapidly. In a study of the revolution's impact, government economist Fernando González Roa found that with the rising cost of food and the decline in real wages the greater part of the rural lower classes were literally dying of hunger throughout Mexico. Similar hardships were faced by persons engaged in mining, commerce, and industry.[2]

Severe shortages of labor in the United States coincided with harsh conditions in Mexico that forced hundreds of thousands of people to leave their native land. The economic mobilization brought on by entry into World War I in April, 1917, accentuated labor shortages in the agricultural Southwest and in many industrial areas in other parts of the country. Over 1,000,000 United States citizens were conscripted for military service. Thousands of poor white and black laborers throughout the South and Southwest trekked northward to cities such as Chicago, Detroit, and New York in search of better-paying industrial jobs created by the wartime boom. In many areas, only old women and children were available for stoop labor in the fields.[3]

Extensive recruitment of Mexican workers was also encouraged by the sharp drop in European immigration brought about by the war and the Immigration Act of 1917. This law imposed an eight-dollar head tax and, for the first time in the history of the United States, a literacy test which excluded many unskilled workers who would otherwise have been admitted prior to 1917. Also excluded were those "who have come in consequence of advertisements for laborers printed, published, or distributed in a foreign country. . . ." This latter provision was designed to halt the inducement of immigration by the indirect assurances made by labor recruiters.[4]

The new law cut deeply into the large numbers of unskilled laborers needed for many western farms, mines, and railroads. Sugar beet growers and refiners in Colorado, for example, were no longer able to hire German and Russian workers. Farming interests in California were deprived of Italian, Slav, Greek, and Portuguese immigrants. The new law immediately cut immigration from southern and eastern Europe by almost 50 percent. This sharp decrease was in addition to the decline caused by the war. In 1914 persons entering the United States totalled 1,218,480; for the remainder of the war the annual number of immigrants hovered around the 300,000 mark. By 1918, after the implementation of the 1917 legislation, the annual number of newcomers was less than 10 percent of that in 1914.[5]

Wages for unskilled and semi-skilled work available in the United States were comparatively higher than those in Mexico and provided another attraction for displaced Mexican workers. In his native land a hacienda peon or migrant farm laborer received a wage of about 15 cents a day; miners earned from 50 cents to $1 daily. In the United States the illiterate, unskilled newcomer could earn $1 to $3 a day in agriculture. Mine work paid even higher wages. Mexican miners in Globe, Arizona, for example, earned $4.50 to $5.50 a day in local copper mines, and such jobs were readily available.[6]

The federal government quickly took steps to remedy the situation faced by farmers. Under the ninth proviso of the new immigration law, Secretary of Labor William B. Wilson, at that time in charge of immigration matters, was authorized to set aside any of the law's provisions if he was convinced of a labor shortage. On May 23, he specifically exempted agricultural workers from Mexico from any and all tests imposed by the Immigration Act of 1917. This waiver lasted until March 1, 1921. Over 72,000 Mexicans registered as entering under the terms of the waiver, but no one knows how many others, unregistered, came in search of work across the border. Throughout the Southwest, anxious employers welcomed countless braceros whether they were registered or not.[7]

Railroad, mining, and industrial interests in the meantime pleaded for Mexican workers in the name of national defense. A spokesman for the United States Railroad administration asked governmental permission to secure 50,000 track laborers from Mexico. One industrialist, apparently expecting a long war, suggested that 1,000,000 Mexicans be recruited by the government to fill factory jobs throughout the United States. Because of the concern expressed by these and other employers, the secretary of labor extended his waiver in July, 1918, to include nonagricultural workers. As temporary contract laborers admitted with no regard for the Immigration Act of 1917, braceros were allowed to work in railroads, mining, and construction. This waiver also lasted until March, 1921.[8]

An unprecedented increase in migration from Mexico took place after the signing of the armistice in November, 1918. Employers sponsored braceros, and the Department of Labor, in view of the economic needs of the Southwest, cooperated with them. From 1918 to 1920 almost 250,000 braceros legally crossed the border in search of employment. Important sectors of the economy had become completely dependent on Mexican migrant labor. It was rare not to find Mexicans working in unskilled and semi-skilled types of employment, often far from the border. The total number of emigrants, legal and illegal, was probably well in excess of 500,000 at a time when Mexico's population was 14,334,000 according to the federal census of 1921.[9]

This massive emigration to the United States was a matter of serious concern to Mexican government officials, employers, and nationalists, even in the midst of many other revolutionary problems. On the one hand, many observers believed that certain benefits accrued to Mexico and her people as a result of contacts with the civilization and culture of the United States. As early as May, 1913, Manuel Bonilla, Madero's secretary of development, pointed out that former hacienda workers found good working conditions across Mexico's northern border. In the United States one did not have to face starvation or brutal treatment by employers. Bonilla concluded that the experience of being in contact with an advanced culture aided emigrants in improving their own life styles. Later writers elaborated on the cultural benefits to which Bonilla had alluded. An editorialist of *El Universal,* one of the leading dailies in Mexico City, believed that the peasantry learned how to be temperate, to dress well, to eat properly, to speak English, and to employ the latest agricultural techniques. When the migrants returned to their homeland with their new skills, they would be cultured persons and a progressive element for Mexico. Anthropologist Manuel Gamio, who viewed the great labor exodus from the vantage point of 1931, echoed similar sentiments when he compared the migrants' stay in the United States to attendance in a "giant university."[10]

On one occasion, even Carranza's government officially praised the cultural benefits and progressive attitudes supposedly manifested by returning nationals. Undoubtedly, this finding favor with labor expatriation was, in part, a defensive attitude. The government was embarrassed by the fact that Mexican citizens, especially those of the peasant class, were forced to go abroad to seek their livelihood. It was an open admission to the world that Mexico reborn could not yet take care of her own people. What benefits had the revolution brought for the humble lower classes? The government could at least reply weakly that emigrants in the United States were enjoying the benefits of temporary refuge.[11]

On the other hand, most available sources of information suggest that the majority of literate Mexicans were totally opposed to emigration. Revolutionary nationalists were convinced that Mexico was underpopulated and that this fact had frustrated economic growth and national security in the past. Emigrants, therefore, were traitors to the fatherland. Just when their own nation was in need of their labor and support, they deserted Mexico and went to provide benefits for the Yankee colossus. Nationalists also believed that the flight of labor had weakened industrial development because of the exodus of much-needed technicians. Agricultural production was in a "very grave" state according to José Inocente Lugo, Carranza's secretary of development, because of the lack of workers needed for proper cultivation. Many other spokesmen lamented the personal hardships imposed on emigrants. Presidential candidate Alvaro Obregón, for example, implicitly criticized the Carranza government in November, 1919, when he railed at the spectacle of freight cars full of Mexicans being taken by labor recruiters from Nogales, Sonora, "like penned cattle."[12]

In spite of conflicting opinions, national political leaders believed that emigration should continue. Carranza's government had to face several pressing realities in formulating a policy that sought to profit from the population exodus and at the same time to control it. Economic conditions in Mexico during the period were obviously deplorable, and most of the lower classes were suffering from elemental wants. Any money sent to relatives from the United States would help to alleviate their poverty. While no government spokesman ever said so publicly, Mexican administrators were inclined to regard emigration as a political safety valve. Miserable have-nots and potentially dangerous rebels and demagogues might support or seek to lead armed protests against the often shaky governments. Furthermore, all political considerations aside, to force braceros to stay at home would only expose them to "absolute misery," as one Mexican border official frankly stated.[13]

Mexican nationalists and employers urged Carranza's government to blockade the northern border. This could have been done on the grounds of fighting United States imperialism. Military incursions into Mexico had taken place on several occasions in attempts to protect United States nationals and to influence the course of the revolution. Many not too subtle attempts to interfere in Mexican domestic matters had been made through diplomatic channels. Carranza, however, could not adopt this proposal. His government faced political enemies on all sides and had few troops which could be spared for border watching. Support and recognition from Washington were sorely needed as props for his revolutionary regime. Furthermore, the Mexican government, pledged to respect constitutional democracy, felt obliged not to contravene article eleven of the Constitution of 1917 which granted citizens the right to enter and exit their country subject only to administrative procedures.[14]

Carranza's government sought a middle course of policy which would placate, at least partially, all interested parties. One basic thrust of this policy began in late 1916 when, on the advice of the governors of the border states, an intensive propaganda campaign was launched to advise would-be emigrants of the prejudice and exploitation faced by Mexicans in the United States. A typical example of this propaganda appeared in the *Diario Oficial* of March 10, 1920. The Mexican reader was told that emigration per se was not harmful, but that braceros were subject to rampant racial discrimination, received lower pay for doing the same types of work as United States citizens, and were treated unfairly by police and court agencies. The article then went on to say that since 99 percent of all emigrants were ignorant of United States immigration laws they were often stopped at the border and forced to congregate in border cities such as Nuevo Laredo and Ciudad Juárez. Once there, without friends, family, or money, the workers formed large "parasitic masses" on the verge of starvation. The natural result of the situation was that many tried to cross the border illegally. If this were attempted, workers ran the risk of being shot by United States border authorities. Those who succeeded in their clandestine efforts then faced multiple instances of ill-treatment and the much greater danger of Americanization. Everywhere in the Southwest, concluded the article, Protestant missionary workers aided by other United States citizens sought to deprive the bracero and his family of their native culture and religion.[15]

The propaganda campaign made selective use of consular reports sent to the secretary of foreign relations. Once a particular report—or parts of it—had been approved by the secretary, it was given wide circulation through newspapers. State governors were also informed of anti-Mexican conditions in the United States and were charged by the federal government to make known to all of their states' inhabitants the "penalties and miseries" which awaited braceros across the border. All federal employees, especially those of the secretary of interior's Department of Migration, were also to give warnings to would-be emigrants. Almost all reports from the secretary of foreign relations placed special emphasis on the broken promises of employers. Arizona cotton companies were singled out as among the prime culprits in this regard. They were accused of inducing workers to cross the border with promises of high wages and good working conditions, and then, with an excess number of workers on hand, exploiting them. The result was a disastrous situation of unemployment or substandard wages wherein hapless migrant workers, far from home in a strange, hostile country, often faced starvation.[16]

United States governmental officials were also attacked for using high-handed methods in dealing with Mexicans. Immigration authorities especially were accused of arresting migrants, dumping them arbitrarily over the border, and leaving them to their own meager resources, which resulted in great hardship. According to published consular reports, police officers, local and state, frequently committed atrocities against Mexican workers. The consul in El Paso, for example, wrote that police agents there killed 391 Mexicans in the period from 1911 to 1919.[17]

In spite of this intensive propaganda campaign, emigration continued unabated. The vast majority of rural Mexicans were illiterate, and it is doubtful that they were much influenced by written government propaganda. What had a decisive influence was the "grapevine." Returning workers painted glowing pictures of better living and working conditions across the border. Besides, the typical worker distrusted the government, whose agents seemed always to exploit him and yet to protect the employer class. Why, now, should one believe in the protective efforts of untried revolutionary regimes? Why stay at home and face possible starvation or violent death? If United States employers and officials occasionally abused Mexicans, the workers' experiences with employers and officials in their own country had taught them how to deal with such treatment. As Consul Cornelius Ferris of Mexico City wrote concerning the propaganda efforts of Carranza's government,

> such representations made by the Mexican authorities make very little impression on Mexicans of the laboring classes. At San Luis Potosí, especially during the year of 1918, I examined hundreds of Mexican applicants for passport visas. . . . Nearly all had friends in the United States. . . . [They] told me that they placed no reliance whatever on representations made by their own government officials, and they felt assured of good treatment in the United States.[18]

Many other consular dispatches recorded the same impressions concerning the propaganda campaign, but perhaps no more eloquent testimony is needed as to its failure than the rising tide of emigration.

Carranza's government also attempted to regulate the outflow of laborers through a series of administrative procedures. One policy decision was to leave in the hands of the state governors the issuance of passports needed by braceros to leave the country legally. Presumably, local politicians were more aware of the effects of the loss of laborers to their states and were better able to enforce the dictates of the central government. Jalisco, one of the Central Plateau states which provided a disproportionate percentage of workers for the United States' agricultural sector, attempted a policy of uniformly denying passports because of the chronic complaints of labor shortages made by local industrialists and agriculturalists. United States consular officials, especially during the acute labor shortages occasioned by World War I, totally defeated the state's intentions by privately encouraging workers to go to the border without passports, knowing that at the port of entry they would be readily admitted.[19]

State governors were also under orders to take active measures to discourage emigration by whatever steps they deemed necessary. Not only did state officials give wide publicity to the propaganda from Mexico City, but some tried to stop labor recruiters who boldly invaded their states during the war in search of braceros. In one case, a representative of Arizona cotton growers who was seeking helpers to harvest crops under authorization from Secretary of State Robert Lansing was forbidden to carry out his work in the state of Sonora by Governor Plutarco Elías Calles. Calles told the recruiter he could contract for workers only if his employers posted a $1,000 bond for every man induced to go to Arizona. In this way, Calles hoped to discourage the recruiting of large numbers of Mexicans, and at the same time ensure that the cotton companies honored all their promises and guaranteed the return passage of workers once the harvesting season was completed. Lansing, when he heard of Calles's demands, refused to intervene through diplomatic channels and presumed that the growers would obtain all the help they needed through the normal flow of braceros once news of the work available in Arizona was made known to Sonorans.[20]

Unable to control the steadily increasing number of emigrants, Carranza's government tried to secure favorable work contracts for Mexican nationals before they left their native land. Beginning in January, 1917, Department of Migration inspectors were ordered to prevent the exit of any worker not having a valid, signed, written contract. The document had to contain specific provisions as to wages and hours and would not be binding on any of the concerned parties unless an officer of the Migration service witnessed its signing. Later in the year inspectors were instructed to tell all emigrants to register with the nearest Mexican consul once they were in the United States. Once this was done diplomatic officers could make sure that employers complied with all of their contractual promises.[21]

The federal government published a model contract in March, 1920, which was intended as a remedy for complaints concerning mistreated Mexicans in the United States. This document also provides a good illustration of the protection which revolutionary leaders hoped to give to the emigrants. No bracero could leave Mexico unless he was protected by this document and accompanied by his family. Presumably, this would act as a brake on attempts to corrupt or Americanize peasants and prevent families from being abandoned in Mexico. Transportation costs to and from the place of employment were to be paid by the employer; the latter was also obligated to pay all entry fees for the family. Detailed working conditions were also spelled out. The minimum wage was set at $2 a day, and free medical care was to be provided for those who became ill or suffered a work-related accident. Any worker disabled in the course of his employment was to be repatriated at the employer's expense. Several enforcement procedures were also stipulated in the contract. Before the worker left his native state, his employer had to sign a notarized agreement in the presence of Department of Migration and state officials and post bond to guarantee compliance on his part. Once the worker was at his place of employment, the nearest Mexican consul was to act as a watchdog over the employer. National railroad companies were also charged with the responsibility of enforcing this contractual relationship. Trains, the major form of transportation to the north and over the border, were to be constantly policed so as to halt workers without contracts.[22]

All of these administrative controls failed to effect the intent of the government. Some individuals were undoubtedly persuaded not to cross the border, but the massive, growing outflow of laborers during the period is evidence of overall failure. Peasant mistrust of government helped cause this failure, but a more basic reason lay in the attitudes of Department of Migration officials. Many, for humanitarian reasons, felt they could not deny their countrymen a chance for a better life. Many more, if not most, according to the accusations which poured out of Mexico City, took advantage of the situation for self-enrichment. They regularly cooperated with labor recruiters and professional smugglers by serving as contact men for workers who wished to cross the border.[23]

The naiveté of the framers of the model contract is striking. In essence they tried to incorporate some of the social provisions of article 123 of the Constitution of 1917 into the document. No political jurisdiction in the United States provided, by law, any of the work guarantees for agricultural workers. It is doubtful that more than a handful of employers would seriously have considered the extension of these benefits to braceros. In fact, no instance of an employer's signing this document has come to light. The easiest and most profitable tactic was simply to ignore the designs of the government in Mexico City.

The protection of the braceros already in the United States was another concern of Carranza's government. So many Mexican nationals found immediate employment across the border that officials were forced to take a realistic view of the situation. As Secretary of Foreign Relations Cándido Águilar expressed it in September 1917: "since it is not possible for the government to prevent emigration, it must make every effort to bring about the least possible suffering for our conationals during their stay in a foreign land." In fact, this policy of consular protection had been in evidence since November 10, 1916. On that date diplomatic representatives in the United States were ordered to use the full powers of their offices and all legal recourses to aid their countrymen. They were to visit jailed migrants and inform them of their rights under local law and see that those rights were respected. This was to be done by contacting police and court agencies to press for nondiscriminatory application of local law, or, when funds were available, through legal representation.[24]

Recourse to diplomatic pressure was to be used only as a last resort. The day after the first set of instructions was sent to consuls, they were told to exhaust all legal recourses in each and every case which came to their attention. If necessary, federal courts were to be used as a device to check abuses committed by state and local judicial bodies. The circular of November 11 went on to say that if justice could not be obtained, the consul was to notify the secretary of foreign relations as well as the Mexican Embassy in Washington, D.C. After each case was studied on its merits, a decision would then be made as to presentation of a formal protest.[25]

There were serious limitations on the implementation of this protective policy. Given the clandestine nature of much of the emigration, few consuls ever had an accurate idea of just how many migrants were in their areas of jurisdiction. Many illegal entrants were fearful of making their presence a matter of public notice. Therefore, many instances of unfair treatment were never reported by braceros who, in any case, tended to distrust the whole of officialdom. Financial resources also imposed a severe limitation on consular effectiveness. Rarely were funds available to pay for legal aid. Moreover, consular districts were so large and office staff so woefully inadequate that only small portions of any given area could be policed. There were never more than several dozen consuls at a time when Mexican nationals in the United States numbered in the hundreds of thousands.[26]

Despite these inherent handicaps, the Mexican diplomatic corps acted vigorously at times. Consuls were generally anxious to promote good relations with the United States under the "Carranza doctrine" of respecting the sovereignty of the laws of all nations. All braceros were urged to register with their nearest consul so the latter could ensure their protection by establishing nationality and providing a legal basis for consular intervention should it become necessary. Migrants were also exhorted to obey all laws of their host country in order to preclude possible difficulties with police and court officials. Zealous consuls also helped illegal entrants by issuing them passports ex post facto so they could regularize their status with United States immigration authorities. The Department of Migration did not chastise consular officials who pursued this highly questionable course of action.[27]

Under the policy of promoting the rights of Mexican labor abroad, aggressive consuls soon became deeply involved in employer-labor disputes. Illustrative of this type of intervention was action by Consul General Teódulo Beltrán in May, 1918, to protect braceros employed by the Spreckles Sugar Company in California sugar beet fields. According to Beltran's report, Mexican migratory laborers were being treated worse than Porfirian peons. He found conditions of near slavery, with open-ended hours, irregular pay, poor food, unfit housing, and armed men in the work camps to ensure submission. Beltrán filed formal complaints with workers' groups, state labor authorities, and the United States Department of Immigration. Then, once the Spreckles Company faced imminent legal action and a barrage of bad publicity during a wartime period when Mexican labor was sorely needed, he began negotiating a new contract for the workers. An agreement was quickly concluded. Workers were to receive a $2.25 wage for a nine-hour day and 25 cents extra for every hour worked overtime. The company further promised better food and lodging, as well as the removal of its armed guards. Finally, the braceros were to enjoy complete personal freedom after work hours and on holidays.[28]

Many other consular activities were related to employer disputes. For example, a road building firm in Hayden, Arizona, went bankrupt in the course of a construction project. This left a large number of Mexican nationals unpaid for work already completed; in the meantime, the owner of the company had disappeared along with most of his liquid assets. The Mexican consul in Tucson promptly sought to obtain some of the wages owed through a lien on the employer's property. In other cases, diplomatic representatives helped migrant workers and their families collect what was due them in the form of unemployment compensation or severance pay and death benefits.[29]

Perhaps the best example of the protection afforded to expatriate laborers by agents of Carranza's government was the handling of the draft problem during World War I. On May 18, 1917, the Selective Service Act became law. Under its provisions all adult males twenty-one through thirty years of age were obligated to register for the wartime draft. The law little affected Mexicans working in the United States as it provided that foreigners who had taken no steps to change their citizenship simply register with their local draft boards and offer proof of their national status. They had no duty whatsoever to serve in the armed forces.[30]

The minimal requirements expected of Mexican laborers had totally unexpected results throughout the Southwest. Apparently state and federal governments had taken no steps to inform Spanish-speaking men of their status. Unfounded rumors and half-truths spread through towns and work camps. Braceros heard that they would be drafted upon presenting themselves to the local draft boards and would be used as cheap cannon fodder while United States citizens stayed at home and took advantage of war-induced prosperity. Few workers hearing these stories were about to risk death for the Yankee Behemoth.[31]

The initial response of Selective Service officials tended to substantiate the rumors. Thousands of braceros who could not prove their place of birth were immediately drafted into the armed forces, and, in the absence of clear guidelines from Washington, many local boards refused to accept consular proof of nationality and insisted on a valid certificate of birth. In some cases, overzealous consuls knowingly issued proof of Mexican birth to Mexican Americans who sought to escape the draft. Where this happened, board officials then refused to accept any proferred consular proofs of citizenship.[32]

Untold thousands of workers responded to the situation by voluntary repatriation. Along the length of the border United States immigration officers viewed with dismay the loss of so many workers needed for the domestic war effort. During the first five days of June alone, 5,451 repatriates streamed across the border; by June 11 another 4,000 had returned. Through the remainder of June and July the daily count of returning workers continued to mount.[33]

Mexican officials cooperated with Secretary of State Lansing's campaign in the southwestern United States to halt the reverse flow of workers. An extensive propaganda effort advised Mexicans of the minimal requirements of the law. On telephone poles, billboards, train station walls, and stores Spanish language posters informed braceros that not one of them would be drafted. All parish priests read a letter of assurance to their Mexican communicants. In many localities priests, together with "friendly Mexican officials," visited farm, mining, and rail camps to explain the position of the United States government. This latter effort had a marked effect in quieting fears about possible difficulties with selective service personnel. By August 17 calm was restored and the number of braceros in the United States approached those of pre-draft times.[34]

Through the course of the war the protective zeal of many consuls was evidenced by their confrontations with local draft boards. In Baltimore, Maryland, for example, when eleven workers were inducted after having failed to present proper proof of their nationality, the local consul rushed to the Department of Justice and the Department of the Army and began a door-knocking, desk-pounding campaign of complaints. The army then discharged the men after they showed satisfactory proof of nationality which the consul had provided. In Jerome, Arizona, Consul Efren Ornelas accompanied six braceros through every stage of the induction process all the way to the training camp, protesting every step of the way. At the same time, Ambassador Bonillas pressed United States officials in Washington for action in the matter. After ten days of such pressure and protest the local board gave in and turned the men over to Ornelas. In the vast majority of those instances where consuls were careful in issuing proof of nationality, friction with local boards was kept to a minimal level.[35]

Despite some success, the Mexican government never solved the dilemma of emigration. Political leaders, particularly the feisty Carranza, wanted to stand up to the United States by allowing the exodus of only fully protected workers. The majority opinion that unregulated emigration was an evil which Mexico could ill afford gave added impetus for Carranza's government to take decisive action. The broader implication of emigration control was obvious: in a real sense it posed a test of political and revolutionary legitimacy. Mexican national interests and the welfare of Mexican citizens had to be given priority—at the expense of the United States if necessary.

This ideal, however, had little chance of realization. The United States government extended virtually no assistance to its Mexican counterpart in the management of the population flow. The wartime waivers, for example, were effected without prior consultation with Carranza's government; United States consular officers and labor recruiters surreptitiously urged defiance of Mexican law by braceros who wished to emigrate. Only when its own national interests were threatened in the draft scare of 1917 did the government in Washington allow its agents to deal with Mexican officials on this matter. The impossibility of any program of mutual, longterm cooperation dictated that Mexico alone had to regulate emigration or nothing would be done.

The disparate economic and political conditions in each nation further negated the ideal scenario hoped for by Mexican revolutionaries. Carranza could not afford the real and potential problems caused by large numbers of unemployed workers in an economy partially destroyed by civil war and inflation. The miserable have-nots were too much revolutionary tinder to be kept at home. The unemployed Mexican easily found work in the United States and sent home money which alleviated suffering and improved his native country's balance of trade position. In a very immediate sense the vigor of the United States' economy with its demand for braceros helped serve as a guarantor of governmental stability in Mexico. There was no valid reason to attempt a total halt to emigration.

Carranza and his bureaucrats largely failed in what they did try to do. Braceros placed little trust in their warnings. Driven by the imperious necessities of food and personal security, it is doubtful that any government could have succeeded in keeping workers at home. Once in the United States, the hundreds of thousands of Mexicans were left largely to their own devices as they coped with new experiences in a new land. Their home government lacked the funds and personnel to extend a full array of protective measures; they had little reason to look to that source for aid in any event. Individual consuls showed the clearest manifestations of zeal and humanitarianism for their fellow citizens. Their efforts to protect workers from employer excesses and the errors of draft officials were surely one of the bright spots in the United States for braceros. When Carranza was ousted from power in May, 1920, some of the principles of the emigration policy of subsequent revolutionary governments had been thought through, if not thoroughly implemented.

NOTES

1. Memorandum, November 17, 1917, [illegible] to Carranza, Archivo Carranza (Fundación Cultural de Condumex, S.A., Mexico City); Charles C. Cumberland, *Mexico: The Struggle for Modernity* (New York, 1968), p. 372. Items in the Archivo Carranza have no classification numbers and are arranged only in chronological order. They are hereafter cited as Carranza Papers.

2. Fernando González Roa, *El aspecto agrario de la Revolución mexicana* (Mexico City, 1919), p. 170; Edwin Walter Kemmerer, *Inflation and Revolution: Mexico's Experience of 1912–1917* (Princeton, 1940).

3. Frank L. Polk to Marion Letcher, January 2, 1918, General Records of the Department of State, File 811.504/85, Record Group 59 (National Archives); Truman G. Palmer to Robert Lansing, August 8, 1917, File 811.504/42, ibid.; U.S., Congress, House, Committee on Immigration and Naturalization, *Temporary Admission of Illiterate Mexican Laborers* (Washington, D.C., 1920), pp. 19, 30, 37, 169–70; U.S., Department of Labor, Bureau of Immigration, *Annual Report of the Commissioner General of Immigration to the Secretary of Labor, 1918* (Washington, D.C., 1919), p. 317. References to Record Group 59 in the National Archives will hereafter be cited as RG 59, NA.

4. Roy L. Garis, *Immigration Restriction: A Study of the Opposition to and Regulation of Immigration into the United States* (New York, 1927), pp. 118, 125 (quotation), 130.

5. Ibid., pp. 159, 164; Enrique Santibañez, *Ensayo acerca de la inmigración mexicana en los Estados Unidos* (San Antonio, 1930), p. 39–40; Paul S. Taylor, *Mexican Labor in the United States: Valley of the South Platte, Colorado* (Berkeley, 1929), p. 102–5.

6. Jesús González, *Nuestros problemas* (Mexico City, 1921), p. 28; *El Universal* (Mexico City), March 3, 1920; House Committee on Immigration and Naturalization, *Temporary Admission of Illiterate Mexican Laborers*, pp. 21, 34, 56, 73; Charles C. Cumberland, *Mexican Revolution: The Constitutionalist Years* (Austin, 1972), pp. 384, 390, 399; Gustavo Hernández to Cándido Águilar, August 17, 1917, Archivo Histórico de la Secretaría de Relaciones Exteriores, (Tlateloco, Mexico City), IV/241.2 (72–73)/13-14-40. The Archivo Histórico de la Secretaría de Relaciones Exteriores is hereafter cited as AHRE.

7. Wilson to Anthony Caminetti, May 23, 1917, File 811.504/28, RG 59, NA; U.S., Department of Labor, Bureau of Immigration, *Annual Report, 1918*, p. 319; Otey M. Scruggs, "The First Mexican Farm Labor Program," *Arizona and the West* (Winter 1960): 319–26. The term "bracero," although not in wide currency in the United States until the 1940s, was the almost universal designation used by Mexicans to describe unskilled and semi-skilled workers who performed arduous physical labor during the period under discussion here.

8. Avery Turner to John Silliman, November 12, 1918, File 811.504/139, RG 59, NA; Charles M. Rork to Lansing, June 17, 1917, File 811.504/104, ibid.; Polk to Embassy, Mexico City, July 26, 1918, File 811.504/120a, ibid.

9. U.S. Department of Labor, Bureau of Immigration, *Annual Report, 1918*, p. 319; U.S., Department of Labor, *Reports, 1918* (Washington, D.C., 1919), pp. 692–93; U.S. Department of Labor, *Reports, 1920* (Washington, D.C., 1921), p. 693; Paul S. Taylor, *Mexican Labor in the United States: Imperial Valley* (Berkeley, 1928), p. 8; James J. Davis to Cyrenus Cole, April 25, 1924, *Congressional Record*, 68th Cong., 2nd Sess., LXVI, Pt. 2, pp. 1366–67; New York *Times*, June 20, 1920; Cumberland, *Mexico*, p. 367; Lawrence A. Cardoso, "Mexican Emigration to the United States, 1900–1930: An Analysis of Socio-Economic Causes" (Ph.D. dissertation, University of Connecticut, 1974), pp. 88–91.

10. Manuel Bonilla, *Apuntes para el estudio del programa agrario* (Hermosillo, 1914), p. 26; *El Universal* (Mexico City), August 13, 1920; Manuel Gamio, "Migration and Planning," *Survey*, LXVI (May 1, 1931), 174 (quotation), 175.

11. *Diario Oficial*, VII (November 7, 1917), p. 395.

12. *El Universal* (Mexico City), December 12, 1916; March 20, 1920 (first quotation);

Gustavo Durán, "Importancia de la agricultura y del fraccionamiento de tierras," paper read to the Antonio Alzate Scientific Society, September 1911, Jesús Silva Herzog (ed.), *La cuestión de la tierra* (4 vols.; Mexico City, 1960–62), I, pp. 190–91; Narciso Bassols Batalla, *El pensamiento político de Alvaro Obregón* (2d ed.; Mexico City, 1970), p. 74 (second quotation).

13. *El Universal* (Mexico City), March 17, 1920. My examination of available archival material in Mexico City suggests no official attempts were made to check emigration from 1910 to 1916.

14. John T. Vance and Helen L. Clagett, *A Guide to the Law and Legal Literature of Mexico* (Washington, D.C., 1945), p. 194. For examples of United States heavy-handedness see Robert Freeman Smith, *The United States and Revolutionary Nationalism in Mexico, 1916–1932* (Chicago, 1972); Robert E. Quirk, *An Affair of Honor: Woodrow Wilson and the Occupation of Veracruz* (Lexington, 1962); Berta Ulloa, *La Revolución intervenida: relaciones diplomáticas entre México y Estados Unidos (1910–1914)* (Mexico City, 1971).

15. *Diario Oficial,* XIV (March 10, 1920), pp. 1089–90; Adolfo de la Huerta to Carranza, September 10, 1916, Carranza Papers; Alfonso Fábila, *El problema de la emigación de obreros y campesinos mexicanos* (Mexico City, 1929).

16. Aguilar to Jesús Acuña, June 17, 1916, AHRE, 17-20-21; *Diario Oficial,* VIII, (April 18, 1918), p. 1139; *El Universal* (Mexico City), April 15, 1918.

17. *Diario Oficial,* XIV (March 24, 1920), p. 1372; Alberto Ruiz Sandoval to Aguilar, undated, AHRE, IV/241 (73-17) (03).I. 11-19-24. For typical examples of Yankeephobia see Querido Moheno, *Cosas del Tío Sam* (Mexico City, 1916), pp. 55–57; Fábila, *El problema de la emigración.*

18. Ferris to Lansing, March 11, 1920, File 811.504/203, RG 59, NA.

19. Silliman to Turner, November 23, 1918, File 811.504/213, ibid.

20. Undated clipping from Baja California *Periódico Oficial,* Lansing to Henry Ashurst, October 6, 1917, File 8. .504/56, ibid.

21. *Diario Oficial,* XIV (March 17, 1920), pp. 1225–26, gives a brief résumé of circulars sent by the government to Department of Migration officials.

22. Ibid. (March 17, 1920), pp. 1225–26; (March 24, 1920), p. 1373.

23. *El Universal* (Mexico City), March 17, June 18, 1920.

24. Ibid., September 21, 1917 (quotation); Circular #13, November 10, 1916, AHRE, 2214-I.

25. Circular #14, November 11, 1916, AHRE, 2214-I.

26. Manuel Gamio, *The Mexican Immigrant: His Life-Story* (Chicago, 1931), p. 216; unsigned memorandum of June 10, 1922, entitled, "Mexicanos emigrantes, medidas sugeridas para controlar sus engergías," in Papepes Presidenciales, Palacio Nacional, Zócalo (Mexico City), expediente 711-M-30; Enrique Colunga to Obregón, March 18, 1921, ibid., expediente 822-M-I. The *Registers* of the Department of State, a yearly publication, give the names and jurisdictions of Mexican consuls in the United States.

27. *Diario Oficial,* XIV (March 17, 1920), p. 1225; Manuel Aguirre Berlanga to Ramón P. Denegri, June 14, 1918, AHRE, 16-24-25. Aguirre Berlanga replaced Acuña as secretary of interior on December 1, 1916.

28. Beltrán to Águilar, May 25, 1918, AHRE, 241 (72:73)/13-14-22.

29. Manuel A. Rico to Andrés García, October 8, 1917, AHRE, 241 (72-73)/13-1355; Aguilar to Raúl R. Domínguez, October 22, 1917, ibid. There is no evidence of how successful the consul was in obtaining the money owed to the workers. Adelaido J. Ortiz to Aguilar, October 1, 1917, ibid.

30. Public Law 12 (May 18, 1917), Selective Service Act, *Statutes at Large,* XL, pp. 78, 80; Gamio, *The Mexican Immigrant,* 56.

31. *El Paso del Norte* (El Paso), May 23, 1917. This newspaper served Mexican residents

throughout the Southwest. Scattered copies are located in the Basave collection in the Biblioteca de México at the Ciudadela in Mexico City.

32. Ives G. Lelevier to Aguilar, August 24, 1917, AHRE, IV/241.2 (72:73)/13-14-3; Denegri to Carranza, July 27, 1917, Carranza Papers; Douglas *Daily Dispatch* (Arizona), August 25, 1917, clipping, ibid.

33. *El Paso del Norte* (El Paso), June—July, 1917; Denegri to Aguilar, May 19, 1917, copy in File 811.504/23, RG 59, NA.

34. Copies of posters, File 811.504/86, RG 59, NA; Matthew E. Hanna to Lansing, May 24, June 4, August 21, 1917, Files 811.504/24, 811.504/29, and 811.504/49, ibid.

35. Rafael Calvo y Arias to Aguilar, September 3, 1918, AHRE, 241.2 (72:73)/1451; Ornelas to Bonillas, September 11, 1917, September 18, 20, 1917; Bonillas to Ornelas, September 13, 19, 1917, ibid., IV/241.2 (72:73):/13-14-3; Hernández to García, August 28, 1917, ibid., 62-R-2; Lelevier to Aguilar, July 20, 1917, ibid.

II

Repatriation During the Great Depression[1]

During the Great Depression, almost half a million Mexican nationals (including American-born children) were repatriated from the United States. Some were deported while others left "voluntarily" under government pressure and still others apparently left completely on their own as job opportunities disappeared. The greatest annual exodus occurred while Herbert Hoover was president but significant numbers continued to depart until the end of the 1930s.

Although Mexican repatriation during the Great Depression was unprecedented in scope, it was not completely without precedent. During 1921–22, there had been another depression and it, too, had caused a substantial return of Mexican nationals to their homeland. In several respects, that earlier repatriation paralleled the later one. For instance, in both cases, public opposition to the use of Mexican labor was fueled by rapidly rising unemployment. Also, during both depressions, municipal governments played an important role in pressuring Mexican nationals to leave the United States. Another parallel lay in Mexico's assistance of repatriates as they left the United States. And neither repatriation movement brought any long-term reduction in the use of Mexican labor in this country.

Once the depression of 1921–22 ended, interests opposed to the use of Mexican labor enjoyed little success. On the contrary, the 1920s brought unprecedented numbers of Mexican workers to this country. While some entered legally, many others entered illegally.

With the onset of the Great Depression in 1929, the balance of power shifted again. The opponents of Mexican employment were able to argue their case even more effectively than they had in 1921, and that probably accounts in part for the more sweeping nature of the latter repatriation movement. In 1929, they could point to unprecedented joblessness and to the presence of record numbers of Mexican nationals. Moreover, by 1929, Mexican workers were less concentrated regionally and less confined to agricultural jobs. Consequently, workers in many jobs and in all major regions of the United States came to feel threatened, and the coalition opposing the government's policy expanded enormously.

Extensive though it was, repatriation during the Great Depression by no means brought a halt to the use of Mexican labor. Many Mexican nationals were not repatriated, because even during the depths of the depression, southwestern growers and other employers continued to claim that Mexican labor was still essential because they simply could not hire American citizens to do certain kinds of work. Moreover, not even the Depression completely shut off the flow of Mexican workers into the United States. In fact, even some of the repatriates soon returned to this country.

United States policy toward Mexican labor during the Great Depression was not designed as a long-range solution to the problem. It was basically an attempt to cope with pressures generated or intensified by the Depression itself. In no sense was it an effort to end permanently the flow of Mexican labor into this country. No new restrictive legislation was passed; old laws were simply applied with new vigor. But that lasted for about a decade at most. By the 1940s, large numbers of Mexican workers would again be entering the United States.

Repatriation was filled with implications for Mexican-Americans. It was sometimes thought that they would be the primary beneficiaries inasmuch as they were supposedly the group with which Mexican nationals had always competed most directly in the job market. However, some of the scholarly literature suggests that repatriation added significantly to the hardships of United States citizens of Mexican ancestry. For instance, naturalized American citizens were sometimes pressured to return to Mexico. Children who were United States citizens by virtue of their birth in this country were often repatriated along with their parents. Moreover, merely having a Spanish surname could subject one to official screening.

The repatriation of Mexican nationals from the United States during the Great Depression provoked bitter criticism in much of Mexico's press. The fifth selection is an example from the newspaper *Excélsior*. It denounces the American action as a violation of legal and humanitarian principles, claiming that repatriation was being conducted ruthlessly, without regard to its impact on existing work contracts or to its role in breaking up families in which Mexican nationals were married to American citizens. The article charges that the rapid return of such massive numbers of hungry people was creating a major crisis for Mexico.

Such scathing attacks in the Mexican press did not go unanswered in the United States. In selection 6, immigration official Walter Carr responds to the widespread criticism of the role played in repatriation by the Immigration and Naturalization Service. Although he admits that there were illegal and inhumane aspects to repatriation, he denies that the Service was responsible for them. He emphasizes that much repatriation occurred informally and thus was beyond the control of immigration authorities. Carr attempts to portray the immigration service as a stalwart defender of Mexican rights during the repatriation era. He argues that it firmly and effectively resisted massive and sometimes hysterical demands to hasten the exodus of Mexicans by resorting to illegal shortcuts.

In selection 7, immigration officer John Zurbrick discusses plans for the repatriation of Mexicans from Michigan during the Great Depression. He argues that such action should not be confused with deportation since many aliens had requested their own repatriation. Zurbrick seems to hope that an emphasis on the "voluntary" nature of the Michigan repatriation would lead many Mexicans to leave the United States on their own—reducing welfare rolls and opening up jobs for unemployed Americans. He notes that the State of Michigan, local governments in the state, the Mexican national government, and state governments in Mexico all had agreed to cooperate with the prospective repatriates.

Selection 8 is a communication from Mexican Consul Ignacio Batiza to Mexican nationals in Detroit, urging them to return to Mexico under the voluntary plan discussed in the previous paragraph. His statement should not be interpreted to mean that Mexico suddenly had become an enthusiastic supporter of repatriation; to Mexico, it had become increasingly clear that repatriation was inevitable. Mexico simply was trying to make the best of a bad situation. For instance, the consul's statement refers to the severe economic plight of Mexicans in Michigan and to Mexico's willingness to help them reestablish themselves in Mexico.

Based heavily on research at the National Archives in Washington, D.C., the selection by George Kiser and David Silverman discusses the rationale developed by supporters of repatriation as well as arguments employed by its opponents. It identifies a variety of participants in the conflict and discusses the political strategies they employed. The article considers policy responses of the Hoover Administration as it faced broad pressure to solve the "Mexican problem." It provides brief accounts of repatriation from Michigan and California and suggests some probable differences between those two cases. It notes that much of the repatriation was decentralized and cautions that this lack of uniformity makes suspect any broad generalizations.

NOTES

1. For accounts of Mexican labor in the United States during the Great Depression and of the repatriation movement, see: Neil Betten and Raymond A. Mohl, "From Discrimination to Repatriation: Mexican Life in Gary, Indiana, During the Great Depression," *Pacific Historical Review* 42 (1973): 370–88; Emory S. Bogardus, "Mexican Repatriates," *Sociology and Social Research* 18 (1933): 169–76; D. H. Dinwoodie, "Deportation: The Immigration Service and the Chicano Labor Movement in the 1930's," *New Mexico Historical Review* 52 (1977): 193–206; Abraham Hoffman, "Mexican Repatriation Statistics: Some Suggested Alternatives to Carey McWilliams," *Western Historical Quarterly* 3 (1972): 391–404; Abraham Hoffman, "Stimulus to Repatriation: The 1931 Federal Deportation Drive and the Los Angeles Mexican Community," *Pacific Historical Review* 42 (May 1973): 205–19; Abraham Hoffman, "The Trinidad Incident," *Journal of Mexican American History* 2 (1972): 143–51; Abraham Hoffman, *Unwanted Mexican Americans in the Great Depression: Repatriation Pressures, 1929–1939* (Tucson: University of Arizona Press, 1974); Norman D. Humphrey, "Mexican Repatriation from Michigan: Public Assistance in Historical Perspective," *Social Service Review* 15 (1941): 497–513; Robert N. McLean, "Goodbye, Vicente," *Survey*, 1 May 1931, pp. 182–83, 195–97.

5

"Deportations Continue"

Excélsior

Thousands of deportees have arrived during the last week through the border port of Nogales, presenting a pitiful and pathetic spectacle, for many of them are hollow-cheeked from hunger.

The problem of the deportees is a dreadful one and the people of this State are becoming quite alarmed for it is assuming the aspect of a na-

---

Translated copy of article from *Excélsior*, May 11, 1931, National Archives, Record Group 85, File No. 55739/674.

tional calamity, urgently requiring the intervention of both the State and Federal authorities.

It is merely that thousands of Mexicans are being thrust or, rather, swept out of the United States without stopping to consider whether it is just in every case. Many of them went to the United States under contract with the notoriously famous labor contract companies . . . , but now that, due to the crisis, they have started a readjustment of all foreign employees and labor in that country, they have broken their contracts and, under the protection of the authorities themselves, are casting them off on Mexico.

If these actions alone are shameful from a legal and humanitarian point of view, it is still worse when an entire country is lacking in the most elementary practices of international law.

Another exceedingly serious aspect of the mass deportation of Mexicans is the lack of consideration shown for marriage contracts. Upon being deported to Mexico, Mexicans are separated from their wives, if the latter are Americans.

Notwithstanding the protests and even entreaties of the unfortunate Mexican husbands, or wives, if the husband is an American, the authorities in question show no consideration and separate husbands and wives under the pretext, it itself, an insult, that Mexicans live in a manner irreconcilable with Yankee customs. Neither labor nor marriage contracts are respected, Mexicans being separated from their wives as if they were animals.

In view of the desperate situation of the deportees, and since it is impossible to help them in the manner desired, meetings are being held between the authorities and inhabitants of the towns with a view to studying the problem in question, which is exceedingly serious even for those having work or a means of livelihood.

The farmers of the (region of the) Yaqui River and especially those in the municipality of Cajeme (Ciudad Obregón) have agreed to give temporary employment to deportees in distress passing through that town and desiring to work for five or six days, by permitting them to substitute for the regular workmen who can easily spare a few days for them without prejudice to themselves.

6

"Immigration Officer Responds to Mexican Newspaper Criticism of Repatriation"

Walter E. Carr

Receipt is acknowledged of your . . . communication, and in reply I may say that I am informed that similar articles have been appearing in the newspapers of various parts of Mexico, evidently based upon the stories told by Mexican arrivals from the United States.

I do not think that the article in question was based on the fact that the Mexican authorities at Mexicali sent some two or three hundred indigents from that point in transit through the United States to Nogales, as that movement was largely made up of Mexicali residents who had not recently been in the United States. I do not think that the parties so conveyed would upon their arrival at points in the interior of Mexico attribute such movement to any United States agencies. No doubt these articles in the Mexican papers are based on stories which have been told by Mexicans who have been scared into leaving the United States by the various propaganda and activities over which this service had no control.

The real underlying cause for this movement is the present depression. Persons cannot live without jobs and the unemployment situation has been excessively acute, resulting in a state of hysteria not only in California but along the southern border and throughout the country. Newspapers and the public generally were looking for measures of relief and the United States citizen out of employment looks with envy upon the job held by a person whom he judges to be an alien. In fact, every one is looking for a cure-all and the idea that an alien deported in reality means one more job and one less mouth to feed by public funds has spread rapidly.

During the last session of Congress there were no end of proposals rumored bearing on the immigration question. The impression prevailed

---

Memo from Walter E. Carr (District Director of Immigration, Los Angeles District) to Commissioner General of Immigration, June 17, 1931, National Archives, Record Group 85, File No. 55739/674.

throughout the country that Congress not only intended to absolutely bar any and all immigration for a period of two years but further that it intended appropriating some fifteen million dollars for the purpose of deportation of illegal entries inaugurating wholesale deportation activities.

The various State legislatures entertained legislation aimed directly at the alien illegally here. . . . In California it was proposed that aliens be segregated and that separate schools be established. Further, in connection with the unemployment situation, State, County and Municipal governments denied any but citizens of the United States work on developments expressly designed for relief purposes. County, State and independent welfare organizations as well as the Chamber of Commerce attempted to bring pressure to bear upon the Immigration Service to immediately deport any and all aliens who happened to be out of employment. Certain counties in California used County funds to pay the railway fare of Mexican indigents to Mexican border points from which points the burden of expense was assumed by the Mexican government, under arrangements perfected by its Consular agents. In addition to the parties which were in a sense sponsored by the Counties themselves the Mexican Consul in Los Angeles has also supervised the departure of many other Mexican nationals.

The Chamber of Commerce in Los Angeles backed a movement to relieve the unemployment situation but which as it was actually handled was designed primarily to scare aliens, especially Mexicans, out of this community. This office was approached and requested to make a statement in the public press to the effect that officers from other districts would be brought here for no other purpose than to deport Mexicans and that all Mexicans illegally here would be immediately deported. This was to be merely a gesture, that is, to give the matter publicity and create the impression that such an activity would immediately start, when, in fact, no such actual activity was contemplated. It goes without saying that such request did not receive favorable consideration. I believe the Secretary of Labor was requested to make a similar gesture. In spite of the fact that this office absolutely refused to lend its name to any publicity along the lines in question and further made every possible attempt to prevent any such publicity, certain articles were placed in the newspapers and copied in the foreign language papers in such a way as to carry the impression that the Mexican people were to be made the target of a deportation drive by this Service. This office, however, made an announcement through the press definitely stating that this Service had no intention of considering any activity aimed solely at Mexicans; that any action which this Service might take would not discriminate against any one race; that in any event, persons legally in the United States had nothing to fear; and that we were interested only in the same classes of aliens that have always demanded our attention, that is, any alien of any race actually subject to deportation under the immigration laws.

The unemployment situation affected Mexicans and persons of Mexican stock to a far greater degree than it did persons of other races. They could not secure employment on public works and I have heard it alleged that even on private enterprises they were denied employment because they looked like aliens.

All of these matters were given wide publicity not only in the public press but through a whispering campaign which gathered strength as time went on until the Mexican population was led to believe, in many instances, that Mexicans were not wanted in California and that all would be deported whether they were legally here or not.

Taking advantage of this situation numbers of unscrupulous persons added their touch to the story and approached many Mexicans who were property owners and, further exaggerating stories of what was likely to take place, managed to swindle them out of their holdings, persuading them the best thing they could do would be to return to Mexico.

No doubt based upon representation made to it by an employee of the Los Angeles Chamber of Commerce, our Department assigned to this district a force of immigrant inspectors under the supervision of Supervisor Watkins and detailed this staff to deportation work. This fact was discussed in the public press and to all appearances added color to the exaggerated statements that had therefore appeared. The fact of the matter is that the total result of the activities of the Immigration Service in this district amounted to practically nothing when compared with the thousands upon thousands of Mexican aliens who have been literally scared out of Southern California through the combination of circumstances above recited. The word "deportation" has been used as applicable to all of those departures and when that word is used, to the ordinary mind, it spells immigration, and therefore the Immigration Service activity is now being looked upon as the actual cause for the repatriation of these thousands of Mexicans when the real responsible parties, if any there be, are the Los Angeles Chamber of Commerce and other agencies above mentioned.

As to the alleged separation of families by this Service, or in fact by any one, I may say that I do not believe there is any foundation in fact. While I of course do not know all that took place in the activities which were conducted by Supervisor Watkins, and no doubt he could best speak in that regard, still from what I did observe I can say with certainty that while from time to time it may have become necessary to deport aliens from families, the other members of which were United States citizens or aliens not subject to deportation, still this was not and never has been by any means an every day occurrence nor have the heartless, inhumane methods depicted in the article quoted ever been resorted to. I believe I am right in asserting that in every instance, wherein actually aggravated circumstances were not present, voluntary departure has been permitted, thus rendering reentry possible. Wives have not been torn from their husbands. Children have not been separated from their mothers. I refer particularly to really legal marriages and actual relationship but may say further that even where less formal and sometimes actually illegal relationships have been found to exist still, in many instances, the privilege of voluntary departure has been accorded.

To sum up, the basic cause for the movement of Mexicans out of the United States has been lack of employment and this movement has been accentuated through fear created by agencies not in any way connected with the Government service and over which the Government of the United States has no actual control. The activities of the Immigration Service in this district have been carried on in exactly the same manner as has always been in vogue. Nothing of the spectacular has been injected into the work by the officers of this Service. The only spectacular features have been the result of an effort on the part of local authorities to substantiate claims which had been made to our Department as to the number of aliens in this community actually subject to deportation and what they could do to assist us in deporting them.

7

"Repatriation From Michigan"

John L. Zurbrick

This office has received a request from the Governor of the State of Michigan, the Honorable Wilber M. Brucker, that we co-operate with the state welfare commissioner in the handling of a number of citizens of Mexico who are desirous of leaving the State of Michigan for the purpose of taking up their homes in the Republic of Mexico. Practically all of these Mexicans are subjects of public welfare, and through a local Mexican artist, Diego Rivera, a society known as the League of Mexican Workers and Peasants was formed for the purpose of making arrangements for the movement. Between 4,000 and 5,000 Mexicans have already signed petitions with this organization requesting that they be returned to Mexico. The association, through the local Mexican Consul, took up the matter with the Governor of the State of Michigan and also arranged with the Republic of Mexico and the twenty-eight states of the Republic for the repatriation of their nationals. The Mexican Government will meet the party or parties at Laredo and El Paso with special trains for the purpose of transporting them into the interior of Mexico. The state welfare commissioner has contacted the various political units of the State, the majority of whom have already signed agreements, as a result of which they will furnish the money for the transportation of these Mexicans at a rate of $15.00 per individual regardless of age, this rate to include railway transportation and food enroute. At the present time over 1,600 Mexicans have signed up with the organization, who are residents of the City of Detroit, as desiring to take advantage of the arrangments. Saginaw, Port Huron, Flint, Mt. Pleasant, Blissfield, Grand Rapids and several other smaller municipalities have all entered the agreement to do their share toward furnishing the funds.

It is expected that a number of Mexicans will be found who are subject to voluntary departure or deportable but at the request of the Mexican Consul the deportation feature has been kept very much in the background and the voluntary removal under the Act of 1917 stressed in order that the Mexicans may not get the idea that this is a deportation movement. This office has assigned one of our inspectors to accompany the state inspector in order that in making a check up he may secure information of any removal or deportable cases. It is felt that if there is an initial movement of 4,000 to 5,000 that the number will increase after the first train has departed, in order that the Mexicans may see that the idea has been worked out to a practical end. It is felt by the writer that, if possible, the Bureau and Department should enter wholeheartedly into this movement and extend the Governor of the State of Michigan all of the co-operation that is possible under the scope of the authority of the

---

Memo from John L. Zurbrick (District Director of Immigration, Detroit District) to Commissioner General of Immigration, October 20, 1932, National Archives, Record Group 85, File No. 55784/585.

Bureau, for the elimination of such a large number of alien laborers and mechanics will work a tremendous benefit not only to the economic situation in the State of Michigan insofar as it concerns the welfare expenditures but will remove from the economic field a group that for some unknown reason is able to get first consideration in employment in the industries of this country and by their removal the openings in industry will be left for residents and citizens of the United States; in fact, one of the large automobile industries has already gone on record as saying that it will give preference to United States citizens in all cases where Mexican mechanics and laborers are removed from their payroll by reason of this repatriation movement.

At a meeting of the representatives of the various railway companies, comprising the central passenger association, tentative plans were laid for the extension of the cheap rates to February or March first in order that these movements may secure the benefits accruing thereunder. Some discussion was had with reference to the supervision of the movement, insofar as its being fed and handled under sanitary conditions is concerned, but no concrete decision was arrived at, as the matter must be taken up with the western passenger association which will meet in Chicago Friday, the 21st, and a committee will report back some time next week. It was suggested by one of the representatives of a transportation company that the Secretary of Labor might have authority to arrange for the supervision of these special trains from the viewpoint of it being an alien movement. The writer feels that this can be done if removal or deportation cases are joined in the party but consideration requested concerning the assignment of an officer to accompany the train in the event no deportation or removal cases are joined thereto. The expense would be minor as the inspector would travel on free transportation.

It is believed that this is the first concerted movement of this type that has been organized in the United States, although for the last year whenever our Service has sent Mexican deportees, in most instances welfare cases have been joined to the party. The state welfare agent remarked yesterday that he believed that approximately 1500 had been sent out of the State since the first of last January under those circumstances. If this movement proves to be a success, there is no doubt but that it will be taken up by adjoining states and possibly may also result in the same system being used to remove indigent Europeans who are not deportable. For instance, the county welfare department has taken up with this office just recently the matter of co-operation in arranging, if possible, for the shipping of approximately 1,500 public charge cases who became such by reason of the depression who are now being lodged at county expense in one of the public institutions adjoining the City of Detroit.

Every effort is being made to make this initial movement a success in order that the idea may spread to other communities and result in a movement of a large number of aliens being removed from the United States, thereby increasing the opportunities for work of the American citizen, and it is earnestly recommended that an intensive study be made of the matter in order that advice can be given just how far the Bureau and Department can go along the line of cooperation.

8

"Mexican Consul Agrees to Repatriation of Detroit Mexicans"

Ignacio L. Batiza

The group called the "League of Mexican Workers and Peasants" having initiated a movement with the objective of accomplishing the return to Mexico of our nationals resident in the United States who desire to return there, has made representations conducive to this end to the Governments of both countries.

The Mexican Consul in Detroit issues a call to all the Mexican residents in this region, without distinction as to their beliefs, and who are desirous of repatriating themselves, that they take advantage of the opportunity presented them by this said Group with the least possible delay. He (the Mexican Consul) advises, as he has been informed by the Secretary of [Foreign] Relations, that for our Government the repatriation of organized groups of persons is easier than with isolated individuals.

As winter approaches, life in this region becomes more and more difficult for persons without work. All of the circumstances which produce the crisis still prevail without possible hope of amelioration in the near

---

Ignacio L. Batiza (Consul for Mexico), Communication entitled "To The Mexican Colony," October 13, 1932, National Archives, Record Group 85, File No. 55784/585.

future; for which reason this Consulate reiterates its call to our Mexican residents that for their own interest they accept this opportunity which is offered them by the Government of Mexico for their repatriation and return to our country. The Mexican Government, within its power, is disposed to aid these repatriates that they may later make themselves important factors in our national economic structure.

9

"Mexican Repatriation During the Great Depression"

George Kiser and David Silverman

Introduction

Throughout most of this century, large numbers of Mexican job-seekers have entered the United States. Most settled in the Southwest, yet the Midwest and other regions increasingly attracted the new arrivals.[1] Although most worked in agriculture, the Mexicans were employed in a broad spectrum of jobs, including skilled ones in commerce and industry.[2]

International migrations of workers are not unusual,[3] yet the Mexican movement is distinguished by the large numbers of migrants involved. Perhaps unequalled anywhere else on earth, it is unfortunate that few scholars have paid serious attention to the coming and going of these Mexican workers. However, the arrival of these people in the United States has attracted more study than has the departure of many who have returned to Mexico.

This selection is concerned with the exodus of Mexicans during the Great Depression. Although they had never left the United States in such large numbers, the event failed to stimulate the scholarly interest which it

---

George Kiser and David Silverman, "Mexican Repatriation During the Great Depression," *Journal of Mexican American History* 3 (1973): 139–64. Reprinted by permission of the editors of the *Journal of Mexican American History*.

deserved. In 1933, Bogardus called for the study of many aspects of this repatriation.[4] Yet, it remains seriously under-studied four decades later. Abraham Hoffman, one of the few scholars to study Mexican repatriation seriously, wrote in 1972 that most aspects of the exodus "have been unexplored, neglected, omitted, or over-simplified."[5]

Because the repatriation movement has been studied so little, there is a great need for filling in even elementary facts.[6] This essay represents a modest effort in that direction. Among other sources, we have relied on records in the National Archives. While this information needs to be made more accessible, we acknowledge its obvious limitation. Official records may gloss over or ignore facts embarrassing to the government.

Mexican repatriation during the Great Depression has been studied so little that any generalizations about it could be dismissed as unjustified.[7] Yet, we believe that it is the responsibility of the researcher to suggest some explanatory order for the events which he discusses. However, our generalizations are offered tentatively and for the purpose of inviting further investigation.

The following section presents historical background relevant to understanding repatriation during the Great Depression. Then the exodus is discussed in terms of common justifications, interests supporting and opposing repatriation, the role of the Hoover Administration and other participants in the repatriation movement, the departure of Mexicans from two American cities, and the fate of the repatriates. The essay ends with a brief summary and conclusions.

Historical Background

Long before 1929, various interacting factors led to a substantial accumulation of Mexican labor in the United States.[8] The northward flow of people was encouraged by the lack of sharp geographical and cultural barriers at the border.[9] Poverty in Mexico and the revolutionary violence beginning in 1910 stimulated large numbers of Mexicans to leave their country. The contrasting peace and economic prosperity of the United States attracted them to come here.

During the late nineteenth and early twentieth centuries, irrigation and other innovations encouraged the development of huge vegetable and fruit farms in the American Southwest. The owners of these farms often preferred the poverty-ridden Mexicans to citizen labor. Accustomed to a feudalistic system in Mexico, the immigrants were often willing to work for less than their American competitors. Growers not infrequently commented that Mexican workers were preferred because they "knew their place." Contributing to the willingness of the immigrants to work long hours for low pay was the fact that many had entered the country illegally and could always be threatened with deportation and return to the hardships from which they had fled.

Until the 1920s there was widespread sympathy for a more or less open border with Mexico. Although immigration laws had been passed there was little effort to enforce them against the northward flow of Mexicans. One reason for the very lax enforcement of the laws was the substantial political influence of the employers of Mexican workers and the relative powerlessness of their American competitors.

It is important to note that sentiment against Mexican immigration did not spring exclusively from conditions of the Great Depression but had been growing since the mid-1920s. Annual efforts were made in Congress to limit rigidly the number of Mexicans who could immigrate to the United States by placing Mexico under the so-called "quota system." As a result of the increasingly nationalistic mood springing from the World War I era, Congress had passed legislation in 1921 and 1924 assigning quotas, or upper limits, for the number of immigrants who could enter each year from different countries. However, various political interests led by employers of Mexican labor succeeded in having Western Hemisphere nations exempted from the requirements of the quota system. Consequently, no limit was placed on the number of immigrants from Mexico so long as they could meet requirements of the general immigration laws such as the ban on illiterates.

The National Archives contain many letters, written before the onset of the Great Depression in October 1929, demanding that the national government do something about the presence of large numbers of Mexicans in the United States. For example, in March 1928, a man from California wrote to the U.S. Commissioner of Immigration:

> For years California has been flooded with white labor and no jobs and at the present time there are thousands of white laborers begging for employment.

The same letter charged that many ranchers in California would hire only Mexicans because they would work cheaper than Americans who "walk the streets hungry."[10]

In December 1928, a letter from southern California to the Secretary of Labor charged that because Mexicans would work for less, "thousands of our American boys that come here with the expectation of getting a job walk out with nothing . . ."[11] Federal officials received many other letters which made the same point.

Even before Herbert Hoover was elected, President Coolidge inaugurated policy changes to cope with these growing demands. His solution was administrative rather than legislative, and it took two forms. First, the Border Patrol stepped up its activities and more Mexicans were apprehended. Secondly, in August 1928, the American consulate in Mexico was instructed to reduce the number of visas issued.[12]

The Depression and Repatriation

The Exclusionist Rationale

Opposition to Mexican immigration increased markedly with the onset of the Depression in October 1929. Many letters and telegrams demanding a solution were sent to the federal government in Washington. Three main themes predominated.

The first theme was job-oriented and blamed American unemployment on the Mexicans. In September of 1932, a letter to the Chief Immigration Inspector in Los Angeles claimed that "there are hundreds of Mexican laborers working in our local and nearby walnut groves . . . while not one American . . ." The writer claimed to have talked to Americans who were denied jobs with the explanation that only Mexicans were being hired.[13]

A letter dated March 4, 1930, from Portland, Oregon, asked the Commissioner-General of Immigration:

> Can we not send back the thousands of Mexicans and give the American working men a chance to make an honest living? It would stop a great deal of want . . . many families are hungry because they cannot get work . . .[14]

From Palms, California, a letter dated February 1930, spoke of "the seriousness of the labor situation here, due to unrestricted Mexican immigration."[15]

A second theme of letters received by the national government expressed opposition to Mexicans on a racial basis although other concerns might also be expressed. For example, a letter from Houston to the Immigration Department in March 1931, referred to the Mexicans as follows:

They are right here to take *white* labors [*sic*] place every time a job shows up . . . They do not let us work in Mexico and why should they be permitted to cut wages and take the bread out of our *white* childrens [*sic*] mouths.[16] [Emphasis added]

Some of the letters emphasizing racial characteristics portrayed the whole problem in terms of civilization as opposed to barbarism. A contractor and builder from Superior, Arizona, explained his sense of alarm in a letter to President Hoover's secretary:

No one who does not live in this country can realize the social and moral ravages in a white civilization made by such a horde of semibarbarous Indians . . .

Do we wish to re-convey to Mexican barbarism . . . and thereby submerge and . . . destroy for all time, white civilization . . .?[17]

The third type of letter spoke of the possibility of rebellion against the government if it failed to provide jobs for Americans by expelling the Mexicans. A letter from California in the fall of 1932 expressed anger that Mexicans held jobs while American citizens were unable to find work:

Such situations make Americans see red and damn the administration, and its [*sic*] no wonder we hear bolshevik talk on all sides.

Personally I hope no such conditions ever prevail in America, but it seems to me that business men had better wake up to the fact that in their small, merciless, cold blooded grasping for the last dollar they are driving Americans to desperation. Do they realize that some American legion members are openly talking rebellion against our government and urging working men can and should take over all business by force and bloodshed if necessary?[18]

Another letter from California complained of foreigners holding jobs while Americans were hungry and unemployed. The writer continued: "Starvation will cause a number of our good citizens to lean toward the Reds."[19]

Exclusionist Forces

During the Depression, much of the American press aligned itself against Mexican immigration, called for the deportation of illegal aliens, or pressed both positions at the same time. Swept up in the movement were publications ranging from the local level to those with a national reputation and circulation.

On May 5, 1930, the *Arizona Silver Belt* editorialized that "We need our jobs for our own people." It called for legislation to stop immigration from Mexico.[20] *World's Work*, a periodical published by Doubleday, charged that Mexican workers were "colored," that they were of low morals, and that they had "the revengeful instinct of the savage."[21] Even respected scholarly journals such as *Current History* raised racial objections to Mexican immigration.[22]

Numerous political interest groups joined the movement to restrict or terminate Mexican immigration. They included such organizations as:

The American Federation of Labor
The American Legion
The California Joint Immigration Committee
The Immigration Restriction League[23]
Lions Club of Los Angeles[24]
East Los Angeles Republican Club
Georgia Federation of Labor[25]
American Eugenics Society[26]
Mission Canyon Chapter of D.A.R. (Santa Barbara)[27]

Various units of state and local government also joined the movement to curtail or end Mexican immigration. Arizona passed legislation requiring that at least 80 percent of the workers in any occupation must be American citizens; the United States Supreme Court held the law to be unconstitutional.[28]

In 1930, the Arizona legislature passed a resolution supporting the so-called Box Bill which was designed to place Mexico under the quota system.[29] The resolution charged that "Mexican peons . . . are in direct competition with American men and women, thus making beggars and tramps of many of our native-born citizens because of an oversupply of labor . . ." It went on to charge that Mexicans were hired in Arizona "at wages which permit of the purchase only of the bare necessities for a temporary existence, thus filling our town and cities during the greater portion of the year with a large and growing army of unemployed, who drain our charities, fill our penal institutions, and many of whom are afflicted with infectious and loathsome diseases, and thousands of whom are saturated with Bolshevik doctrines, thus become an actual menace and danger to our institutions and Government . . ."[30] Various other state legislatures, including those of California, Oregon, and Georgia, also passed resolutions calling on Congress to enact legislation limiting immigration from Mexico.[31]

Hoffman notes that Las Animas County's (Colorado) sheriff set up a roadblock at the New Mexico-Colorado border and refused to permit migrant workers (apparently those which he thought were "Mexicans") to enter the county. Others who had already entered were put "back across the state line into New Mexico, where they were left to their own devices as to matters of food and shelter."[32] In 1936, Ed Johnson, Governor of Colorado, called out the National Guard to bar migrant workers from coming into the state.[33]

Pro-Mexican Interests

Although less numerous than the restrictionists, there were organizations and individuals who opposed efforts to repatriate the Mexicans. Foremost among these were growers and other employers who used Mexican labor. Some of the literature gives the misleading impression that when the Depression arrived, employers no longer had any use for Mexican labor so they joined the exclusionist forces. For example, Bogardus wrote:

> In times of prosperity Mexican immigrants have been "invited" by large scale employing concerns to come to the United States. They have come, furnishing an alleged "cheap labor" supply. In times of depression when they are no longer an economic asset but a liability, they are sent back to their native communities . . .[34]

Although there may have been such cases, the predominant pattern was apparently one of consistency on the part of employers; even in the depths of the Depression, they continued their historical opposition to restricting the flow of Mexican labor in any way.

Both before and after October 1929, federal officials received numerous letters and telegrams from growers warning that any reduction of Mexican labor would have serious consequences. At its annual meeting in 1929, the California Farm Bureau Federation passed a resolution declaring that the farm labor shortage was growing worse and that farmers in that state were already suffering substantial crop losses.[35] In January 1930, the American Fruit and Vegetable Association declared that there was a serious shortage of common farm laborers in some parts of the United States and expressed fear that legislation curbing Mexican immigration would be enacted.[36] Similar resolutions were passed by the American Chamber of Commerce in May 1930,[37] and the Arizona Cattle Growers' Association in February 1930.[38]

Some elements of the mass media spoke out against efforts to reduce the Mexican labor supply. The publisher of the *Los Angeles Times* was particularly outspoken.[39] In May 1930, an article in *The Review of Reviews* claimed that:

> There will be a serious shortage of harvest labor this summer, unemployment in cities notwithstanding. Labor was short last fall.[40] They [the Mexican immigrants] did not displace other farm labor. On the contrary, they created new jobs for white men because without the Mexican seasonal worker, the great expansion of southwestern agriculture would have been impossible.[41]

In February 1930, a *New York Times* editorial expressed reservations about the congressional effort to restrict Mexican immigration. The paper claimed that patrolling the Mexican border effectively was almost impossible. It also expressed the belief that Mexican labor was probably needed in the Southwest.[42]

In the April 1930, issue of *Survey Graphic*, Robert McLean raised questions about the justice of the effort to rid the country of illegal Mexicans. He noted that these people had done much of the hard work necessary to make the American Southwest prosper, and that so long as they were needed "we forgot our own immigration laws." However, with the coming of the Depression, they faced expulsion and hardship although "most of them have been conscious of doing no wrong . . ."[43]

Not surprisingly, some of the most vigorous opposition to restricting Mexican immigration and repatriation came from Mexico. By the time of the Depression, she was only beginning to recover from the destructiveness of the Revolution. Immigration to the United States had served as a safety valve to drain off some of the most poverty-ridden population. Just when recovery was already seriously threatened by the arrival of the Depression, Mexico's economy was unprepared for absorbing large numbers of returnees.

The Mexico City press was particularly outspoken. On May 28, 1930, *Excélsior* wrote that Mexican workers were needed in southwestern agriculture and that new restrictive immigration laws would harm relations between Mexico and the United States.[44] *La Prensa* editorialized that if Congress acted to curtail Mexican immigration, Mexico should boycott all American products.[45]

Perhaps the most bitter comments came from the Mexico City newspaper *El Universal*. It called the proposed legislation for placing Mexico under the quota system a "policy of economic conquest by the United States of the weaker peoples of the American continent." It went on to charge:

> We consider that the Americans . . . have no right to . . . deny us entry into their country after having taken without pity the last ounce of energy of hundreds of thousands of our compatriots who contributed with their strength, their health and even their blood to cementing that superb structure of North American prosperity from which they obtained not even a modest benefit.[46]

Hoover Administration Policy Toward Mexican Immigration

Although the policy of the Hoover administration toward "the Mexican problem" contained unique elements, it was partly a continuation of policies established by the previous administration. On March 5, 1928, Coolidge's Secretary of State had testified before a Senate committee against legislation which would have extended the quota system to Latin America. He claimed that the proposed law would harm United States relations with these countries which in turn would seriously undermine American business interests in Latin America.[47]

The Hoover administration also opposed extension of the quota system to Latin America.[48] As we have seen, the Coolidge government preferred to control Mexican immigration by reducing the number of visas issued. The Hoover administration continued this basic policy. However, the president ordered an even more rigid curtailment of Mexican visas as an unemployment measure. In September, 1930, the State Department, acting in his name, directed American consuls in Mexico to increase the rate at which visas were being denied.[49]

The decision of the Hoover administration to control Mexican immigration through denying visas rather than through congressional extension of the quota system was important. Congressional changes in the law are likely to be more permanent whereas mere changes in administration of the law leave the executive branch more room to make policy immediately responsive to changing conditions. Had Congress extended the quota system to Mexico, these administrative options would have been closed. As it happened, all efforts to include Mexico under the quota system failed.

Executive discretion was desirable to the Hoover administration because of its need to satisfy two major political interests which were vehemently opposed to the quota solution. First was the Mexican government. While it expressed understanding of the American need to cope with widespread unemployment during the Depression, it opposed the quota system as a threat to the increasingly friendly relations between the two countries.[50] Cutting immigration through visa denials was preferable because it was less likely to be permanent and this administrative policy could be readily reversed once the economic conditions prompting it had ended.

Apparently one reason for Hoover's opposition to the quota system so disliked in Mexico was his interest in bettering relations with the Latin American countries. Bryce Wood notes that through a number of policy changes between 1928 and 1933, the president was successful in improving the United States image in Latin America.[51] This priority was simply inconsistent with support for "permanently" limiting Mexican immigration through the quota system.

The visa solution was also preferred by southwestern growers, a second important political interest. While not wanting to lose their Mexican labor, doing so through presidential action left more hope for a rapid reversal once the economic emergency had passed.

The third major political interest to which the administration had to respond was the increasingly vocal group calling for rigid control over Mexican immigration. By drastically reducing the number of visas issued, the Hoover administration was able to give the impression that the immediate goal of quota supporters had been achieved without the dangers involved in that solution.

In summary, the administration found a partial solution to the "Mexican problem" which was more or less acceptable to all three of the most involved political interests: southwestern growers, the Mexican government, and American exclusionists. Although the quota solution would have pleased most of the latter, it would have been bitterly resented by the former two. The administration appears to have maximized its political standing by responding to the rapidly increasing pressure of the exclusionists while not irreparably harming its relations with the growers or with the Mexican government.

The solution of the Hoover administration, however, suffered from one serious shortcoming. It did not deal with the problem of the large number of Mexicans who had already entered the United States illegally. Although some deportations were based on the deportation act of March 4, 1929,[52] massive expulsions by the federal government would certainly have led to serious setbacks in United States-Mexican relations. However, the unfolding of events enabled the Hoover administration to accomplish the equivalent of massive deportations while appearing to be practically uninvolved in the exodus of Mexicans. There was obviously political capital in this solution. Expulsion of the Mexicans reduced political opposition from the exclusionists, yet pro-Mexican groups found it difficult to clearly pin-point blame on the national government.

The Decentralized Nature of Repatriation

During the Great Depression, many of the Mexicans left the United States under pressure from local welfare departments. Relief rolls had increased dramatically while tax bases shrank. The rapidly reached conclusion in many areas was that returning the Mexicans to Mexico was the answer. Although it was widely believed that they were taking all the jobs from unemployed Americans, many charged that the Mexicans had swollen the welfare rolls. Assuming that the Mexican nationals were on relief, many local governments simply calculated the welfare payments for all resident Mexicans for a year, estimated the amount it would cost to provide them free transportation to the border, and concluded that repatriation would bring large savings. It was also widely believed that short-term alien laborers had no right to receive welfare.[53] Also, some state and local governments prohibited aliens from working on relief type projects. Examples were the California state government and various city and county governments within that state.[54] An apparently common pattern was for welfare officials to notify Mexicans that they must agree to return to Mexico or their relief checks would be terminated.[55] Further pressure to leave was the frequent offer of free transportation to the Mexican border.[56] A diverse assortment of municipal, county, and state governments sought to pressure immigration authorities to deport summarily large numbers of Mexicans.[57]

The role of private citizens in getting Mexicans to leave should not be underestimated. In Los Angeles, the District Director of Immigration stated in a memo written in June 1931:

> Taking advantage of this situation numbers of unscrupulous persons added their touch to the story [of deportations] and approached many Mexicans who were property owners and, further exaggerating stories of what was likely to take place, managed to swindle them

> out of their holdings, persuading them the best thing they could do would be to return to Mexico.[58]
>
> Through a whispering campaign which gathered strength as time went on . . . the Mexican population was lead to believe, in many instances, that Mexicans were not wanted in California and that all would be deported whether they were legally here or not.[59]

The Hoover administration deemphasized the deportation aspect of repatriation. Apparently it decided that there was enough pressure at the state and local levels to accomplish the task, so it could appear to stand relatively aloof. Also, Mexican officials asked the American government to make possible voluntary repatriation even for wetbacks. The request was probably motivated by the realization that the exodus was inevitable and that those who left "voluntarily" would probably be in a better position to return to the United States once the Depression had ended.

Two Case Studies

One of the problems in generalizing about the repatriation movement is that it apparently varied extensively from area to area in terms of motivation, initiation, the role of various levels of government, and other factors. We believe that case studies of repatriation from specific cities, counties, and states are greatly needed. Although in-depth studies are not possible here, some brief illustrations from the cases of California and Michigan follow.

The greatest concentration of Mexicans in California was in the Los Angeles area. Shortly after the onset of the Depression, various organizations in that city sought to involve the federal government in the "Mexican problem." In April 1930, the Lions Club of Los Angeles wired the congressman representing that area:

> We have more Mexicans in Los Angeles County than we can take care of now. The burden on Los Angeles County for Mexican charity is tremendous. Thousands out of work here now.[60]

In February 1931, the Los Angeles County Welfare Department sought to reach an agreement with the Mexican government whereby the Department would pay the transportation costs of repatriates to the border from where Mexico would transport them to their homes in Mexico. According to records in the National Archives, local officials hoped that not only many illegal aliens could be repatriated by this means but also that many "undeportable aliens" would choose to take advantage of free transportation.[61]

Also during February, other organizations and officials were intent upon solving the "Mexican problem" in the Los Angeles area. The supervisor of the local immigration office met with the sheriff, the chief of police, the District Director of Immigration and the coordinator of the local Citizens' Committee on Unemployment Relief. The Citizens' Committee apparently took the initiative at the meeting. It proposed that immigration authorities apprehend a token number of Mexicans with calculated and dramatic publicity. This "example" was expected to frighten great numbers of aliens into leaving the United States without the necessity for deportation proceedings. According to records in the National Archives, both the local and national officials present wanted to take a more correct and restrained approach without publicity. They proposed that careful investigations determine the deportable and that the law be enforced without fanfare. The sheriff and police chief pledged that they would aid in apprehending deportable Mexicans who would be turned over to the immigration authorities.[62]

Within a few days, the immigration authorities in cooperation with Los Angeles law enforcement officials had questioned several thousand "Mexicans" to determine their immigration status. After the first two weeks, the number apprehended began to decline as newspapers dramatized the events and other aliens learned of them by word-of-mouth.[63]

In addition to these deportations, arrangements were made for "voluntary repatriation" from the Los Angeles area and other sections of California. In *Southern California Country*, Carey McWilliams reports that Los Angeles County paid the transportation charges for repatriates leaving there. He notes that the Southern Pacific Railroad received $14.70 for each passenger.[64] In April 1931, the *New York Times* reported that transportation charges were being paid by "various organizations seeking to relieve unemployment."[65]

In Los Angeles, a local relief organization named *Comité Mexicano de Beneficencia* was actively involved in channeling requests for repatriation to the proper authorities.[66] Also playing an important role in the exodus was the Mexican government. Undoubtedly its commitment to care for the repatriates upon their arrival in Mexico played some part in stimulating the movement.[67]

Various sources have described the organized movement of Mexicans out of Los Angeles and other areas of California. McWilliams has written:

> I watched the first shipment of "repatriated" Mexicans leave Los Angeles in February, 1931. The loading process began at six o'clock in the morning. "Repatriados" arrived by the truckload—men, women, and children—with dogs, cats, and goats; half-open suitcases, rolls of bedding, and lunchbaskets.[68]

Apparently many of the repatriates from California did not channel their return through local officials and did not ask for any kind of assistance. Some simply left by automobile. In April 1931, the *New York Times* reported that "immigration authorities report hundreds of automobiles with Mexican occupants and their meager belongings crossing the line at various highway points on the border."[69]

Diverse factors caused these people to return to Mexico. The *Times* reported that "arrests by [immigration] agents have terrified the Mexicans. They dread being sent to jail."[70] Another factor was growing anti-Mexican sentiment in California as indicated by the so-called Bliss bill, which would have required the segregation of Mexican children in the public school system. Also, various employers began denying employment to Mexicans.[71]

The *New York Times* called attention to the suffering which repatriation from California was causing:

> In their hasty migration . . . Mexican families often make considerable sacrifices in real and personal property to obtain money for traveling. In scores of cases equities in homes have been transferred for little return, household and personal effects have been sold for small change and meager savings of years used.[72]

Upon leaving California in 1931, some of the Mexicans simply left their property behind receiving nothing for it.[73]

Although statistics on repatriation from California vary, Meier and Rivera report that on the average a trainload of Mexicans was sent from Los Angeles each month during the 1931–1933 period. The authors estimate that some 50,000 to 75,000 were repatriated from California in 1932. Approximately 35,000 of the repatriates lived in Los Angeles County.[74]

McWilliams reports that some of the returnees did not stay long in Mexico but returned to the Los Angeles area:

> . . . When the harvest season once again came around, the growers dispatched their "emissaries" to Mexico, and again recruited thousands of Mexicans. Many Mexicans have been "repatriated" two and three times, going through this same curious cycle of entry, work, repatriation.[75]

Another state with substantial repatriation was Michigan. As in the California case, the Mexican government was actively involved. Although many of the Mexicans had entered the United States illegally, Mexico requested American immigration authorities to minimize the deportation aspect. The theme suggested was "voluntary removal."

Secondly, the Mexican government encouraged an *organized* return to Mexico. The explanation given by the Mexican consul in Detroit was "that for our Government the repatriation of organized groups of persons is easier than with isolated individuals." On October 13, 1932, he appealed to "the Mexican colony" to return to Mexico:

> As winter approaches, life in this region becomes more and more difficult for persons without work. All of the circumstances which produce the crisis still prevail without possible hope of amelioration in the near future for which reason this Consulate reiterates its call to our Mexican residents that for their own interest they accept this opportunity which is offered them by the Government of Mexico for their repatriation and return to our country. The Mexican Government, within its power, is disposed to aid these repatriates that they may later make themselves important factors in our national economic structure.[76]

A local Mexican organization in Detroit took much of the initiative for encouraging Mexicans to accept repatriation. Spearheaded by renowned Mexican artist, Diego Rivera, the organization was called the League of Mexican Workers and Peasants. Through the Mexican consul in Detroit, the League arranged the repatriation movement with Mexico's government and each of her state governmnts. The Mexican government agreed to furnish trains to meet the returnees at Laredo and El Paso and return them to the interior of Mexico. It encouraged persons desiring repatriation to register with the League.

In Michigan, the state government played a role in repatriation. It was primarily one of coordination. Michigan's governor, Wilber M. Brucker served as a kind of mediator between the Immigration Service and state and local officials. He took the initiative in approaching the immigration authorities to cooperate with the state's commissioner of welfare.

Michigan's welfare commissioner urged local governments to sign agreements to pay transportation expenses to the Mexican border for returnees from their respective communities. By October 20, 1932, the funding agreement had been signed by officials in Grand Rapids, Port Huron, Saginaw, Flint, Blissfield, Mt. Pleasant, and several smaller towns.

Although on various occasions, immigration officials claimed to have played almost no role in the repatriation effort, a memo from the Detroit District Director of Immigration to the Commissioner-General suggests that they were eager to cooperate:

> It is felt by the writer that, if possible, the Bureau . . . should enter wholeheartedly into this movement and extend the Governor of . . . Michigan all of the co-operation that is possible under the scope of the authority of the Bureau, for the elimination of such a large number of alien laborers and mechanics will work a tremendous benefit not only to the economic situation in . . . Michigan insofar as it concerns the welfare expenditures, but will remove from the economic field a group that . . . is able to get first consideration in employment . . . and by their removal the openings in industry will be left for residents and citizens of the United States.[77]

The most vocal opponent of repatriation from Detroit was an organization named the International Labor Defense. It distributed Spanish-language circulars in Mexican areas of the city. Although undated, most of the pamphlets were apparently distributed in late November or early December 1932. They charged that most of the Mexicans living in Michigan had been brought there by the automobile industry "so that they might work . . . at the least possible salary."

Noting that the repatriates had been promised land, agricultural tools, and food by Mexico, the circular charged that "this lie is evident. Actually in that fatherland thousands of workers will die of hunger." The pamphlets charged further that families were being broken up as Mexican members were deported while close relatives of American citizenship remained. The organization charged that it had asked for the trains' itinerary but was told that it was classified. The pamphlet continued:

> We must oppose this exploiting project of the rich to abandon thousands of Mexicans to die of hunger. . . . The American Government exploited the Mexicans and the duty of giving them an opportunity to live actually lies with it. . . . This is only a part of the capitalistic system to deceive and terrorize the workers . . . UNITE, WORKERS, OF ALL RACES TO STRUGGLE AGAINST OUR EXPLOITERS! Unite with us![78]

The first group of repatriates left Michigan by train on November 15, 1932. It consisted of 442 persons, only two of whom were deportees. Although the trip was financed by Michigan municipalities, an inspector from the U.S. Immigration Service went along "for the purpose of seeing that the persons were taken care of en route."[79]

In a series of articles, the *Detroit Times* detailed the events of repatriation. The Great Depression had brought massive unemployment to the Mexicans, and a repatriate was quoted as saying that "there was nothing else we could do." The Mexican government was concerned about them, and it had allotted 10,000 acres of land for the repatriates in Nuevo León. Although apparently sympathetic with the alleged need for repatriation, the *Times* did not appear to be anti-Mexican. One picture depicted children crying as they were taken from school and their friends to be returned to Mexico.[80]

Immigration inspectors accompanying the trains to the border filed reports with the District Director of Immigration in Detroit. An inspector, Gangewere, reported that the American trains moved across the border to Nuevo Laredo where Mexican health officials inoculated the returnees. They were then unloaded and the train returned to the United States. His report on a Saginaw-to-Laredo trip indicated that the Mexicans were well treated en route. He noted that they were well fed, children received milk whenever they wanted, and special arrangements were made for the comfort of invalids.

Gangewere acknowledged that some of the Mexicans were taken to Nuevo Laredo against their will, although the repatriation was supposedly voluntary. About a dozen of the returnees changed their minds about repatriation en route and asked to be permitted to leave the train in San Antonio. Railroad officials claimed that they were unauthorized to grant permission. Gangewere's report noted that two young Mexican men leaped from the train windows at Laredo and could not be found until the following morning.[81]

Inspector Harry Yeager filed a report on a trainload of repatriates which left Detroit on November 15, 1932, for Nuevo Laredo. In addition to himself, the returnees were accompanied by a representative of the office of the Mexican Consulate. Yeager reported that the Detroit Department of Welfare hired a medical doctor to go on the train "owing to the fact that several of these Mexicans were taken from the hospitals or had been removed from the hospitals shortly before this trip . . ."[82] Events such as this and the refusal of railroad officials to permit the departure of passengers in San Antonio cast doubt on the official claims of the immigration authorities that the repatriation was "voluntary."

In a report dated November 23, 1932, John Zurbrick, District Director of Immigration, Detroit District, described another of the rail trips from

Michigan to the Mexican border. Of 430 repatriates, only two were deportation cases. In addition to ten passenger cars, the train pulled four baggage cars to accommodate material possessions of the returnees. Zurbrick noted that the railroad interpreted "baggage" quite liberally as illustrated by the fact that one repatriate took along three barber chairs.[83]

Some of these reports indicate that the Mexican government did not completely honor its commitments to the repatriates. As the Mexican Consulate in Detroit had encouraged the people to return to Mexico, it had promised them comfortable transportation from the border to their destinations. However, in his report of November 23, 1932, Zurbrick expressed concern about "information" or "rumors" concerning the first trainload of returnees to pass through the Laredo Port of Entry. He explained that he had heard that "on arrival at the Mexican side the engine was cut off and the people required to remain on the train all night without light or heat and that no arrangements were made by the Mexican National Railways to furnish food the next day and that they were sent to the interior of Mexico in box cars."

Zurbrick's report frankly acknowledged his reason for concern about the alleged mistreatment of the repatriates:

> If this promise [of good treatment by Mexico] has been carried out, it is felt that there will be a large number of applications for repatriation following these two movements, but in the event that rumors are correct, it is not believed that there will be any further applications to any great extent.[84]

The Mexican Consulate advised the American Immigration Service that due to a storm the train in question had arrived in Nuevo Laredo some nine hours behind schedule. According to the Consulate, this unanticipated development had indeed disrupted the plans for dispatching the repatriates immediately and comfortably to their destination. However, it assured United States officials that the problem would not reoccur.[85]

We have briefly outlined some of the details of repatriation from Michigan and California. The two cases share obvious similarities such as involvement by the Mexican government, the interest of local welfare departments, and the cooperation of the immigration authorities. However, our information suggests some possible differences. In Michigan, state officials appear to have played a more significant role than was the case in California. The movement from California appears to have been more decentralized, perhaps because of the proximity to Mexico and the relative ease with which the repatriates could independently leave the United States.

Our limited information suggests that the role of semi-vigilante groups such as the Citizens' Committee in Los Angeles may have been of less significance in the exodus of Mexicans from Michigan. For this reason and because repatriation from Michigan was more governmentally supervised, that movement appears to have been somewhat less inhumane than the exodus from California.

Summary

During the early 1930s, a variety of arguments urged repatriation of Mexicans living in the United States. The popularity of these arguments was primarily a result of economic crises during the Great Depression. Many Americans saw Mexicans as actual or potential competitors for scarce job opportunities. Economic crises stimulated many Americans to apply their belief in Mexican inferiority to racist arguments justifying Mexican deportation. Still another popular belief was the fear that American labor would be more inclined to bolshevism if public authorities did not take active measures to repatriate Mexicans. All these views can be found in letters from private persons to government officials and in the media of that era.

Though pro-deportation arguments and interests were widespread, there were less popular but powerful interests during the 1930s which opposed Mexican repatriation. Among the most formidable of these were the growers and ranchers of the southwestern states. Many of them saw repatriation as a threat to cheap and plentiful sources of Mexican labor for their ranches and farms. They continued their earlier opposition to curtailing Mexican immigration through extension of the quota system.

The Hoover administration modified governmental policies in response to the bitter conflict between groups supporting and opposing repatriation. Although it deported some Mexican nationals, the federal government maintained a low profile and permitted state and local governments great latitude in handling repatriation. Thus the process was a very decentralized one. The Hoover administration probably feared that intense and obvious involvement by the national government would alienate southwestern farming interests and would damage diplomatic and economic relations between the United States and Mexico.

It is very difficult to generalize about the repatriation of Mexicans in the 1930s because its administration was so decentralized. Our discussion of the exodus from Los Angeles and Detroit has suggested that important differences have occurred from one area to another. Before definitive conclusions can be reached, many more studies at the local level need to be made.

NOTES

1. Matt S. Meier and Feliciano Rivera, *The Chicanos: A History of Mexican Americans* (New York: Hill and Wang, 1972), p. 131.

2. "Increase of Mexican Labor in Certain Industries in the United States," *Monthly Labor Review*, 33 (January 1931): 81–83.

3. For example, workers tend to migrate from southern to northern Europe: "Guest Workers," *National Review*, 2 May 1967, p. 476. Workers also move from some countries to others within Latin America. See, for example, *Hispanic American Report*, January 1957, pp. 570–71.

4. Emory S. Bogardus, "Mexican Repatriates," *Sociology and Social Research*, 18 (1933): 175.

5. Abraham Hoffman, "Mexican Repatriation Statistics: Some Suggested Alternatives to Carey McWilliams," *Western Historical Quarterly*, 3 (1972): 404.

6. Hoffman makes this point in his article. He calls particularly for studies of repatriation from individual cities. *Ibid.*, pp. 391–404. Hoffman's Ph.D. dissertation also deals with Mexican repatriation: "The Repatriation of Mexican Nationals from the United States during the Great Depression," (University of California, Los Angeles, 1970). See also idem, *Unwanted Mexican Americans in the Great Depression: Repatriation Pressures*, 1929–1939 (Tucson: University of Arizona Press, 1974).

7. Hoffman claims that generalizations about repatriation are premature at this time. Idem, "Mexican Repatriation Statistics," p. 404.

8. Because one of the present authors has dealt with pre-1929 Mexican labor in the United States in another article, our coverage is brief. Much of the following information is from George C. Kiser, "Mexican-American Labor Before World War II," *Journal of Mexican American History*, 2 (1972): 122–34.

9. Carey McWilliams, *North from Mexico* (New York: Greenwood Press, 1968), p. 58.

10. Letter from M. D. Clay, 1 March 1928, National Archives (cited hereafter as N.A.), Record Group 85 (cited hereafter as R.G.), File #55639/616.

11. Letter from E. L. Baldwin, 6 December 1928, N.A., R.G. 85, File #55639/616A.

12. *Congressional Record*, 71st Congress, 1st Session, Part 3, (1929), p. 3368.

13. Letter from H. D. Beatty, 12 September 1932, N.A., R.G. 85, File #55639/616.

14. Letter from J. A. Latimer, N.A., R.G. 85, File #55639/616.

15. Letter from J. C. Krien, 4 February 1930, N.A., R.G. 85, File #55639/616.

16. Letter from W. G. Klien, 18 March 1931, N.A., R.G. 85, File #55639/616.

17. Letter from J. C. Brodie, 28 September 1930, N.A., R.G. 85, File #55639/616.

18. Letter from H. D. Beatty, 12 September 1932, to Office of Chief Immigration Inspector, Los Angeles, N.A., R.G. 85, File #55639/616.

19. Letter from Darrell W. Pabst, N.A., R.G. 85, File #55639/616.

20. *Congressional Record*, 71st Congress, 2nd Session, Part 8 (1930), p. 8748.

21. C. M. Goethe, "Peons Need Not Apply," *World's Work* 59 (1930): 48.

22. Remsen Crawford, "The Menace of Mexican Immigration," *Current History* (1930): 904.

23. Ibid., p. 902.

24. *Congressional Record,* 71st Congress, 2nd Session, Part 7 (1930), p. 6843.
25. Ibid. p. 7226.
26. Letter to President Hoover, 5 June 1930, N.A., R.G. 85, File #55639/616.
27. Letter to President Hoover, 14 March 1930, N.A., R.G. 85, File #55639/616.
28. *Congressional Record,* 71st Congress, 2nd Session, Part 7 (1930), p. 7226.
29. Ibid.
30. Ibid.
31. Ibid. p. 6843.
32. Abraham Hoffman, "The Trinidad Incident," *Journal of Mexican American History,* 2 (1972): 145.
33. Ibid. p. 148.
34. Bogardus, "Mexican Repatriates," p. 174.
35. For a copy of the resolution, dated November 1929, see N.A., R.G. 85, File #55639/616.
36. Letter from the Manager of the Association to Secretary of Labor, 1 February 1930, N.A., R.G. 85, File #55639/616.
37. Telegram of 22 May 1930, N.A., R.G. 85, File #55639/616.
38. Dated 19 February 1930, N.A., R.G. 85, File #55639/616.
39. *New York Times,* 25 January 1930, p. 17.
40. Walter V. Woehlke, "Don't Drive out the Mexicans," *The Review of Reviews,* (May 1930): 67.
41. Ibid., p. 68.
42. *New York Times,* 28 February 1929, p. 22.
43. Robert N. McLean, "Tightening the Mexican Border," *Survey Graphic,* (Spring 1930), reprinted in *Congressional Record,* 71st Congress, 2nd Session, Part 6 (1930), p. 6616.
44. *New York Times,* 29 May 1930, p. 10.
45. Ibid.
46. Ibid.
47. *Congressional Record,* 71st Congress, 1st Session, Part 3 (1929), p. 3367.
48. *New York Times,* 13 March 1930, p. 9.
49. *New York Times,* 10 September 1930, p. 1.
50. *New York Times,* 21 May 1930, p. 11.
51. Bryce Wood, *The Making of the Good Neighbor Policy* (New York: W.W. Norton and Co., 1967), p. 127.
52. *Congressional Record* 71st Congress, 1st Session, Part 3 (1929), p. 3368.
53. Meier and Rivera, *The Chicanos,* p. 160.
54. Memo from Los Angeles District Director of Immigration to Commissioner-General of Immigration, 17 June 1931, N.A., R.G. 85, File #55739/674.
55. Carey McWilliams, *Factories in the Field* (Boston: Little, Brown and Co., 1944), p. 129.
56. Bogardus, "Mexican Repatriates," p. 174.
57. Memo from Los Angeles District Director of Immigration to Commissioner-General of Immigration, June 17, 1931, N.A., R.G. 85, File #55739/674.
58. Ibid.
59. Ibid.
60. *Congressional Record,* 71st Congress, 2nd Session, Part 7 (1930), p. 6843.
61. Letter from W. F. Watkins, Supervisor, Office of Inspector in Charge, Los Angeles Office, 8 February 1931, to Robe Carl White, Assistant Secretary of Labor, N.A., R.G. 85, File #55739/674.
62. Ibid.
63. Letter of 21 February 1931, From W. F. Watkins, Supervisor, Office of Inspector in

Charge, Los Angeles Office, to Robe Carl White, Assistant Secretary of Labor, N.A., R.G. 85, File #55739/674.

64. Carey McWilliams, *Southern California Country* (New York: Duell, Sloan and Pearce, 1946), pp.316–17.

65. *New York Times*, 25 April 1931, p. 21.

66. *New York Times*, 12 April 1931, p. 5.

67. *New York Times*, 25 April 1931, p. 21.

68. McWilliams, *North from Mexico*, p. 193.

69. *New York Times*, 12 April 1931, p. 5.

70. Ibid.

71. Ibid.

72. Ibid.

73. *New York Times*, 19 April 1931, III, p. 6.

74. Meier and Rivera, *The Chicanos*, p. 161.

75. McWilliams, *Factories in the Fields*, p. 129.

76. Communication entitled "To the Mexican Colony," 13 October 1932, from Ignacio L. Batiza, Consul for Mexico, Detroit, N.A., R.G. 85, File #55784/585.

77. Memo from John L. Zurbrick, District Director of Immigration, Detroit District, to Commissioner-General of Immigration, 20 October 1932, N.A., R.G. 85, File #55784/585.

78. Pamphlet entitled "Down with Diego Rivera," N.A., R.G. 85, File #55784/585.

79. Letter from Zurbrick to Commissioner-General, 16 November 1932, N.A., R.G. 85, File #55784/585.

80. Clippings from the *Detroit Times*, 16 November 1932, N.A., R.G. 85, File #55784/585.

81. Report dated 29 November 1932, from Gangewere to District Director of Immigration at Detroit, N.A., R.G. 85, File #55784/585.

82. Report from Yeager to District Director of Immigration at Detroit, 21 November 1932, N.A., R.G. 85, File #55784/585.

83. Letter from Zurbrick to Commissioner-General, 23 November 1932, N.A., R.G. 85, File #55784/585.

84. Letter from Zurbrick to Inspector in Charge, U.S. Immigration Service, Laredo, 23 November 1932, N.A., R.G. 85, File #55784/585.

85. Letter from Zurbrick to Commissioner-General, 23 November 1932, N.A., R.G. 85, File #55784/585.

III

The Second Bracero Era (1942–1964)[1]

After the United States entered World War II in 1941, increasing numbers of southwestern growers claimed that they were plagued with a severe and deteriorating labor shortage. Just as in the First World War, they said that their workers were being lost to the military and to higher paying jobs in defense industries. And once again they stressed the necessity of uninterrupted farm production for military success. At their urging, the United States government established in 1942 its second bracero (Mexican labor) program. Although it was later extended to other workers, initially it was limited to farm workers.

Although the bracero program was modified occasionally and even allowed to lapse briefly, it was not finally terminated until 1964. Under its auspices, over 4.5 million Mexican nationals were recruited and brought to the United States for temporary jobs, mostly in agriculture. Like the World War I bracero program, these men were limited to the performance of certain jobs for approved employers, and upon completion of their contracts they were to be returned to Mexico. And once again their entry was not subject to the regular provisions of the United States immigration laws.

Unlike the World War I program, which was established unilaterally by the United States, the second one was the product of careful and sometimes painful negotiations with Mexico. When United States spokesmen first raised the possibility of a new program, Mexican officials pointedly reminded them of the long history of exploitation of Mexican labor by American employers. Unless the United States was prepared to depart radically from that tradition, any new program was completely out of the question.

In the negotiations, Mexico insisted firmly that her workers could go to the United States as braceros only if they were given contracts guaranteeing them a host of rights and benefits. Due to their distrust of American employers, the Mexican officials insisted that the United States government itself serve as the formal employer and guarantee the faithful fulfillment of contract terms; the United States government could then contract the braceros to individual employers. That arrangement lasted until 1947 when the United States refused to continue in its wartime role as the formal employer. With great reluctance, Mexico then agreed to employers contracting directly with braceros.

In the negotiations of 1942, Mexico was particularly concerned that her workers not become stranded in the United States as they had during the Great Depression. Consequently, the agreement provided that they would receive round-trip transportation. Other benefits to be guaranteed in contracts included adequate housing, a minimum number of working days, minimum wages or "prevailing wages" if the latter were higher, and protection against discrimination.

Whereas American labor had no input into the World War I bracero program, the 1942 agreement included provisions designed to protect American workers. To protect them from unfair competition, the "prevailing wages" provision was included. There was also a guarantee that braceros could be contracted only when domestic labor was unavailable.

The second bracero program was continuously controversial. Much of the criticism came from farmers who resented what they considered to be undue government interference with their "right" to use Mexican labor. They claimed that provisions of the program were excessively favorable to Mexico and the braceros. Yet, organized labor and other interests often accused the government of violating the spirit of the agreement with Mexico by administering it with a pro-grower bias. For instance, "prevailing wages" often turned out to be whatever wages the prospective users of Mexican labor in a particular area agreed upon *before* the season began. Ordinarily in a free enterprise system, if wages offered do not attract sufficient labor, they are raised until they do. However, if the farmers' arbitrarily set wage offers did not attract enough domestic workers, the United States government customarily declared a "labor shortage" and approved the use of braceros.

From the beginning, the second bracero program was depicted as a means of coping with war-induced labor problems. Therefore, it was widely assumed that once the war had ended, it would be phased out. However, as happened at the end of World War I, new reasons were found for extending it into peacetime. Once again many growers argued that their former employees, having had a taste of higher wartime wages, would be most unlikely to return to farm work. They also stressed the fact that the government was urging record farm production as part of its plan to assist nations devastated by the war. After the war ended, the bracero program was not only kept alive but it brought unprecedented numbers of braceros to the United States.

Numerous as they were during the postwar period, braceros apparently comprised only a minority of all Mexican nationals working in this country. The number of illegal entrants also reached unprecedented levels.

After the war ended, both the bracero program and the accumulation of illegal Mexican workers were protested vigorously by a growing number of interests. By 1950, it appeared that they were on the verge of winning major concessions from the United States government. However, that hope was dashed by the outbreak of the Korean conflict. Once again growers could tie their labor needs to the fate of their nation in war.

The bracero program finally fell victim to the New Frontier and the Great Society. Both Presidents Kennedy and Johnson thought it had been used to undermine American farm workers. They maintained that if growers were not assured of a Maxican labor supply, they would attract workers the same way other employers do: increasing benefits until they reach the point where they attract enough applicants.

Paradoxically, termination of the second bracero program was the prelude to even greater reliance on Mexican labor. Since 1964, the entry of illegal Mexican workers into the United States has apparently skyrocketed. As the bracero program was being phased out, some of its supporters warned of the imminence of such a development. They argued that so long as Mexico was relatively poor and the United States wealthy, large numbers of Mexican workers would enter this country whether or not the bracero program was extended.

When American scholars have studied the second bracero era, they have focused overwhelmingly on its development within the United States rather than within Mexico. This uneven treatment has been unfortunate because Mexican labor in the United States cannot be understood without reference to its complementary dynamics in Mexico. The first selection, from David Pfeiffer's much-cited graduate thesis, considers the bracero program as an output of Mexico's political system. According to his interpretation, the Mexican government's bracero policies were ambivalent because they attempted to reconcile a host of sharply conflicting demands made by competing interests. Pfeiffer explains, particularly, how Mexico could continue to supply the United States with braceros when so many Mexican interests sharply opposed such action. His answer lies largely in the nature of Mexico's presidency and of the dominant political party. He considers the impact of Mexican opposition political parties, labor unions, agriculturalists, industrialists, the border patrol, and the army on Mexico's bracero policies. Pfeiffer also turns his attention to the impact of graft on the selection of braceros for the United States.

Almost from the beginning, Mexico sought to use the second bracero program as a wedge to reduce discrimination against Mexican-Americans in the United States. The selection by Otey Scruggs provides a fascinating case study of Mexico's use of this strategy in Texas during World War II. Mexico's position was that no braceros would be sent to Texas until that state took effective steps to alleviate discrimination against persons of Mexican ancestry. The Scruggs article focuses on a series of steps then taken by the Texas government and on Mexico's response to them.

In selection 12, Ellis Hawley examines the bracero program in terms of American interest groups. He identifies the program's major supporters and opponents, the rationale developed by each side, and the relative political strengths and weaknesses of the two coalitions. According to the article, the balance of power solidly favored the users of Mexican labor during the 1950s but shifted away from them during the Kennedy years. Hawley seeks to explain the mystery of how a program which benefited so few could have been continued for so long, especially when it flew in the face of the national interest of the United States.

When the United States House of Representatives voted in 1963 to end the bracero program, Mexico's ambassador conveyed his government's misgivings to the Secretary of State. His note is reprinted as selection 13. In it the ambassador argues that Mexican labor still was needed in the United States and that to end the program only would aggravate the problem of the illegals. He claims that the bracero program had given significant protection to Mexican workers, that it had helped improve labor conditions in the United States, that it had fostered better relations between the two countries, and that it had helped to reduce discrimination against Mexican-Americans.

Each year Mexico's president delivers a "State of the Nation" address to his country's congress. These addresses commonly contain brief accounts of why no new bracero program is possible. The final selection contains the relevant excerpts from President Luis Echeverría Alvarez's last three addresses.

NOTES

1. On the second bracero era, see: Henry P. Anderson, *The Bracero Program in California, with Particular Reference to Health Status, Attitudes and Practices* (New York: Arno Press, 1976); Richard B. Craig, *The Bracero Program: Interest Groups and Foreign Policy* (Austin: University of Texas Press, 1971); James F. Creagan, "Public Law 78: A Tangle of Domestic and International Relations," *Journal of Inter-American Studies* 7 (1965): 541–56; Ernesto Galarza, *Merchants of Labor: The Mexican Bracero Program* (Santa Barbara: McNally and Loftin, 1964); Ernesto Galarza, *Strangers in Our Fields* (Washington: United States Section, Joint United States-Mexico Trade Union Committee, 1956); N. Ray Gilmore and Gladys W. Gilmore, "The Bracero in California," *Pacific Historical Review* 32 (1963): 265–82; Richard H. Hancock, *The Role of the Bracero in the Economic and Cultural Dynamics of Mexico* (Stanford: Hispanic American Society of Stanford University, 1959); and John G. McBride, *Vanishing Bracero: Valley Revolution* (San Antonio: The Naylor Co., 1963).

10

"The Bracero Program in Mexico"

David G. Pfeiffer

During the twenty year history of the MFLSP (Mexican Farm Labor Supply Program or Bracero Program) the Mexican government has been willing to let the program continue, providing that certain guarantees are met. However, Government officials evidence an ambiguous attitude toward the MFLSP. On the one hand they encourage their citizens to go to the United States to work because the Mexican economy has grown to depend upon them as a source of foreign exchange and because there are no jobs available; on the other hand they hate to admit that the Mexican economy cannot take care of these workers. What has enabled the Mexican goverment to continue the program even though many officials and some private interest groups oppose the MFLSP? Which groups have opposed the MFLSP? It is these two questions which this chapter seeks to answer.

From David G. Pfeiffer, "The Mexican Farm Labor Supply Program—Its Friends and Foes" (Master's Thesis, University of Texas, Austin, 1963), pp. 90–117. Reprinted by permission of the author.

The Government's Position

During World War II the Mexican government considered the MFLSP as its contribution to the war effort. It also saw it as a boon to its economy. Since World War II only cotton and tourists have brought more dollars to Mexico than the earnings of agricultural workers (legal and illegal). Perhaps the ranking would be changed if more than a rough guess could be made as to the amount of dollars brought back to Mexico by the wetbacks. These are the reasons why the Mexican government has continued to allow Braceros to come to the United States even when shortages of labor existed in Mexico and when Mexico, itself, has participated in negotiations to import agricultural labor.[1] They are also the reasons why for such a long time Mexico made little effort to stop the wetback flow. Yet it is the powerful position of the official Revolutionary Institutional Party (PRI) and the Mexican president which allowed the government's policy to be carried out over the ojections of opposing interest groups.

The PRI and Presidential Power in Decision Making

The Mexican government's policies have been made possible in a large measure because of the dominance of the one official political party. In 1929 President Plutarco Elías Calles created an official party and thus brought stability to the machinery of political control. Though this party has changed its name several times since 1929, it has remained throughout the dominant party. It has never lost a major election. Although in 1952 the combined opposition presidential vote was 26 percent, the official party's vote rose to 90.4 percent in 1958.[2]

The PRI contains the major pressure groups in Mexico. In the 1930s President Lázaro Cárdenas made the National Peasant Confederation one of the PRI's primary supports. It was an organization of the country's communal landholders who in turn were products of Cárdenas's land reform of the same decade. Also in the 1930s Cárdenas aided the development of the Mexican Confederation of Labor (CTM). These two groups—the peasants and the unions—together with the military composed the three important sectors of the official party.[3] In 1943 the various groups of smaller merchants, industrialists, and farmers, the women's and youth groups, the civil service unions, the professions, and the intellectuals were all organized into the National Confederation of Popular Organizations to form a fourth sector of the PRI. The military were dropped as a sector in 1946. The only groups at present not formally included in the PRI are the military, the Catholic clergy, the large landowners, the foreign capitalists, and big business and industry.[4]

Another thing which has made it possible for the government to take an unpopular stand on the outward flow of agricultural labor has been the institutional position of the presidential office in Mexico: "The president is the government, and all discussion of Mexican politics must assume that fact."[5] His position is extraordinarily strong, yet he is limited by the fact that he is dependent upon the groups which compose the PRI. It is true that the PRI presidential candidate is usually the one the president personally chooses, but he would not pick a man who would cause an irreparable split in the party. It is true that the president has little opposition in Congress, but again he would not undertake a legislative program far out of sympathy with the people's desires.[6] All things considered, the presidency in Mexico is a very strong office, by far the most powerful in the nation.

As a result of a hierarchical government and party organization, decisions about important matters such as the MFLSP and the wetback problem are made at the top level. The lower levels usually support these decisions once they are reached. The government agency handling the Mexican end of the MFLSP is the Contract Labor Office in the Ministry of Government. The Secretary of Government is the leading member of the cabinet and several holders of the office have become president. The Secretary plays a primary role in handling presidential patronage and acts as liaison between the president and Congress.[7] His attitude toward the MFLSP can be crucial. During World War II Miguel Alemán held the post. He supported the World War II program, and after becoming president in 1946 he was probably decisive in the decision to continue the program. Other Secretaries of Government have supported the program and taken over direct supervision of the Contract Labor Office.[8]

Alemán's predecessor as president, Miguel Avila Camacho (1940–1946), and his successor, Adolfo Ruiz Cortines (1952–1958), both supported the program as he did.[9] So also did Cortines's successor, Adolfo López Mateos, one-time Minister of Labor.[10] Their belief in its beneficial effects upon the economy of Mexico accounts for their continued support of the program. Mexico's abrogation of the international agreement in 1948, its acquiescence in its termination in 1954, and its frequent threats of ending the program have been tactical moves. In the long run the Mexican government wishes to retain the MFLSP.

In addition to support from the Ministry of Government, the Ministry of Foreign Relations has lent its backing to the program. This was especially true under Foreign Secretary Ezequiel Padilla Nervo during World War II. Congress has endorsed the program, but that is to be expected because of party discipline.

Pressure has come from within the PRI to end or at least modify the MFLSP. The CTM in conjunction with U.S. trade unions has taken a stand against the program.[11] In 1946 the Ministry of Labor unofficially declared that it wished the program to end.[12] Most likely this was an expression of CTM opposition, but since the CTM is a part of the PRI and the Ministry of Labor is a governmental branch, presidential endorsement of the program effectively stifled it.

The Ambivalent Attitude of the Government

As has been noted, the Mexican Government has adopted an ambivalent attitude toward the MFLSP. It has continually insisted upon the enforcement of the contract guarantees for its citizens and asked for the enactment of a law penalizing wetback employers.[13] At the very same time it has done little to impede the flow of agricultural laborers to the north, many of whom become wetbacks and complain of the loss of manpower for its expanding economy.

Some Mexican government officials have claimed that since their constitution and migration laws guarantee Mexican citizens freedom of movement, the government cannot prevent these agricultural laborers from traveling to the United States border.[14] However, a simple government information campaign about the injustices and privations (even murder) suffered by wetbacks might reduce the number. Such stories have been carried by newspapers, but the official weight of the government would make them more effective. In addition the government could jail convicted wetback smugglers for nine years or penalize wetbacks on their return.[15] The only time the Mexican government has used or threatened to use these laws to any extent was in early 1954 when the United States was unilaterally recruiting braceros at the border.

Why has the Mexican government been ambivalent in its attitude? Because it is torn on the horns of a dilemma: on the one side there is the population pressure, economic disturbances, the need for dollars, and the shortages of jobs; on the other side there stand the opposition political parties crying shame on the PRI for its inability to provide its citizens enough jobs in an expanding economy. Government officials see a need for the program in the Mexican economy, but they are loath to admit that such a need exists because it hints of failure in the economic policy of the PRI.

The Opposition Political Parties

Election campaigns in Mexico today are relatively fair but vote counting is frequently fraudulent. During the campaigns there is quite vigorous electioneering, but only occasional violence. The opposition press does have the freedom to criticize though this privilege is sometimes abridged. This situation, plus an almost instinctive anti-Americanism among the opposition party politicians, makes the MFLSP and the wetback problem a prime campaign issue. Aspects of racial prejudice and exploitation are dwelt upon. In the heat of oratory—or demagogy—the truth is often strained and exaggerated. Misinformation and deliberate falsehoods have appeared. The criticism of the PRI and the government in regard to the MFLSP has often been severe.

The extremist parties, expectedly, have offered the most criticism. The Sinarquista Party in Mexico—reactionary, nationalistic, pious, pro-Hispanic, anti-Communist, and anti-American—was very vociferous especially during World War II when it was at its peak strength.[16] Believing the United States to be imperialistic, materialistic, and atheistic, it violently opposed the 1942 and 1943 international agreements.[17] During 1944 it loudly proclaimed the braceros were being drafted in the U.S. Army, that the program had ruined Mexican agriculture, that the dollars flowing into Mexico had caused the country's great inflation, and that graft was ever rampant in the program. Since the end of World War II the Sinarquistas have become much less effective and in 1949 the government cancelled their ballot rights.[18] Their numbers and influence have dropped sharply.

At the other end of the political spectrum are the Socialist People's Party (PPS) and the Communist Party. The PPS is an off-shoot of the PRI. In 1948 the once popular labor leader Vicente Lombardo Toledano led a group which broke away from the PRI with charges of corruption hurled at the official party. This group then formed a new party claiming that the PRI had forsaken the ideals of the Revolution. The PPS domestic platform calls for improvements in the educational system, more social security services, and extended agrarian reform,[19] but in international relations it follows the Soviet line unswervingly. During World War II Lombardo Toledano, following the Moscow line to support the war effort at all costs, supported the MFLSP and was friendly toward the United States. After World War II he became violently anti-American as the Cold War set in.

Toledano ran as his party's candidate for the office of president in 1952. The Communist Party gave him full support. During the six-month campaign he attacked the United States bitterly. His main targets were, in this order, the U.S.-Mexican defense pact, U.S. economic imperialism, and the MFLSP joined with the wetback problem.[20] Toledano called for an immediate renunciation of the MFLSP in February of 1952.[21] In later speeches he claimed the program was graft-ridden, harmful to Mexican agriculture, and rife with racial discrimination and exploitation.[22]

The Communist Party has also used the MFLSP issue to the fullest extent since World War II. It, however, has always been hampered by low membership. The party failed to qualify for the 1952 election on the grounds of too few members.[23] During World War II it did not attack the program since the USSR and the United States were allies.[24] After World War II it bitterly assailed the United States, the MFLSP, and the wetback movement. In 1952 when supporting Toledano in his race for president, the party made the MFLSP the main issue for their speakers.[25] In 1956 the party charged in its newspaper that braceros had to agree to serve in the U.S. Army before they could be admitted to the United States. Later in the year the party proclaimed that an extension of the program would be a national disgrace.

The parties of the middle have been less extreme than the PPS, the Communists, and the Sinarquistas. The strongest of these moderate parties is the Partido Acción Nacional, or PAN. It is composed of people from the middle and upper classes who are conservative with its leaders being drawn from the business and professional class. PAN is Roman Catholic-oriented with some elements of Sinarquismo in it.[26] It has not said very much about the MFLSP because of its membership and its moderate approach.[27] On the other hand it has accused the government of suppressing information about the plight of the wetback in the United States.[28]

It is not difficult to assess the importance of the opposition parties in influencing the MFLSP. Since the PRI is so strong and so well entrenched, the government can afford to disregard their criticisms. It has also come to be recognized that often the anti-American campaigning has opportunistic motivation.[29] Nevertheless, the criticism continued from the Sinarquistas during World War II and from the PPS and the Communists after the war. The government has been pressed time and again to explain why Mexican citizens have to leave the country to find jobs and higher wages when Mexico is underdeveloped. The pressure at times has become acute.

The Labor Unions

The Mexican Confederation of Labor (CTM) has taken a very definite stand on the MFLSP. However, since 1943 the Popular Sector of the PRI has held the most power within Congress and the party but the CTM's influence has waned. In 1946 it expressed its desire, through the Ministry of Labor, to end the program, but it was not successful. Since 1946 the CTM has worked with U.S. unions in an attempt to make the MFLSP guarantees effective and to protect both bracero and U.S. domestic agricultural labor. It has urged that the recruiting stations remain in the more populated interior provinces. It has also urged that wherever discrimination is found braceros be barred from the area. The CTM has also fought the graft (discussed below) connected with the MFLSP.[30] During the 1954 meeting of the Inter-American Regional Organization of Workers the CTM guided through a resolution asking that the Mexican government penalize farmers who leave their land and become wetbacks. Another of its resolutions demanded that the bracero be given detailed information about the location, climate, and conditions of work when offered a contract.[31]

At times the CTM has asked for guarantees in the MFLSP which are not politically possible and may not be economically feasible. For example, in 1949 it wanted to raise the 75 percent guarantee of work to 100 percent. Most of its objectives have been more practical. It has requested more U.S. Labor Department compliance officers, better bracero housing, a better way to determine the prevailing wage (i.e., other than accepting that offered by the growers' association), and the braceros' right to form their own unions or to join existing U.S. unions.[33]

One reason the CTM wanted to end the MFLSP in 1946 was its fear that braceros would be used as strikebreakers (as they were in 1948 and 1949). Attitudes such as these have created a close feeling between U.S. and Mexican trade union leaders.[34] Together they have charted plans in connection with the MFLSP. In December of 1954 the Joint United States-Mexico Trade Union Committee was formed to give a continuous, formal framework for this cooperation.

After the Popular Sector of the PRI won a majority of seats in the Chamber of Deputies in 1943 and then elected its own candidates, Miguel Alemán and Ruiz Cortines, to the presidency, the influence of the CTM declined. The government has not followed the CTM's counsel on the MFLSP nor did it include the CTM representatives on the Joint U.S.-Mexican Migratory Labor Commission created by the two governments in March of 1954.[35] Thus, even though the CTM, as a part of the PRI, can act as watchdog over the MFLSP, it also has had to accept its role within the official party. In this position it is not free to act independently nor to speak out freely. It has occasionally had to modify its positions and demands.

Agricultural Interests: Growers and Ejidos

The Mexican Revolution had land reform as one of its keystones. This reform virtually destroyed the large landowners and has kept the remainder out of the PRI. Nevertheless, they can still be described as an important pressure group within Mexican society. Most of them are located in the northern states where they have been able to expand the production of cotton, sugar cane, and vegetables since World War II through extensive irrigation. Since they, too, depend upon migrant labor for harvests, they have taken a decided interest in the MFLSP and the wetback problem.

The growers in the southern states of Chiapas, Guerrero, Oaxaca, and Veracruz are also dependent upon migratory labor. They have correspondingly been interested in the MFLSP. Most of the workers for their harvests come from the highlands and then return.[36] The coffee growers in Chiapas, on the border of Guatemala, have their own Bracero Program in which some 4,000 Guatemalans are annually imported for the harvest. They have a wetback problem as does the United States, but on a smaller scale. In 1956 the Confederación Nacional Campesina protested vigorously to the government that 50,000 Guatemalan wetbacks had entered Mexico to work on coffee plantations putting thousands of Mexicans out of work in the state of Chiapas. The wages of the few able to obtain work are forced down to starvation levels, they said.[37] The same answers have been given and the same issues have been raised in both contexts.[38]

In 1952 the Mexican growers' associations invited the American Farm Bureau Federation representatives to a three-day conference in Mexico City to discuss their common problems. The two groups met on January

7-9 and decided that the wisest strategy would be to cooperate. In exchange for Mexican growers' associations' support of the MFLSP, the U.S. growers agreed to plug for interior recruiting planned in advance and coordinated with the Mexican agricultural cycle and to oppose the use of wetbacks.[39]

On the whole, the influence of the Mexican growers on the MFLSP has not been very effective. It could be significant that the growers and the unions have similar proposals in regard to the MFLSP. Real coordination of effort might produce some effects; but such an event is unlikely. The growers might be able to obtain from the government some voice in the program's operation in exchange for increased agricultural production which the government sorely wants.[40]

Besides growers, about one half of the agricultural population of Mexico, working about one half of the cultivated land, is organized into *ejidos* (communal farms). The members of these *ejidos* comprise the National Confederation of Peasants (Confederación Nacional Campesina) which since 1938 has been a very important part of the PRI and embodies one of the basic ideals of the Revolution. The National Confederation of Peasants does not exert much influence on the program. Probably one reason is that few *ejidatarios* leave their land for the United States;[41] secondly, the *ejidos* are very dependent upon agricultural credit which the government issues through the *ejido* banks;[42] and, thirdly, the MFLSP takes off the burden of oversupply of labor on *ejidos*. In any event the National Confederation of Peasants declared during the negotiations on the 1951 agreement, TIAS 2331, that they agreed with the government on the benefits of the MFLSP to the Mexican economy.[43]

The Industrialists

Mexican industry has always had a ready supply of cheap labor and has experienced little difficulty with workers leaving industrial jobs to become wetbacks. One might suppose that industry was then noncommittal about the movement of wetbacks and the MFLSP, but in fact Mexican industrialists have shown much concern and interest in them. Their concern centers around the creation of a scarcity of labor, but also on the treatment of the Mexican national in the United States.

During the summer of 1945 the president of the Mexican Confederation of National Chambers of Commerce visited the United States. On his trip he toured several of the areas where braceros were being used. Upon his return to Mexico he roundly criticized the fact that some braceros were being cheated in their wages. The official organ of the Confederation published articles in 1947 and again in 1948 claiming that economic dislocation was resulting from the MFLSP.[44] By 1952 the industrialists were exerting great pressure upon the Mexican government to stand up to the demands of the U.S. growers.[45] They supported enthusiastically the Mexican government's stand when negotiations with the United States broke down in January of 1954.

Due to the great emphasis upon industrial expansion in Mexico since 1945,[46] the industrialists have had general influence on government policy even though they are outside of the PRI. Even though they are dependent on the government for investments, credit, tariffs, and tax concessions, the industrialists have been greatly relied upon by the government for advice as might be expected in a country trying to expand and improve its economy.

The industrialists have a ready-made channel of access to the government through their various chambers of commerce. The government often consults the chambers upon legislation and policy matters and the industries are required by law to maintain membership in them.[47] A mutual exchange of ideas and opinions occurs.

The Effect of Graft

One of the greatest obstacles to the carrying out of the ideals of the Revolution in Mexico has been graft which is so firmly rooted in Mexican society as to be all but institutionalized.[48] The MFLSP is particularly susceptible to graft because of the competition to be chosen a bracero and the requirement that certain conditions be met. This in turn has created a vested interest in minor government circles to continue the MFLSP.

The aspiring bracero must first obtain a permit from his Municipal President signifying that he neither holds property rights in an *ejido* nor in his own name. At first the officials took whatever tip was offered for their services. However, as the competition to go to the "fabulous" United States increased, the officials saw a golden opportunity. Only those applicants able to pay the price were issued the permits—regardless of whether they were entitled to them.[49] Upon reaching a recruiting center the aspiring bracero finds at least ten qualified workers for every contract and many unqualified ones as well.[50] In order even to be considered he must pay some official a bribe.

This situation results in two serious consequences. First, in order to get to the United States the bracero must pay out around 600 pesos or about 50 dollars. Often he has borrowed this money, but in any event he must recoup it. This is possible to do if he obtains a contract, but in order to remain in the United States he becomes a very docile worker at times enduring many abuses.[51] The other consequence of the graft is that it encourages many workers to become wetbacks in order to avoid the costs.

Other bribery occurs. If the worker is eligible for the draft, he has to pay the military inspector to pass him through the recruiting center.[52] When braceros were recruited at the border, the U.S. growers often had to pay a bribe to get qualified workers.[53] Sometimes as many as a third of the wetbacks recently returned by the United States to Mexico have "escaped" from the Mexican train carrying them to the interior by bribing the guards while it was still near the border.[54] Even members of the Mexican Chamber of Deputies have been involved. In 1945 in the first incident in twenty years of such a nature, three deputies were indicted for counterfeiting exit permits and selling them. An extraordinary session of the Chamber of Deputies was convened by President Miguel Alemán to remove their parliamentary immunity so that they could be arrested.[55] All three deputies were members of the PRI.

Newspapers have roundly condemned this graft and accused specific officials of accepting it. Both the PRI and opposition candidates have used it as a campaign issue. President Adolfo Ruiz Cortines (1952–1958) made a real effort to eliminate this graft.[56] It continues partly because of tradition, partly because of low governmental salaries, partly because the Mexican people seem willing to tolerate it, and partly because more economic prosperity makes more money available for such a use.[57] Party hacks are used to staff the recruiting centers and they take advantage of the situation.[58] Local politicians are especially powerful in the PRI and can demand a bribe with impunity. Those officials who demand and receive graft in the MFLSP have become so numerous that they have emerged as a vested interest exerting influence on the government to continue the program.

The Border Patrol and Army

The responsibility for guarding the U.S. border is placed upon both the Mexican Army and the Border Patrol. They have in the past been remarkably ineffective in controlling the illegal flow of wetbacks in and out of Mexico. This inability is caused in part by the lack of equipment and small funds of the Border Patrol and the small number of army troops used. For a busy sixty-mile stretch between Camargo and Río Rico on the Texas border in 1950, where many wetbacks and other illegal border crossers passed between the two countries, the Mexican Border Patrol had only sixteen men and one jeep.[59] Just as important a contributing factor is the lack of coordination and cooperation between the Mexican and U.S. Border Patrols.[60]

Undoubtedly, the most important reason for this inability to control the border is the fact that until recently the Mexican government has never taken a definite stand that the wetbacks should be prevented from crossing. The Mexican Border Patrol and the army have reflected this ambivalent attitude of the Mexican government toward the wetback movement and the MFLSP.

NOTES

1. In 1949 Mexico and Italy entered into negotiations to arrange for 5,000 Italian laborers to come to Mexico to put previously uncultivated land into agricultural production. Cf. *Hispanic World Report*, November 1949, p. 8; ibid., December 1949, p. 7; and ibid., January 1950, p. 10. In 1952 a private financial society was formed in Mexico with a 350,000 dollar capital fund to carry out such a program with Italy. The living and working conditions of the Italians would be governed by a treaty. Cf. *Hispanic American Report* (October 1952): 10. In 1956 the Confederación Nacional de Campesinos reported that 50,000 Guatemalan wetbacks had entered Mexico. Cf. ibid. (February 1956). It is not known if any Italians ever came under these arrangements.

2. *Hispanic American Report* 11 362 (1958): 362 and ibid. (1958): 484.

3. William P. Tucker, *The Mexican Government Today* (Minneapolis: University of Minnesota Press, 1957), pp. 52–56.

4. Ibid., p. 58.

5. Frank Tannenbaum, "Personal Government in Mexico," *Foreign Affairs* 27 (1948): 46.

6. Ibid., pp. 45–47.

7. Tucker, *The Mexican Government Today*, pp. 173–74. For a detailed discussion of this ministry see Virginia Pauline Stullken, "Keystone of Mexican Government—The Secretaría de Gobernación," (Master's Thesis, University of Texas, Austin, 1954).

8. José Lázaro Salinas, *La emigración de braceros: Visión objetiva de un problema mexicano* (Mexico City, 1955), pp. 167–69.

9. Cf. *El Universal* (México, D.F.), 21 April 1943, p. 9, for Avila Camacho's favorable comment on the program; see also *Hispanic American Report* 10 (1959):452.

10. Cf. *Hispanic American Report* 11 (1958):11.

11. Cf. H. L. Mitchell, "Unions of Two Countries Act on Wetback Influx," *American Federationist*, January 1954, pp. 28–29; and Serafino Romualdi, "Hands Across the Border," ibid., June 1954, pp. 19–20.

12. Robert D. Tomasek, "The Political and Economic Implications of Mexican Labor in the United States Under the Non Quota System, Contract Labor Program, and Wetback Movement" (Ph.D. diss., The University of Michigan, Ann Arbor, 1957), p. 158.

13. U.S., Congress, Senate, Committee on Labor and Public Welfare, Subcommittee on Labor and Labor-Management Relations (82d Congress), *Migratory Labor: Hearings, February and March 1952* (Washington, D.C.: Government Printing Office, 1952), p. 707.

14. Tomasek, "Mexican Labor," p. 160, based on an interview with Rafael Aveleyra, Mexican Minister Counselor, Washington, D.C. (He cites Chapter I, Article II of the 1917 constitution.)

15. Ibid., pp. 160–61, for a discussion of these laws.

16. Nathan Whetten, *Rural Mexico* (Chicago: University of Chicago Press, 1948), pp. 484–522.

17. Enrique L. Prado, "Sinarquism in the United States," *New Republic*, 26 July 1943, p. 98.

18. Tucker, *The Mexican Government Today*, p. 62.

19. Ibid., pp. 60–61.

20. Tomasek, "Mexican Labor," p. 167, based on an analysis of Lombardo Toledano's speeches as printed in the PP newspaper *El Popular* during the six-month campaign.

21. *El Popular* (México, D.F.), 17 February 1952, p. 1.

22. Ibid, 23 February 1952, p. 3; 17 June 1952, p. 1; and 22 June 1952, p. 1.

23. Tucker, *The Mexican Government Today*, p. 61.

24. Joseph Werlin, "Mexican Opinion of Us," *South Atlantic Quarterly* 43 (1944):241.

25. *El Popular* (México, D.F.), 15 January 1952, p. 2.

26. Tucker, *The Mexican Government Today*, pp. 59–60.

27. Tomasek, "Mexican Labor," p. 166, based on an interview with Rafael Aveleyra, Mexican Minister Counselor, Washington, D.C.

28. *New York Times*, 26 April 1951, p. 8.

29. Flora Lewis, "Why There is Anti-Americanism in Mexico," *New York Times Magazine*, 6 July 1952, p. 10.

30. Romualdi, "Hands Across the Border," p. 20.

31. *El Nacional* (México, D.F.), 1 January 1954, p. 5; and *Hispanic American Report* (January 1954):10.

32. "Braceros," *Américas*, March 1949, p. 17.

33. Tomasek, "Mexican Labor," p. 171, citing the minutes of the Fourth International Conference of the Joint United States-Mexico Trade Union Committee, 2–4 April 1957, Appendix I. During World War II Lombardo Toledano tried to get President Avila Camacho to insist that braceros be able to join U.S. unions. Cf. Jorge del Pinal, "Los Trabajadores Mexicanos en los Estados Unidos," *Trimestre Económico* 12 (April 1945):26. However, Tomasek says that the Mexican government had not pressed for this right because it felt that this would be interfering in the domestic troubles of the United States and might cause the MFLSP to be ended. Cf. ibid., p. 59 fn. 2, based on an interview with Rafael Aveleyra, Mexican Minister Counselor, Washington, D.C. The bracero has always had the right to elect one of his own number to serve as a bargaining agent with the employer as long as the agreement and contract were observed in any decisions. TIAS 3054 (6 August 1954) allowed the member of any bona fide labor organization to be elected as agent, but to my knowledge no U.S. union member has been so chosen.

34. U.S., Congress, House, Committee on Agriculture, Subcommittee on Equipment, Supplies, and Manpower (84th Congress), *Mexican Farm Labor Program: Hearings on H.R. 3822, March 16, 17, 21, and 22, 1955* (Washington, D.C.: Government Printing Office, 1955) pp. 153–54.

35. *New York Times*, 16 May 1954, p. 71.

36. Whetten, *Rural Mexico*, pp. 262–64.

37. *Hispanic American Report* 9 (1956):9.

38. *Excélsior* (México, D.F.), 1 January 1954, p. 9.

39. U.S., *Congressional Record* (82d Congress), 98:1342–43 (25 February 1952).

40. *Hispanic American Report* (October 1953): 9; ibid., (November 1953): 10; ibid. (February 1954): 9; and Tucker, *The Mexican Government Today*, pp. 284–85.
41. *El Nacional* (México, D.F.), 19 January 1954, pp. 1, 4.
42. Tannenbaum, "Personal Government in Mexico," p. 55.
43. *El Nacional* (México, D.F.), 17 July 1951, p. 2.
44. "Debe Impedirse la Emigración de Braceros," *Carta Seminal: Organo Oficial de la Confederación de Cámaras Nacionales de Comercio*, 17 May 1947, p. 12; and Pablo Castellano, "El Problema de 'Bracerismo,' " *Carta Seminal*, 6 November 1948, pp. 5–6.
45. *New York Times*, 24 July 1952, p. 24.
46. On this see Howard Cline, *The United States and Mexico* (Cambridge, Mass.: Harvard University Press, 1953), chapter 17.
47. Tucker, *The Mexican Government Today*, pp. 58, 217–19.
48. Whetten, *Rural Mexico*, p. 546.
49. *Down in the Valley: a Supplementary Report on Developments in the Wetback and Bracero Situation of the Lower Rio Grande Valley of Texas Since Publication of "What Price Wetbacks?"* (Austin: Texas State Federation of Labor, 1955), p. 6.
50. Salinas, *La emigración de braceros*, pp. 101–61.
51. U.S., Congress, House, Committee on Agriculture, Subcommittee on Equipment, Supplies and Manpower (84th Congress), *Mexican Farm Labor Program: Hearings on H.R. 3822, March 16, 17, 21, and 22, 1955* (Washington, D.C.: Government Printing Office, 1955), p. 167; and *Hispanic American Report* 10 (1957): 520.
52. Salinas, *La emigración de braceros*, pp. 63–97.
53. U.S., Congress, House, Committee on Agriculture, Subcommittee on Farm Labor (81st Congress), *Farm Labor Investigations: Hearings, October 2, 1950, at Greenville, Mississippi, October 4, 1950, at Memphis, Tennessee, and December 18, 1950, at Midland, Texas* (Washington, D.C.: Government Printing Office, 1951), pp. 160–61.
54. *New York Times*, 27 January 1953, p. 32.
55. *New York Times*, 17 January 1945, p. 5.
56. Manuel R. Morris, "Revolution in Mexico: The Battle 'de la Mordida,' " *American Mercury*, July 1953, pp. 83–89.
57. Whetten, *Rural Mexico*, pp. 550–52.
58. Salinas, *La emigración de braceros*, p. 109.
59. Lyle Saunders and Olen Leonard, *The Wetback in the Lower Rio Grande Valley of Texas* (Austin: The University of Texas, 1951), p. 92; and *New York Times*, 13 August 1952, p. 22.
60. Tomasek, "Mexican Labor," p. 184, based on an interview with Paul Crosby of the U.S. Border Patrol, INS, Washington, D.C.

11

"Texas and the Bracero Program, 1942–1947"

Otey M. Scruggs

Of the 291,420 braceros (contract farm laborers from Mexico) entering the United States in 1961, 117,368 went to Texas. That was more than to any other state. This proportion, however, has not always existed. For the first five years of the bracero program—from the signing of the United States-Mexico executive agreement on farm labor on August 4, 1942, to the end of 1947, when the wartime farm labor supply program was terminated—none of the 220,000 Mexican farm workers imported went to Texas. The efforts of Texas farmers to obtain labor and the Mexican government's ambivalent attitude toward the problem are a neglected chapter in the history of a program that has become an enduring part of American agriculture and an important link in the chain of United States-Mexico relations.[1]

The agreement of August 4, 1942, grew out of the fear of both southwestern growers and the United States government that there would be an insufficient supply of labor to harvest the crops during the war. It placed the administration of the bracero program in the hands of the Department of Agriculture and guaranteed that the immigrants would have at least minimum working and living conditions. Many farmers, however, greeted the undertaking with undisquised hostility. They had hoped for a program modeled after the one developed during World War I. In that program, the United States, after relaxing its restrictions on the admission of contract laborers, had left operations largely in the hands of the farmers, and Mexico, involved in more pressing domestic problems, had played an even more passive role. Moreover, the growers disliked intensely the guaranties in the agreement, especially the provision of an hourly minimum of 30 cents, correctly fearing that the safeguards were part of an effort to bring all farm labor, domestic as well as foreign, within the orbit of existing federal labor legislation. For these reasons, only a

---

Otey M. Scruggs, "Texas and the Bracero Program, 1942–1947," *Pacific Historical Review* 32, no. 3 (August 1963): 251–64.

handful of growers—none from Texas—participated in the program in 1942.[2]

In the spring of 1943, two significant developments led growers near El Paso, who had long had easy access to large supplies of labor from Mexico, to attempt to circumvent the agreement. First, on April 26, 1943, the two governments exchanged notes on a new agreement which replaced the old. Instead of liberalizing the terms of employment, as farmers would have liked, the new accord tightened them slightly to meet some of the Mexican government's objections to the program's operation in 1942. Then three days later, Public Law 45, in which Congress for the first time gave its approval to the program, was entered on the statute books. During the bill's progress through Congress, large farm groups led by the powerful American Farm Bureau Federation had worked hard to tailor the program to the farmers' specifications. In conference, Section 5 (g) was added, giving the commissioner of immigration authority to lift the statutory limitations on the entry of farm labor from Western Hemisphere countries when he deemed it essential to the war effort. The desire for an "open border," such as had existed during World War I, appeared to have been realized. Workers entering under P.L. 45 regulations would not be protected by the wage and working condition provisions of the agreement of April 1943, nor would supervision be by the War Food Administration, which had superseded the Department of Agriculture in charge of all farm labor programs. However, since Section 5 (g) was contrary to the spirit if not the letter of the bilateral agreement which had just been concluded, any attempt to proceed under this section of the law would lead to a crisis if the Mexican government adhered to its oft-stated position that workers would be allowed to emigrate only in accordance with the agreement.[3]

The crisis was not long in coming. Border farmers, angered at being denied direct access to labor in Mexico, had been appealing to the Immigration Service since the initial agreement of August 1942, to "let down the bars" on the entry of labor from Mexico. Their appeals had become more insistent as hundreds of workers poured into Mexican border towns hoping to be contracted under the agreement. These pressures eventually proved too strong for the immigration authorities. On May 11, 1943, the commissioner of immigration issued regulations under Section 5 (g) of P.L. 45 authorizing his subordinates to supply laborers at the border with cards permitting them to enter for one year. Shortly afterward, the Immigration Service's El Paso office informed the head of the local water users' association of the regulations, and the rush was on. Jubilant farmers, harried by fears of insufficient labor to meet spring needs, rushed across the border to recruit the necessary workers. Meanwhile, Mexicans from Ciudad Juárez, who had permits to cross to the American town opposite to shop and to work on certain nonagricultural jobs, promptly applied for identification cards under the May 11 regulations. Others without cards crossed at nearby unguarded points. Before the border was closed at El Paso three days later, 2,040 workers had been distributed to farmers on both sides of the Texas-New Mexico line.[4]

The Mexican government's reaction to the El Paso episode was what the State Department had anticipated. Under fire from the start from powerful groups in Mexico hostile to any form of labor emigration, the government quickly made known its intention of abrogating the agreement of April 26, 1943, unless all farm labor emigration from Mexico was placed under its provisions. On May 28, following a series of conferences in Washington at which some of the participants bluntly advocated disregarding Mexico's wishes, the State Department announced that Section 5 (g) of P.L. 45 did not apply to Mexico. However, to avoid the immediate problem of having to transport the workers back to their homes, the Mexican government allowed those to whom cards had been issued to remain one year.[5]

Section 5 (g) of P.L. 45 and the subsequent regulations issued under it were, in fact, parts of a concerted effort by farmers, emboldened by fears of labor shortage, to undermine the United States-Mexico farm labor agreement. As Ambassador George S. Messersmith wrote Secretary of State Hull from Mexico City in the midst of the uproar:

> In other words, in spite of the hue and cry from some of the border states about their need, they have not requested any certification of workers for that area. This is an indication to you that some of the states are not interested in getting workers under the agreements but are more interested in trying to break down the agreements so as to get workers under arrangements which are quite impossible.[6]

The movement across the border under P.L. 45 temporarily lessened the demand for farm labor in the upper Rio Grande Valley. But Mexico's unyielding attitude must have convinced most growers that in order to obtain labor from Mexico they would have either to accept the bilateral agreement or take their chances with "wetbacks," illegal entrants from Mexico.

Texas farmers did not get around to requesting labor under the agreement until late in the summer of 1943, a year after the original notes were signed. By then, however, the Texas farmers' problem of obtaining labor from Mexico had become complicated by the injection of an issue that was ultimately to prevent the dispatch of workers. In June 1943, under prompting from its consuls in Texas, the Mexican government had announced that it would not authorize braceros for Texas "because of the number of cases of extreme, intolerable racial discrimination." Though the pronouncement came as something of a surprise, a discerning observer could have detected the straws in the wind.[7]

Mexicans on both sides of the border had long been sensitive to discrimination against Latins in the United States. Texas particularly aroused their indignation, for there discrimination against Mexicans was more overt than elsewhere in the country. But the war, in which Mexican-Americans were required to give their services, led to increased demands among Mexicans in the state for decent treatment. Moreover, by the spring of 1943, the American government, through the Office of the Coordinator of Inter-American Affairs (OCIAA), had become sufficiently concerned about the effect discrimination was having on its Good Neighbor policy to underwrite a program of education on the problems of the Spanish-speaking in the Southwest.[8]

Aware of the need to take action to improve a situation made more acute by acts of discrimination against Mexican-Americans in uniform and visiting Mexican dignitaries, Governor Coke Stevenson had induced the Texas legislature to pass the so-called "Caucasian Race" resolution, which he had approved on May 6, 1943. The resolution affirmed the right of all Caucasians within the state to equal treatment in public places of business and amusement and denounced those who denied such privileges with "violating the good neighbor policy of our state." Doubtless, this manifesto of good intentions added to the surprise that greeted the Mexican announcement that braceros would not be allowed to go to Texas.[9]

With the cotton harvest fast approaching, many Texas farmers, now reconciled to obtaining Mexican nationals under the agreement, became alarmed that the ban would leave them without an adequate labor supply. It thus became necessary to get the state off the Mexican "blacklist." To do so the Texas Farm Bureau hired Cullen W. Briggs, a Texas judge, who brought the matter to the attention of the American consul general in Ciudad Juárez. Accompanied by representatives of the Ambassador of Mexico and of the OCIAA, the consul called on Governor Stevenson and explained that steps would have to be taken to satisfy Mexico's complaints before labor would be made available. Thereupon, on June 25, 1943, the governor issued a proclamation, which though more specific, in that it pointed to the need for closer cooperation between Mexico and Texas, was essentially a reaffirmation of the "Caucasian Race" resolution. He then departed on a "good will" tour of Mexico, where he gave assurances that upon his return home he would take steps to assure Mexicans fair treatment.[10]

Before issuing his proclamation, the governor on June 12 had drafted a formal letter to Mexican Foreign Minister Ezequiel Padilla. After pointing to the need for several thousand workers for the coming cotton harvest and expressing the wish that it might be met under the agreement, he acknowledged the existence of discrimination and listed the steps already or about to be taken to eliminate it. He promised to order state law enforcement officials to deal severely with those found discriminating against Mexicans and to consider the appointment of a commission to handle complaints of illtreatment. In his reply of July 20, 1943, Señor Padilla expressed the view that the governor's program of action was unequal to the magnitude of the problem. Effective action, he suggested, would include "laws, wholesome propaganda, and penalties."[11]

The contents of the interchange were published in the press of both countries on July 28, and the next day a copy of the governor's instructions to the appropriate enforcement agencies was likewise made public. The governor further notified the Mexican government that the following week he would announce the appointment of a commission to study and take action to end acts of prejudice against Mexicans.[12]

In the meantime, the United States government was also hopefully making efforts that would result in the dispatch of braceros to Texas. On July 22, 1943, following appeals from the Texas congressional delegation, it approved and prepared to send on to the Mexican government a request for 5,000 Mexican nationals for Nueces and San Patricio counties in the coastal bend of Texas. The State Department continued to press for the removal of the ban, which would be necessary before the official request for 5,000 workers could be transmitted. These efforts appeared to have been successful when, on August 6, 1943, the Foreign Office informed the State Department that in view of Governor Stevenson's evident desire to help solve the "thorny problem of discrimination," Mexico would entertain a request for 5,000 workers as soon as the governor announced publicly the creation of his proposed commission to deal with questions involving discrimination against Mexicans. Mexican leaders, still in doubt about the wisdom of the move, suggested that braceros going to

Texas either be selected from those already in the United States or be recruited in Mexico City for the "southern" states, but with the understanding that they would go to Texas.[13]

This unenthusiastic endorsement of the venture was prophetic; no farm laborers went to Texas under the agreement in 1943. The governor did not grant the Good Neighbor Commission of Texas authority to organize until September 4, 1943, when he learned that federal funds would be forthcoming through the OCIAA to support it. Whether a formal request for labor was ever made to the Foreign Office is not known. In all likelihood it was not. In any event, it would not have affected the outcome, for by this time the Mexican government had concluded the time inopportune to approve such a request.[14]

From the start the Mexican government was anxiously concerned about the repercussions of the contract labor programs on Mexican politics. President Manuel Avila Camacho had consented to the undertaking as part of Mexico's contribution to allied victory in the war. The program was also part of an effort to cement closer ties with the United States, and thereby strengthen the president's program to hasten Mexico's economic development. But in allowing workers to emigrate, the government opened itself to the criticism of powerful and vocal elements within the country. Labor leaders were disturbed by the president's middle-of-the-road policy for economic growth which courted business as well as labor support. Agrarians were uneasy over the slowdown in the government's land distribution programs and over the wartime inflation. Large commercial farmers in the north opposed any program that might add to their problems of obtaining needed labor. There were nationalists of all hues, from those like the *sinarquistas*, who were averse to almost any form of cooperation with the United States, to those who believed that Mexican manpower should remain at home to help in the economic development of Mexico. Mindful of the large reservoir of anti-American feeling throughout the Republic, these groups could be expected to point to any evidence of difficulty in the operation of the emigration programs in an effort to embarrass the government. The exigencies of internal politics were often as compelling as concern for the braceros' welfare in dictating Mexico's course of action on problems arising out of sending labor to the United States.[15]

Under these circumstances, nothing exercised the government more than the reports of discrimination against braceros in the United States that continued to drift back to Mexico. Indeed, the Mexican public was apt to regard nearly all of the difficulties as some form of discrimination.

The most serious instances of illtreatment involved workers recruited under the railroad labor agreement of April 29, 1943, an accord similar in most respects to the earlier farm labor agreements. The protest of a group of braceros employed on the Santa Fe line near Fullerton, California, early in July 1943, against being paid wages lower than those paid American workers threatened to agitate the political waters in Mexico. Acting quickly to forestall any cries of discrimination, the government temporarily suspended recruitment under the railroad labor agreement. After protracted negotiations, a settlement was concluded in favor of the workers.[16]

A month after the Santa Fe "incident," Mexican nationals working on railroads in central Texas complained of discrimination in two towns, and the Mexican government was forced to request their immediate removal to areas where discrimination was not likely to occur. This and other instances of discrimination against Mexicans in Texas prompted a member of the Mexican legislature, a former consular official in that state, to urge adoption of a resolution setting up a committee to meet with Governor Stevenson and to investigate conditions. In the face of these developments, the government chose to say nothing more about sending farm labor to Texas in 1943, and the State Department, aware of the government's predicament, did not further press the issue. Texas growers finished the season with student volunteers, a handful of prisoners of war, the traditional but much reduced Mexican-American migratory labor force, and an increasing number of wetbacks.[17]

The Mexican government continued to vacillate in 1944. Indeed, in spite of domestic opposition, President Avila Camacho and Foreign Minister Padilla were anxious to have farm workers go to Texas. They feared that persistent refusal to send them would not only antagonize the United States, but might undermine the steps already taken by Governor Stevenson to wipe out discrimination. Thus, the government announced on December 26, 1943, that braceros would be allowed to go to Texas in 1944. However, when Ambassador Messersmith approached the foreign minister several weeks later, Padilla stated that while he was personally sympathetic to permitting workers to go to certain counties, he could not defy public opinion by allowing them to emigrate.[18]

In the meantime, Governor Stevenson was being pressured to have the ban removed. The workers who entered under Section 5 (g) of P.L. 45 were due to be repatriated by May 15, 1944, and El Paso County growers were anxious either to contract them under the agreement or to import others under its terms to replace them. Together with state officials, they devised a plan that would give El Paso County preferred treatment. Officials of two El Paso farm groups, accompanied by a representative of the OCIAA, would journey to Mexico City to urge that contract labor be allowed to go to Texas counties with records of favorable treatment of Mexicans, the first so selected to be El Paso County. The plan was believed to have the two-fold advantage of demonstrating to Mexico that discrimination was not inevitable and of stimulating counties with poor records to reform conditions. The deputation arrived in the Mexican capital in mid-March and conferred with officials of the American embassy. Although Ambassador Messersmith did not wish to jeopardize the two labor emigration programs "by an inopportune insistence on a point which is politically impossible in Mexico at the present time," he again took up the matter with the foreign minister and received Padilla's promise to authorize labor for El Paso County upon receipt of a formal request.[19]

The request was made on April 25, 1944, and though the period of critical need for labor was cited as of May, the month passed without further word from Mexico. Nor apparently was any promise made at a three-day conference on border problems in Mexico City beginning May 29. The meeting was called by Mexico primarily to consider ways of coping with the mounting volume of unlawful emigration, both those who crossed unnoticed and those who used Form 5-C cards to leave to perform farm work in the United States. The Mexican delegation also stressed its government's growing concern over the several hundred P.L. 45 workers not yet returned and its desire that they be repatriated without further delay in accordance with the original understanding. Despite the insistence of the American delegation that the United States was reluctant to see Texas stripped of labor, the Mexicans remained noncommittal about labor for El Paso County. However, the informal agreement of June 2, 1944, pledged the United States to strengthen its border force, to cease issuing Form 5-C cards to farm workers, and to repatriate all those in the country contrary to the expressed wishes of Mexico.[20]

United States border authorities acted quickly to meet these commitments, speedily returning the remaining P.L. 45 entrants and embarking on a campaign to round up and deport wetbacks in south Texas. This evidence of American willingness to cooperate was probably a major factor in the Mexican government's decision of June 16 to authorize the recruitment of between two and four thousand braceros for El Paso County, provided Governor Stevenson publicly reaffirmed his intention to combat discrimination. There followed a month in which assurances were once again given by the governor regarding discrimination and by the United States that the contractees' interests would be amply protected. Then followed still another month of silence from Mexico.[21]

While the Mexican government continued its hedging, instances of discrimination continued to reach the Mexican public. In August 1944, the *Comité Mexicano contra el Racismo* was formed, and its publication, *Fraternidad*, ran a column, "Texas, *Buen Vecino?*" ("Texas, Good Neighbor?"), in which were listed acts, names, and places of discrimination. The Inter-American Bar Association, meeting in Mexico City the same month, discussed the issue of discrimination as an obstacle to better hemisphere relations. Significantly, the foreign office notified the American embassy near the end of August that it had again changed its mind, believing that it could not accede to the request for labor for El Paso County and still expect the emigration programs to continue functioning smoothly. "This," said the embassy, in informing Washington of the decision, "is the long and the short of it. It is useless to again raise the question. . . ." The note of finality was significant, for the attempt to obtain labor for El Paso County marked the last concerted effort by the United States during the history of the Emergency Farm Labor Supply program to induce Mexico to lift the ban on labor to Texas. The United States had concluded that to persist in the matter would only jeopardize existing labor programs and mar efforts at closer cooperation between the two countries.[22]

Pressure in Texas to have the ban removed abated after 1944. This was partly due to previous failures, but it was also due to developments only indirectly related to the ban. In January 1945, the Texas State Extension Service, with the cooperation of the Good Neighbor Commission, inaugurated a program to make greater use of resident workers by improving on-farm housing and educating local communities in the need for better treatment of Mexican-Americans who followed the crops. Moreover, when the war ended, greater numbers of Mexican-Americans returned to the fields.[23]

The most significant accretion, however, came through illegal entry from Mexico. In May 1944, Mexican officials had contended that there were 25,000 wetbacks in American border areas, most of them in Texas. Early in 1947, they placed the number at 100,000. At least half of this number was believed to be in the lower Rio Grande Valley of Texas. Because they were in the country unlawfully, hence subject to immediate deportation in the event of arrest, these unfortunates were forced to work for painfully low wages and to accept miserably poor living conditions.[24]

By 1947, the mounting volume of unlawful migration over-shadowed all other border problems. As in 1944, officials of the two governments met in Mexico City to consider ways of solving the problem, and out of their discussions came two agreements on March 10, 1947. The principal accord permitted wetbacks to be returned to Mexico and issued contracts enabling them to re-enter the United States legally as farm workers. The other extended the terms of the accord to workers picked up in Texas.[25]

The official reasons for the separate agreement pertaining to Texas are set forth in the document. It declared that Mexico remained "firm in its determination not to permit, under the protection of existing conventions, persons of Mexican nationality to be contracted to work in States of the United States where there may exist discrimination against Mexicans. . . ." Hence, the agreement "was not to constitute a precedent and was only to be temporary." Mexico, it said, in effect, was making the concession in appreciation "of the repeated proofs of friendship and of good will" displayed by the Texas government in attacking the problem of discrimination. Finally, the Texas agreement pointed out, with reference to the wetbacks, that Mexico was "confronted with a factual situation which was not created by the Government of Mexico, but which it is desirable to solve in benefit to the Mexican workers."[26]

The Mexican government's motives were several. It wanted to lend as much support and encouragement as it could to the Texas authorities in combatting discrimination. It wanted to provide greater protection for the workers. Prompted by a real concern for the workers' welfare, it was also motivated by political considerations. An American embassy official reported that during the discussions some of the Mexican delegates admitted as much. In other words, "confronted with a factual situation," the government was compelled to present to the Mexican people evidence of its concern to improve the lot of the workers, the greatest number of whom were in southern Texas. At the same time, it wished to make clear that it was not abandoning its position on the discrimination issue, although in fact it was taking the first concrete step toward doing so. The Texas agreement was intended to emphasize to interested parties in both countries, but especially in Mexico, that the Mexican government, with respect to farm labor emigration, continued to regard Texas in a different light from the other border states.[27]

These accords supplemented but did not replace the agreement of April 26, 1943. Thus, the contract subsequently drafted by the Mexican government was similar but not identical to the bracero contract. It included guarantees of minimum working and living conditions. But instead of being enforced by an agency of the United States, it was to be policed by a commission on labor emigration set up by Mexico. The parties to the contract were to have recourse to American courts, and, in the final analysis, the Mexican government could deny workers to offending employers.[28]

The contract was even less palatable to the growers than the bracero contract had been five years earlier. With the war over, they were more than ever convinced of the superfluity of worker guarantees. Consequently, the majority, especially in the lower Rio Grande Valley, chose to ignore the new management, and many of those who had their workers "legalized" failed to comply with the terms of the contract. As a result, following a dispute with the El Paso Cotton Growers Association over wage rates, the Mexican government on October 15, 1947, abrogated the Texas agreement.[29]

In the years after 1947, due largely to the continuous influx of wetbacks, Mexico gradually removed its ban on the emigration of braceros to Texas. As early as 1943, the availability of illegal entrants had made it unnecessary for the farmers of southern Texas to worry unduly about the ban on braceros. As long as they could obtain wetbacks, they could ignore braceros, whose use required the farmers' acquiescence in conditions of employment which they detested.

However, Mexico's policy of using the braceros as a lever to force Texas to take steps to end discrimination against Mexicans was not devoid of results. More than any other factor, it was responsible for the creation of the Good Neighbor Commission, which in 1947 became a permanent agency of the Texas government. Moreover, the publicity attending Mexico's stand, and the work of the Good Neighbor Commission, helped bring out into the open a problem long in need of searching examination.

Mexico's approach to the question of sending labor to Texas in the years from 1942 to 1947 well illustrates its approach to the larger question of farm labor emigration over the years. That approach has been dictated by a host of economic, political, and humanitarian considerations. The relative importance that Mexican leaders have attached to each at any given time has determined their course of action. Indeed, if Mexico's program of economic diversification, begun in earnest under President Avila Camacho, were to keep pace with its rapidly increasing population, which is unlikely for some time to come, they would probably act quickly to end the bracero undertaking. American farmers would then have to look elsewhere for sources of labor.

NOTES

1. W. Carl Holley, Office of Farm Labor Service, U.S. Department of Labor, to the author, 16 Oct. 1962; Wayne D. Rasmussen, *A History of the Emergency Farm Labor Supply Program*, 1943–47 (Washington, D.C., 1951), pp. 199, 226.

2. See the author's "The First Mexican Farm Labor Program," *Arizona and the West* 2 (1960): 319–26; idem, "The Evolution of the Mexican Farm Labor Agreement of 1942," *Agricultural History* 34 (1960): 140–49; idem, "The Bracero Program under the Farm Security Administration, 1942–1943," *Labor History* 3 (1962): 149–68.

3. Scruggs, "The Bracero Program," p. 160 fn.

4. American Consul at Ciudad Juárez to American Embassy (Mexico City), 12, 18 May 1943, Files of the Department of State (hereafter referred to as S.D.); El Paso *Times*, 5 Feb. 1944.

5. Memo of conversation, Division of American Republics, 12 May 1943; memo., Division of American Republics, 28 May 1943; Department of State to American Embassy, 28 May 1943, S.D.

6. George S. Messersmith to Cordell Hull, 24 May 1943, S.D.

7. Carey McWilliams, *North From Mexico* (Philadelphia and New York, 1949), p. 270.

8. Ibid., pp. 259–263, 269–270; Nellie Ward Kingrea, *History of the First Ten Years of the Texas Good Neighbor Commission* (Fort Worth, 1954), pp. 30–31.

9. Kingrea, *Texas Good Neighbor Commission* 27.

10. Ibid., 32–34.

11. Coke R. Stevenson and Ezequiel Padilla, "The Good Neighbor Policy and Mexicans in Texas," 17 *National and International Problems Series* 17(1943): pp. 7–13, 17–22.

12. Memo of conversation, Department of State and American Embassy, 28 July 1943, S.D.

13. Hull to Messersmith, 22 July 1943; American Embassy to Department of State, 6 Aug. 1943, S.D.; Philip Bruton, Office of Labor to Marvin Jones, Administrator, War Food Administration, 22 July 1943, in General Correspondence Record Group 224, National Archives, Washington, D.C.

14. Kingrea, *Texas Good Neighbor Commission* 34.

15. Howard F. Cline, *The United States and Mexico* (Cambridge, Mass., 1953), pp. 261–82; Donald M. Dozer, *Are We Good Neighbors?* (Gainesville, Fla., 1959), pp. 233, 235–36; Stephen S. Goodspeed, "The Role of the Chief Executive In Mexico: Policies, Powers and Administration" (Ph.D. dissertation, University of California, Berkeley, 1947), pp. 332–50; Messersmith to Hull, 11 Aug. 1943; American Embassy to Department of State, 18 May 1944, S.D.

16. Messersmith to Hull, 29 Oct. 1943; Department of State to American Embassy, 22 April 1944, S.D.

17. American Embassy to Department of State, 15 Sept. 1943, S.D.; McWilliams, *North From Mexico*, p. 271.

18. Messersmith to Hull, 20 July 1943; American Embassy to Department of State, 7, 15 March 1944, S.D.; El Paso *Times*, 27 Dec. 1943. Interestingly, Padilla resigned his post a year later to launch his campaign for the presidency, a campaign which he lost in part, it is commonly believed, because of his well-known friendship for the U.S. See Robert F. Scott, *Mexican Government in Transition* (Urbana, Ill., 1959), p. 215; also Austin F. MacDonald, *Latin American Politics and Government*, 2d. ed. (New York, 1954), p. 251.

19. American Embassy to Department of State, 15 March 1944, S.D.

20. American Embassy to Department of State, 6 June 1944, S.D.

21. American Embassy to Department of State, 16 June 1944, 18 July 1944; memo. of conversation, American Embassy and Department of State, 29 June 1944, S.D.

22. McWilliams, *North From Mexico*, pp. 263–64; American Embassy to Department of State, 29 Aug. 1944, S.D.
23. Pauline R. Kibbe, *Latin Americans in Texas* (Albuquerque: University of New Mexico Press, 1946), pp. 182–90.
24. American Embassy to Department of State, 6 June 1944, S.D.; *U.S. Stat.*, 80 Cong., 1 sess. (1947), Vol. LXI, Part 4, p. 4098.
25. American Embassy to Department of State, Feb. 7, 1947, S.D.; *U.S. Stat.*, 80 Cong., 1 sess. (1947), Vol. LXI, Part 4, pp. 4097–4100, 4106–7.
26. *U.S. Stat.*, 80 Cong., 1 sess. (1947), Vol. LXI, Part 4, pp. 4106–7.
27. American Embassy to Department of State, 7 Feb. 1947, S.D.
28. Otey M. Scruggs, "The United States, Mexico, and the Wetbacks, 1942–1947," *Pacific Historical Review*, 30 (1961): 160.
29. For a more detailed description of the Texas agreement in operation, see ibid., pp. 161–62.

12

"The Politics of the Mexican Labor Issue, 1950–1965"

Ellis W. Hawley

The politics of agriculture, as a number of recent studies have pointed out, is a highly complex subject.[1] The farm leaders and their organizations quarrel with each other, clashes between regional and commodity groups are frequent, and political alignments differ from one issue to another. The so-called "farm bloc" is in reality a loose coalition of widely diverse and often conflicting groups. While these groups share certain attitudes and draw upon common sources of power, each of them has tended to develop its own program and devise its own methods of working out compromises, acquiring allies, subordinating internal differences, and building the political coalition necessary to keep the program intact. Some of them, moreover, have been remarkably successful. In defiance of all logic, they have been able for long periods of time to maintain special programs that benefit only a tiny segment of American agriculture.

Ellis W. Hawley, "The Politics of the Mexican Labor Issue, 1950–1965," *Agricultural History* 40 (1966): 157–76. Reprinted by permission of the Agricultural History Society and the author.

The present article is a case study of one such group—the small contingent of farm employers who were able to secure and maintain the Mexican labor program from 1951 to 1965. In the late 1950s, something over 94 percent of these imported workers went to some 50,000 growers in five states, where they were used almost exclusively in such crops as cotton, sugar beets, fruits, and vegetables. Over 98 percent of the nation's commercial farmers received no workers at all.[2] Yet, prior to 1960, extensions of the program moved through Congress with relative ease. Repeatedly, these employers demonstrated an amazing ability to hold their coalition together, manipulate the appropriate symbols, and apply pressure at key points in the governmental structure. Then, in the early 1960s, the tide turned against them, and the program came to an end. Apparently, they had lost their political magic, and, presumably, an examination of their initial successes and later failures will cast some light on the general nature and methods of agricultural pressure groups. Hopefully, it will reveal something, not only about their strong points and limitations, but also about the political and ideological milieu in which they operate.

In the form that they took in the 1950s, the arrangements for importing Mexican farm workers were largely a by-product of the agricultural labor shortage during World War II. Under an executive agreement in 1942, followed by supplementary legislation in 1943, the federal government, acting originally through the Farm Security Administration and later through the Extension Service and the War Food Administration, proceeded to recruit Mexican workers, bring them to the United States, and supply them to farm employers. It also attempted to enforce a number of protective clauses, most of which were included either at the insistence of Mexico or to pacify labor opposition. For example, employers could not discriminate against the Mexicans; they could not secure labor for the purpose of displacing American workers or depressing their wages; and they were required to pay the prevailing wage, guarantee work for at least three-fourths of the contract period, and provide the Mexicans with the same social benefits available to American farm workers.[3]

By 1947 the number of Mexican workers imported under the wartime agreement had reached nearly 220,000, most of them employed in California, Arizona, and the Northwest, since overt discrimination in Texas led the Mexican government to deny legally imported workers to that state. The employers, moreover, in spite of periodic complaints about impractical requirements, seemed relatively well satisfied. In any event, when the wartime program expired in 1947, there was strong agitation for some sort of substitute. Again, government officials listened sympathetically, and the result was a new set of arrangements allowing the employers themselves to recruit contract laborers and, after making the same general guarantees as were made during the war, to bring them into the United States whenever the Employment Service determined that a need for them existed. This was the general procedure under the agreements of March 1947, April 1947, February 1948, and August 1949. All of these agreements, too, except that of 1948, allowed employers to make contracts with illegal entrants or "wetbacks" that were already in the United States.[4]

In some respects, the employers regarded the postwar arrangements as being even more satisfactory than the wartime program.[5] Mexico, however, complained about employer abuses and the drainage of vitally needed labor from her border areas.[6] In 1951, as the date for the expiration of the 1949 agreement approached, the Mexican government refused to renew it unless the United States guaranteed the performance of work contracts, penalized the employers of wetbacks, and agreed to some system of interior recruiting. Federal legislation, it seemed, was imperative, particularly in view of the new labor shortage engendered by the Korean War.[7] And once again the users of Mexican labor mobilized their forces to secure an acceptable program.

The employers, moreover, were remarkably successful. Congress ignored almost completely the proposals of labor groups and liberal congressmen for stringent safeguards and new curbs on the wetback traffic.[8] It paid little attention to the recommendations of the President's Commission on Migratory Labor.[9] And it refused to go along with the proposals of the Department of Labor for the recruitment, transportation, and protection of domestic as well as foreign workers. Such an approach, the farm spokesmen insisted, was impractical, bureaucratic, and unneeded. The government should stay out of the "motel business," and legislation dealing with foreign labor. Consequently, the administration bill received little attention during the congressional hearings and was almost totally ignored in the committee reports.[10]

The bill finally adopted was that sponsored by Senator Allen J. Ellender of Louisiana and Representative W. R. Poage of Texas. Throughout the hearings and debates, this measure had the strong endorsement of the employers' organizations; as Public Law 78, it was to provide the basis for the Mexican labor program for the next fourteen years. The only dissent among farm groups came from the Farmers Union, which claimed that the measure ran counter to the interests of small farmers, and from Northwestern farm employers, who wanted the government to establish reception centers in the interior and absorb more of the transportation costs. In the final showdown, the bill passed both houses of Congress by comfortable margins, and President Truman, after stressing the need for stronger measures to curb the wetback traffic, reluctantly rejected the advice of the Department of Labor and added his signature.[11]

As finally passed, the new law authorized the Secretary of Labor to recruit Mexican farm workers, bring them to reception centers near the border, assist them in negotiating contracts, and guarantee that the contracts would be carried out by the employers. Wetbacks who had been in the United States five years or longer might also be placed under contract. Again, however, there were to be a number of restrictions and safeguards. The workers could not be imported until the Secretary of Labor had certified that there was a need for them. The government was to be reimbursed for transportation costs and legal losses, and, in accordance with the executive agreement of 1951 and its later extensions, employers must pay the prevailing wage, guarantee work for 75 percent of the contract period, provide compensation for occupational injuries and diseases, and furnish adequate housing, sanitary, and transportation facilites.[12]

During the 1950s, in spite of persistent criticism on the part of labor groups, Mexican-Americans, and humanitarian reformers, the program established by Public Law 78 remained substantially intact. Repeatedly, to be sure, the critics called for reform. They wanted, among other things, to establish minimum wages, determine labor shortages in public hearings, and require that employers offer domestic workers the same fringe benefits as were guaranteed to Mexicans. They failed, however, to achieve anything of this sort. On the contrary, most of the changes that were made were relatively minor ones. In 1955, for example, there was an amendment requiring the Employment Service to consult with laborers as well as employers. In 1956 the Interstate Commerce Commission was empowered to regulate the transportation of migrant workers. And, in the late 1950s, the Employment Service did force a raise in minimum piece rates and issue a new and stricter set of administrative rules.[13]

Under the circumstances, one might expect nothing but praise from the employers, but this was hardly the case. They continued to complain about excessive safeguards, bureaucratic red tape, "one-sided" contracts, and needless surrenders to the wily Mexicans. They deplored the Employment Service's appointment of a Labor Advisory Committee, were alarmed over the efforts of reformers to project the agreements with Mexico into the domestic situation,[14] and would have preferred to see the program in friendlier hands, in those of the Extension Service, for example, rather than the Department of Labor.[15] Yet, when all was said and done, not many of them would change the basic system. The defects, they insisted, could be corrected through negotiation and administrative changes. Accordingly, when the program came up for renewal in 1953, 1955, 1958, and 1960, the interested farm groups merely called for and pushed through an extension of Public Law 78.[16]

The one major change during the 1950s was the gradual substitution of legally imported labor for Mexican wetbacks. This was due in part to new legislation penalizing the importation, transportation, and concealment of illegal entrants,[17] and in part to "Operation Wetback," the massive enforcement campaign that followed Attorney General Herbert Brownell's tour of the border areas in 1953. Under the direction of General Joseph M. Swing, the Immigration Service opened a concerted drive in the spring and summer of 1954. It strengthened the border patrol, conducted special drives in California and Texas, and made every effort to enlist employer support. As a result, the number of wetbacks apprehended declined rapidly from 1,075,168 in 1954 to 242,608 in 1955 and 30,196 by 1959. At the same time, the number of braceros or legally imported workers grew from 201,380 in 1953 to 445,197 in 1956 and remained at 437,643 in 1959. Some employers, particularly in the Rio Grande Valley, protested sharply about the federal "army of occupation." Yet most of them seemed willing to cooperate. Those remote from the border areas had long complained about unfair competition, and others recognized that failure to deal with the problem could seriously alienate public opinion, that their best strategy now was to forget about wetback labor at ten cents an hour, concentrate on defending the bracero program, and work for permanent acceptance of Public Law 78.[18]

This strategy, moreover, seemed to get excellent results. Repeatedly, the employers and their allies were successful in pushing aside the agitation for reform, blocking proposed amendments, and convincing Congress that a further extension of the program was in the national interest. Their success often astonished their critics; to understand it, one must examine and analyze their activities in some detail, particularly the sources from which they drew their support and the symbols and arguments that they found useful.

One key to success was organization; typically, the users of Mexican labor acted not as individuals but as members of labor associations. They belonged, in other words, to such groups as the Imperial Valley Farmers

Association, the Trans-Pecos Cotton Association, and the Tarzan Marketing Association, all examples of the type of organization that had taken over the job of recruiting, transporting, distributing, and rationalizing the use of Mexican labor. Frequently, such groups could decide upon a "prevailing wage," and almost inevitably they became deeply involved in political lobbying. Through a network of private and semi-official users' committees, organizations like the county and state advisory boards, the Employment Service's Special Farm Labor Committee, and the National Farm Labor Users' Committee, they could formulate a common policy and coordinate their efforts to put it into effect.[19]

As lobbyists, moreover, the employer associations could take advantage of close ties with other farm and business organizations. As a rule, the same group of farmer-businessmen that spoke for them doubled as leaders of the farm bureaus, the agricultural councils, the marketing cooperatives, and the special groups that looked after the interests of individual commodities.[20] Such men were influential in the national farm organizations, particularly in the American Farm Bureau Federation and the National Council of Farm Cooperatives. And usually, they could count on the strong support of the processing, refining, and canning companies, a number of whom had hundreds of contracts with "captive farms" and were naturally interested in keeping the cost of labor and raw materials to a minimum.[21] The result in many rural areas was an axis of power that ran from the growers' organizations to the processing companies to the local chambers of commerce; and it was only natural that local officials, county agents, and state administrators should go along with the established order, particularly when it was reinforced by rural over-representation and backed up by the conservative orientation of most of the agricultural colleges and state farm agencies.[22]

In Congress, too, farm groups had long occupied a favorable position, one that stemmed partly from the very make-up of that body, partly from the fact that congressional redistricting was often in the hands of rural-dominated state legislatures, and partly from the nature of the congressional committee system. Many rural congressmen came from politically safe, one-party districts. Years of accumulated seniority had moved them into key committee chairmanships. This, coupled with the practice of assigning rural representatives and senators to the agricultural committees, usually insured that farm pressure groups would receive a highly favorable hearing. The typical rural congressman, moreover, tended to share the attitudes of farm leaders. He enjoyed their company, accepted their evaluation of "grass roots" feeling at home, and was readily susceptible to "education" on farm issues. The result, especially among the "old hands" in Congress, was a sort of club atmosphere, a feeling of comradeship that cut across party lines and facilitated interregional bargaining.[23]

During the 1950s, there was also a loose alliance between the congressional farm bloc and a number of conservative urban Republicans. Both groups wanted to curb the power of organized labor and block urban social legislation, and cooperation in these areas naturally carried over into such matters as the Mexican labor issue. In 1951, for example, 70 of the 103 urban representatives that voted for Public Law 78 were Republicans, while another 28 of them came from urban districts in the South or Southwest. And again in 1953, 82 of the 122 urban representatives who voted for extension of the program were Republicans, while 28 were Southern Democrats. At the same time, rural and small-town representatives voted overwhelmingly for the program. Only 41 of them opposed it in 1951, only 21 in 1953, and of these the great majority came from rural districts in the Northeast.[24]

The power of agriculture was less apparent in the administration than in Congress. The president, after all, was elected by a process that tended to magnify the political strength of the large urban states; consequently, the more conservative farm leaders distrusted the federal bureaucracy and advocated measures that would enhance the power of Congress or deliver farm programs into the hands of local interests. This is not to say, however, that the users of Mexican labor had to contend with a hostile administration. Their program had the general endorsement of the departments of State, Justice, and Agriculture, and their spokesmen were not without influence at the White House. During the Truman administration, they could approach the president through such men as Tom Baker of Missouri and Clinton Anderson of New Mexico, and, under the Eisenhower administration, they were able to develop similar channels.[25]

One might suppose that the Department of Labor, the agency that actually administered the program, would be a hostile agency. Yet even here appearances were deceptive. The United States Employment Service was only a coordinating agency for the state services and their farm placement divisions. The crucial day-by-day decisions were made on the local and state levels, where employer influence was strong, and, since the whole farm placement system had once been a part of the Department of Agriculture, the men who ran it continued to think in terms of supplying farm labor, not in terms of protecting or finding jobs for farm workers. Repeatedly, such men showed a disposition to accept the employers' own determination of "labor shortages," agree to whatever "prevailing wage" the employer associations were willing to pay, and then to recruit a foreign labor force. During the mid-1950s in particular, the program was run to suit the employers. In the words of Secretary of Labor James Mitchell, it became a sort of "lefthanded adjunct" to the Labor Department, a program that was presumably temporary in nature, of minor importance, and therefore of little concern to the higher officials there. It was not until the late 1950s, when Mitchell became deeply concerned about the abuses in the program, that the growers began agitating for administrative changes.[26]

The ability of farm pressure groups to exert political power was also enhanced by a favorable set of public attitudes and symbols. Agriculture, so it was said (and widely believed), was the nation's basic industry, the foundation for all others, and farmers were the nation's chosen people, the guardians of its most cherished virtues, and the defenders of individual freedom, republican simplicities, and old-fashioned morality. Such men deserved every consideration. Farm laborers, on the other hand, enjoyed no such special status. On the contrary, many Americans still thought in terms of the old and largely mythical agricultural ladder. The status of a farm worker, they felt, was a temporary one. He was an entrepreneur in training, an individual who would soon rise to the rank of farm owner. Consequently, he needed no unions and little or no governmental protection.[27]

To a considerable extent, then, the users of Mexican labor could take advantage of a ready-made apparatus of power, a going system of farm lobbies, political connections, potent symbols, and favorable attitudes. At the same time, farm workers were almost completely unorganized. Such support as they received from urban labor was largely perfunctory. Since they were rarely eligible to vote and had no way of undertaking political reprisals, they possessed little or no political power. Their spokesmen came mostly from the ranks of social workers, religious leaders, and humanitarian reformers, people who had to rely primarily on an appeal to the national conscience; when it came to getting action, conscience was often a poor substitute for power.[28]

The coalition that backed the Mexican labor program, however, was far from a monolithic one. Theoretically, it might be split in various ways, along regional, commodity, class, ethical, or ideological lines. Consequently, the politics of the issue was largely a matter of working out arrangements and devising a rationale that would subordinate these internal differences, discredit the critics, and hold the coalition together.

One possibility of division, that along regional and commodity lines, stemmed from the fact that the bulk of the braceros were used in one section of the country and in a relatively few commodities. Why, the opponents of the program asked, should farmers in the East, Midwest, or Northwest pay taxes to subsidize the farmers of the Southwest? Why should wheat, corn, or dairy farmers subsidize the growers of cotton, sugar beets, fruits, and vegetables? And why should a vegetable grower in New Jersey allow his Texas and California competitors to undercut him by importing cheap foreign labor?

Occasionally, such arguments were effective, but during most of the 1950s, they seemed to meet with little success. Complaints from the Northwest virtually ceased after the growers there learned that Mexican labor in California would add to the supply of domestic migrants in Washington and Oregon. Other employers went along for much the same reason: Those in the upper Midwest felt that any tampering with the foreign labor program would disrupt their own supply of Texas-Mexicans; and those on the Atlantic Coast were afraid that a labor shortage in the Southwest would mean increased competition for the labor that they drew from the Southeast, Puerto Rico, and the British West Indies.[29] The advocates of imported Mexican labor also benefited from the process of agricultural logrolling. Their program enjoyed the support of a united regional group, and, since there was no active opposition from other regional farm groups, most of the national farm organizations and most of the politicians from the wheat, corn, or tobacco regions were willing to support it.[30] After all, the support of the Southwest might come in handy when Congress began considering wheat, corn, or tobacco legislation.

A second effort to divide the farm forces was along class lines. Most of the Mexican workers, so this argument ran, went to corporate growers and plantation owners. The great majority of small farmers hired no labor at all; since their income was primarily labor income, they suffered from an arrangement that forced them to compete with braceros and to accept prices that were profitable only to the exploiters of cheap labor. The only ones to benefit, so the critics implied, were the processing companies and the "factories-in-the-field," and if family farmers really wanted to improve their position, they would help to abolish such programs, turn their attention to marketing organization, and force processors and distributors to pay decent prices for farm goods.[31]

These arguments, appealing as they did to such potent symbols as the yeoman farmer and the greedy monopolist, were not without some effect. They were convincing to Western liberals like Hubert Humphrey and

George McGovern. They became the standard line for the Farmers Union, which claimed to speak for "family farmers." And occasionally, a small farmer or one of the more progressive growers would use them before a congressional committee. They failed, however, to bring any organized protest from low-income farmers. Typically, such farmers did not belong to farm organizations, and those that did usually thought of themselves as entrepreneurs rather than laborers. They were willing, in any event, to leave policy formulation to their more prosperous neighbors, to men with the time, inclination, and education to engage in it. So-called "farm opinion" came mostly from the representatives of upper-income farmers; the testimony of the Farmers Union, the one organization that did present a different point of view, was largely ignored. The union, after all, was relatively weak and, in any case, was reluctant to become deeply involved in an issue that was not of really vital concern to its members.[32]

The supporters of the Mexican labor program were also able to develop counter-appeals that blunted the whole effort to divide farmers along class lines. On the one hand, they deplored the efforts of urban rabble rousers to stir up class conflict and make trouble for the nation's more "productive" farmers. On the other, they paid homage to the small farmer and insisted that a cut in imported labor would hurt him more than it would the large one. The idea that the little farmer hired no outside help, they argued, was misleading. It might be true in the wheat and corn belts, but it was certainly not true in such labor-intensive crops as cotton, sugar beets, and vegetables. Here a farmer simply could not operate without extra help. And, since the ability of the small farmer to mechanize or attract domestic labor was considerably less than that of his larger neighbor, he was dependent for his very existence on the importation of braceros. The critics, to be sure, challenged the statistical validity of this argument; they claimed that even in the vegetable field the great bulk of hired labor was used by a minority of the farmers. However, farm representatives seemed willing to discount these statistics, and most of them would deny that they were voting for class legislation.[33]

A third attempt to divide the farm forces was along lines of morality and ethical conduct. The appeal here usually began with a recitation of the deplorable conditions under whirh farm workers lived, of the squalor, poverty, and social evils that resulted from low wages, long hours, bad housing, and irregular employment. It then noted how the Mexican labor program had accentuated these conditions. Finally, it attempted to distinguish between the bad employers and the good. The former were those who treated their workers like animals and were motivated solely by the desire for economic gain; and the latter were those who wanted to improve working conditions but were held back by competition from the first group. The obvious inference was that the good employers should welcome remedial legislation, measures that would protect them from unfair competition, provide them with a more stable and dependable labor force, raise the purchasing power of their workers, and help their communities to overcome a variety of social evils. Actually, said Senator Wayne Morse, the decent farmers themselves should be the leading supporters of reform, and they would be, once they understood the relationship between a decent standard of living for farm workers and permanent prosperity for agriculture.[34]

This appeal to social justice did not have much effect in dividing the farmers themselves, but it did pose a threat to their public image, particularly in urban areas and among urban congressmen. Consequently, the advocates of the Mexican labor program tried their best to counter the appeal and discredit the people who used it. In reality, they argued, the so-called "studies" of farm labor were grossly exaggerated distortions written by urban do-gooders, labor propagandists, and "pseudo-socio-agricultural experts." As a matter of fact, conditions were quite good. In his home state of Michigan, declared Representative Clare Hoffman, the workers ate "good food," slept in "good beds," drank "pure water," and got plenty of "God's sunshine and clear air." They liked it, he assured the House of Representatives. Otherwise, they would not do it. And the "folks from New York and the other cities" would do well to clean up their own slums and send some of their people to the "great outdoors," where they would receive not only material benefits, but a "little more religion and patriotism."

To some extent, too, the employers were able to offset the image of the downtrodden laborer with that of the long-suffering farmer, the poor, struggling soul who was constantly harried by the vagaries of weather and insects, subjected to the iron grip of a cost-price squeeze, haunted by the specters of unionism, rotting crops, and bankruptcy, and beset by comissions that were "totally ignorant" of the subject they were investigating. The famers, so their spokesmen argued, simply could not afford to raise wages, maintain workers on a year-round basis, or provide fringe benefits. Such things would never pay for themselves; besides, they were apt to spoil the workers and do more harm than good. In the words of one Texas employer, "As soon as you begin to Americanize a Mexican he's no longer any good. He just won't work any more."[35]

The supporters of the program also maintained that a genuine labor shortage did exist, and, therefore, the importation of foreign labor hurt no one and had nothing to do with the issue of social justice. Such labor, they insisted, was "expensive," and employers turned to it only because they could not find enough domestic workers able and willing to do farm work. The latter would no longer pick cotton, make use of a short-handled hoe, or engage in other "stoop labor"; and the few that the Employment Service could supply were so lazy, shiftless, and spoiled that no employer should be required to use them.

During the 1950s, such arguments were effective. The critics, of course, denied that they were true. They noted the failure of wages to rise proportionately in areas that used Mexican labor; they charged that the employers preferred the more docile and more easily managed Mexicans; and they claimed that domestics would do the work if employers would only provide decent wages and working conditions, that it was not a matter of "stoop labor," but rather one of hard labor at "stupid wages." Yet a majority of congressmen seemed to buy the idea of a labor shortage. Many of them were appalled at the prospect of crops going to waste because of the lack of harvest hands. Consequently, the effort to abolish the foreign labor program by an appeal to social justice failed to make much headway.[36]

A fourth attempt to discredit the Mexican labor program and divide its supporters took the form of an appeal to such traditionally conservative symbols as nativism, nationalism, and anti-Communism. The importation of Mexican workers, so this argument ran, was un-American. It brought in substandard "foreigners" to take "American jobs," drained off "American dollars" to Mexico, and made "American farmers" dependent on a foreign labor supply, one that could be cut off at the whim of a foreign government. It was also a boon to Communist agitators and an avenue whereby enemy agents, dope peddlers, and other undesirables could enter the United States. Clearly, the critics implied, no "real American" would sanction such a policy, and, among rural politicians, such arguments often had more appeal than any plea based on social justice. During the early 1950s, a conservative legislator like H. R. Gross of Iowa felt that the program could develop into an "open gate for assorted subversives." Instead of taking American jobs, he declared, the Mexicans should "go over and do some of the fighting and dying in Korea."[37] If too many rural congressmen began thinking along these lines, the whole arrangement would be in jeopardy; therefore, the spokesmen for the program took great pains to explain why the users of Mexican labor were just as patriotic as anyone else.

Actually, the employers and their allies declared, the bracero program helped to protect the American system, especially when one realized that abandonment of it would mean a new influx of wetbacks. Under existing arrangements, the workers were subject to strict controls; they took jobs that Americans simply would not fill; and, since they were then returned to Mexico, they created no serious social problems and posed no threat to "American" values or the "American" stock. Nor was there any justification for raising the Communist bogey. The real breeding ground for Communists was in the urban centers, among "educated fellows" who did not like to "get their hands dirty," and the real threat to Americanism came from those who would "socialize" agriculture, turn farm workers into wards of the government, and subject farmers to a useless, unworkable, and suffocating blanket of controls.[38] Repeatedly, too, the farm spokesmen depicted the program as an exercise in international good will and were thus able to take advantage of the favorable symbol of Pan-Americanism. Under it, they claimed, the bracero could come to the United States, earn several times as much as in his native land, learn American agricultural techniques, and then return with a "nest egg" that would give him a chance in life. The whole process amounted to a type of indirect foreign aid, and, since it not only made friends for the United States but also stimulated the Mexican economy, it was clearly in the interests of both nations.[39]

Like most pressure groups, in fact, the users of Mexican labor insisted that their program benefited everyone and, therefore, could not fail to be in the national interest. The United States benefited from an ample supply of food and fiber, the creation of international good will, and the economic utilization of its resources. Mexico benefited from the alleviation of her unemployment problem, the influx of bracero dollars, and the acquisition of new skills and practices. Farmers benefited from their ability to secure the necessary labor at a reasonable price. Businessmen benefited from the farmers' prosperity and the plentiful supply of raw materials. Laborers benefited from the elimination of the wetback traffic, the abundance of food, and the upgrading of American jobs. And consumers benefited from "reasonable" prices, something they would not have if farmers had to pay the same wages as industrialists.[40] Instead of eliminating such a beneficial program, some of its proponents argued, public policy should be moving in the opposite direction, toward encouraging domestic migrants to find other jobs and then substituting Mexicans who were willing to do farm work and return home when the jobs were done. Such an approach, they thought, was distinctly preferable to the idea of encouraging American workers to uproot their families and "take them a thousand miles to accept temporary employment."[41]

Thus, during the 1950s, the defenders of the Mexican labor program were able to develop an elaborate rationale, one that reinforced their political power, identified their cause with the national interest, and held their alliance together. At the end of the decade, the program that they had put through in 1951 remained basically intact, and not many observers were predicting that it would soon be abolished. On the contrary, most of them, even those who were strongly critical, seemed to feel that the importation of braceros was likely to become a permanent feature of the farm labor picture.[42]

In 1961 the advocates of the bracero program were successful in extending it for two more years. Yet there were indications now that further extensions might run into much more difficulty. In the Senate, a liberal-labor coalition succeeded, for the first time, in adding an amendment that would require prospective users of Mexican labor to pay a minimum farm wage based upon state and national averages; while this amendment failed to survive the conference committee, the new act did require that employers offer domestic workers the same wages, hours, and physical conditions as were offered to Mexicans and that they refrain from using braceros for year-round jobs or in connection with power-driven, self-propelled machinery.[43] At last, it seemed, the stark poverty of migrant farm workers was beginning to trouble the national conscience. The social and political climate was changing, and this, coupled with the declining power of the farm bloc, made it increasingly difficult to convince urban congressmen that Mexican labor was needed.

The new concern with migrant labor was a part of the broad changes that produced the New Frontier and the Great Society. Yet it also had specific antecedents of its own. It began in the late 1950s when an interdepartmental committee headed by Secretary of Labor James Mitchell, a group of prominent citizens organized as the National Advisory Committee on Farm Labor, and a special senatorial subcommittee all focused attention on the problem and publicized a variety of needed reforms.[44] In 1959 Mitchell appointed a group of expert consultants to review the foreign labor program: out of this review came a report that pointed up the adverse effects on domestic workers and suggested a number of new safeguards, especially a provision for minimum wages and a requirement that employers offer domestics the same conditions and benefits as were required for braceros.[45] This report soon became the rallying cry for a number of labor, religious, and welfare organizations. In the 86th Congress these groups tried without success to secure the passage of the McGovern bill, a measure based directly on the consultants' recommendations. In late 1960, they benefited from the public indignation aroused by the television documentary, "Harvest of Shame," and in 1961, although they were still unable to secure any basic changes, they did win the support of the Kennedy administration and demonstrated more strength than ever before.[46]

During the next two years, the strength of the reform bloc continued to grow. No longer, it seemed, were urban labor leaders willing to sacrifice the farm workers in return for rural acquiescence in the passage of urban labor measures. Religious, welfare, and liberal organizations, groups like the National Council of Churches, the Catholic Rural Life Conference, the National Consumers League, and Americans for Democratic Action, were also demonstrating more and more concern. From all of these groups came a renewed effort to educate the public, identify the bracero program with agribusiness, split the farm bloc, and point up the "incredible anomaly" of importing foreign workers to produce farm surpluses at a time when several million American laborers were looking for work. Increasingly, too, the critics of the program tried to make its existence a moral issue. In their eyes it became a "slave labor" program, a social and moral "outrage," and a "disgrace" to American democracy and the Christian religion.[47]

To some critics, the process seemed painfully slow, but at long last, in a Congress in which urban liberals were exercising greater influence, they were winning converts. A growing number of urban congressmen agreed that the bracero program was immoral, reactionary, and unnecessary. Veteran liberals made its elimination a part of the liberal creed, and, even among rural groups, support for Public Law 78 was declining. Some farm leaders were probably worried about the threats of Eastern legislators to withdraw their support from the more basic farm programs; others seemed anxious to dissociate themselves from an unpopular cause; and still others, particularly the spokesmen for the cotton farmers, were less concerned once they found that mechanization could replace the braceros. The Farm Bureau continued to endorse the program, but the Grange gave it only qualified support, the Farmers Union opposed it, and a number of rural congressmen began voting against it.[48] In 1961 only 23 percent of all rural representatives did so, but by October 1963 this number had grown to 33 percent.[49]

The growers also faced an increasingly skeptical administration, one that discounted their talk of labor shortages and seemed bent upon putting teeth into the law. When he signed the 1961 extension, President Kennedy directed the Department of Labor to use the full scope of its powers to protect domestic workers, and, in the months that followed, Secretary Arthur Goldberg and his successor, Willard Wirtz, took the directive seriously. In the executive agreement of 1962, a new clause and joint interpretation appeared, allowing the Secretary of Labor to set bracero wages high enough to avoid "adverse effect" on domestic workers. Under this authority, the Department of Labor established a schedule of minimum wages, running from sixty cents an hour in Arkansas to a dollar in California, and, in spite of bitter protests from the employers, it continued to enforce the schedule. It insisted, too, that the clauses forbidding the use of braceros in year-round jobs or machine operations meant exactly what they said. And these policies, coupled with increased mechanization, did reduce the number of braceros from 315,846 in 1960 to 194,978 in 1962. Under Orville Freeman, moreover, the Department of Agriculture officially backed the policies of the Department of Labor. In 1963 both departments took the position that the program should come to an end unless employers were required to offer domestic workers the same housing, transportation, and insurance benefits as were provided to the Mexicans.[50]

In 1963, in spite of the growing opposition to the program, its advocates pushed for another two-year extension. Again they stressed the stoop labor argument, depicted the program as an exercise in international good will, and raised the specters of rotting crops and rising prices. Again they warned that failure to extend the law would result in a mass influx of wetbacks and permanent immigrants. And again they argued against "impractical" reforms and claimed that most of the criticism was grossly unfair, that actually there was "no class of people in the whole world" who were "more decent" or who had "a greater sense of anxiety about being their brother's keeper than the farmers of this country." It was obvious, however, that such appeals had lost much of their power. In May the House rejected a two-year extension. In August the Senate passed a measure that would require employers to offer domestic workers the same fringe benefits as were guaranteed to the braceros. Only by heroic efforts did the growers' lobby succeed in reversing these decisions and obtaining a simple one-year extension. Key members of the farm bloc, like Senator Ellender of Louisiana, now promised that they would not support a further extension, and a number of the congressmen who changed their positions did so on the basis of such pledges or because they felt that it was only fair to allow a year for an orderly phase-out.[51]

Some growers undoubtedly hoped that a further extension might be obtained or that some sort of special program might be set up under the Immigration Act of 1952.[52] Such hopes, however, failed to materialize. There was no major effort to extend the law in the congressional session of 1964, and, as the date for its expiration approached, Secretary Wirtz made it clear that he had no intention of continuing it in another form. In his opinion, "getting rid of the bracero program" was "one of the most important social and economic developments" of the 1960s, and government action should now concentrate on rationalizing the farm labor market and improving conditions so as to attract sufficient domestic workers. After a series of hearings in late 1964, the Department of Labor announced that employers, in order to be eligible for any foreign workers, must offer a minimum wage ranging from $1.15 an hour in Arkansas to $1.40 in California. And, in addition, they must provide a written contract containing the same fringe benefits as were previously guaranteed to braceros under Public Law 78.[53]

The policies of the Department of Labor brought strong protests, particularly from the California growers, who claimed that much of their crop would rot in the fields. Yet Wirtz refused to relent. After a personal inspection of California farms in the spring of 1965, he indicated that only in very exceptional cases, none of which existed at present, would there be any importation of Mexican labor. The bracero program, he said, was "dead," and most of its proponents would concede that the chances of reviving it were not very bright. The growers, to be sure, had not lost all of their political punch. They continued to apply pressure, both in Congress and at the White House, and, in September 1965, their attempt to amend the farm bill so as to transfer the controls over foreign workers from the Secretary of Labor to the Secretary of Agriculture failed by only one vote. Yet it seemed unlikely that any new program would be set up, and in the future the demand for one was likely to diminish. Mechanization would further reduce the need for farm labor, and there were indications that once the growers realized that the Department of Labor meant business, they would take steps to recruit and attract domestic workers.[54] The change would necessitate some painful readjustments, but these were to be expected when any economic group was deprived of the vested interest that it had developed in a special governmental privilege.

In retrospect, it appears that the bracero program was a casualty of the reform spirit that pervaded the Kennedy and Johnson administrations. In the generally conservative climate of the 1950s, the users of Mexican labor could take advantage of a built-in structure of power and devise a rationale that would keep this structure intact, salve the national conscience, and win the necessary urban support. But in a climate that produced the Civil Rights Act and the war on poverty, the perpetuation of Public Law 78 became a moral issue and urban support became much harder to secure. Urban liberals were now exercising greater influence, both in Congress and in the administration, and, once the Department of Labor had raised the cost of importing and using braceros, mechanization increased and some farm groups lost interest. Those who still wanted braceros became an increasingly isolated group, one with a bad public image, a rationale that was no longer convincing, and a set of values that ran counter to the current conception of "progress." The end result was a loss of bargaining power, and this fact was reflected in the political decisions of 1963 and 1964.

One can only speculate, of course, as to whether the fate of the bracero program has any relevance to other farm programs. The circumstances surrounding it may be unique. Yet it is also possible that its demise may foreshadow the end of other special farm subsidies. If the farm bloc continues to splinter into small segments, each primarily concerned with its own narrow program, and if these groups become identified in the public mind with agribusiness and with an obstructionist rural conservatism, then it seems likely that an increasingly urbanized democracy, one with fewer and fewer farmers, will look upon government aid for such groups with more and more suspicion. Under these circumstances, the rationale behind the farm program will lose much of its appeal, aid for "underprivileged farmers" and salvation of the "family farm" will cease to be a part of the liberal creed, and a variety of farm groups may find themselves fighting an isolated, rear-guard action against reformers who have come to regard them as entrenched "special interests." If such is the case, a study of the politics associated with the Mexican labor program may prove instructive, both to those who would perpetuate the existing network of farm subsidies and market controls and to those who would revise or eliminate it.

NOTES

1. See Charles M. Hardin, "The Politics of Agriculture in the United States," *Journal of Farm Economics* 32 (1950): 571–83, and idem, "The Tobacco Program: Exception or Portent?" ibid. 28 (1946): 920–35; Ernest A. Englebert, "The Political Strategy of Agriculture," ibid. 36 (1954): 375–86; "Politics of Agriculture," *CQ Weekly Report* 20 (15 June 1962): 1020–22.

2. The five states using the most Mexican laborers in 1959 were: Texas, 205,959; California, 136,012; Arkansas, 27,837; Arizona, 24,630; and New Mexico, 18,290. House Agriculture Committee, *Extension of Mexican Farm Labor Program,* 86th Cong., 2d sess., 1960, pp. 221, 378–80, 386, hereinafter cited as HAC Hearings with appropriate date.

3. For the executive agreement and subsequent law see U.S., *Statutes at Large,* vol. 56, p. 1759 and ibid., vol. 70. The wartime program is discussed in Otey M. Scruggs, "Evolution of the Mexican Farm Labor Agreement of 1942," *Agricultural History* 34 (1960): 140–49; George O. Coalson, "Mexican Contract Labor in American Agriculture," *Southwestern Social Science Quarterly* 32 (1952): 228–31; Wayne D. Rasmussen, *A History of the Emergency Farm Labor Supply Program* (Washington, 1951); and President's Commission on Migratory Labor, *Migratory Labor in American Agriculture* (1951), pp. 37–38, hereinafter cited as *PCML, Rept.*

4. U.S., *Statutes at Large,* vol. 61, pp. 37, 38, 4097; ibid., vol. 62, p. 3887; U.S. *Treaties,* vol. 2, pp. 1048–67; *PCML Rept.*, pp. 38–44, 52–54; Coalson, "Mexican Labor," pp. 231–34. Mexico renounced the 1948 agreement after American authorities at El Paso admitted several thousand Mexicans illegally and then "paroled" them to employers that wanted their services. See *Time,* 1 November 1948, p. 38; and "The 1948 Agreement," 11-15, Mexican Labor File, David M. Stowe Papers, Truman Library.

5. The farm labor investigations in 1950 produced a variety of employer complaints, but there was no support for a return to the wartime system of governmental contracting. The ideal arrangement, most employers seemed to think, would be a simple crossing-card system. HAC Hearings, *Farm Labor Investigations,* 81st Cong., 2d sess., 1950, 10, 17, 42–43, 54–55, 159–62, 169–73, 191–94, 228–30. See also Memorandum, Roger Jones to James Sundquist, 30 March 1950, Official File (OF) 407-E, Truman Papers, Truman Library.

6. The treatment of Mexican workers was a matter of heated debate, but labor representatives and the Mexican consuls compiled a long list of grievances and some employers would admit that they did not live up to the letter of the law. Some, however, claimed that the Mexican protests were due to selfish interests in Mexico who wanted to keep "a surplus of labor" there. HAC Hearings (1950), pp. 159, 225; *PCML Rept.*, p. 45; Ernesto Galarza, *Strangers in Our Fields* (Washington, 1956), pp. 18–58; Senate Agriculture Committee, *Farm Labor Program,* 82d Cong., 1st sess., 1951, pp. 110–12, hereinafter cited as *SAC Hearings* (1951); Senate Labor Committee, *Migratory Labor,* 82d Cong., 2d sess., 1952, pp. 146, 259, herinafter cited as *SLC Hearings* (1952); Chart, "Mexican Nationals Complaints in Region VIII in 1949"; PCML Hearings, 31 July 1950, both in PCML Records, Truman Papers.

7. *Mexican-American Review,* May 1951, p. 15; *SAC Hearings* (1951), pp. 40–42, 111–12; *Congressional Record,* vol. 97, pp. 4417, 7521; "The Executive Agreement: 1951–53," pp. 2–5, Mexican Labor File, Stowe Papers.

8. Senator Dennis Chavez of New Mexico and Representative Samuel Yorty of California both sponsored measures to protect domestic workers, but these received little consideration from the agricultural committees in Congress. The attempt to place new curbs on the wetback traffic had stronger support, but it, too, eventually ended in failure. HAC Hearings, *Farm Labor,* 82d Cong., 1st sess., 1951, pp. 1–3, 98–99, 114–18. SAC Hearings (1951), pp. 1–3, 133–34, 139–40; *Congressional Record,* vol. 97, pp. 4603, 4608–10, 4952–53, 4961–71, 7168–75, 7264, 7519–23; Memoranda, Eleanor Hadley to PCML, April 12, 18, 20, 30, 1951, PCML Records, Truman Papers.

9. The President's Commission on Migratory Labor was appointed in June 1950, largely because the Department of Labor felt that such a commission could absorb some of the "political heat" and provide a factual foundation for future policy decisions. After conducting extensive hearings, the commission concluded that employers were exaggerating the need for foreign labor, that it was being used to depress farm wages, and that steps should be taken to improve working conditions and make more efficient use of domestic labor. Rural

spokesmen, however, promptly discounted the report as the work of social reformers, urban do-gooders, and union people. Its findings, they claimed, were "ridiculous," "quite devoid of justifiable evidence," and illustrative of the "erroneous" thinking that had once appeared in the Farm Security Administration, *PCML Rept.*, pp. 58–61, 177–85; HAC Hearings (1950), pp. 174, 190–91; *Congressional Record,* vol. 97, pp. 4511, 4588, 4591; SLC Hearings (1952), pp. 15–18, 482, 510–16; Memorandum, Roger Jones to James Sundquist, 30 March 1950, OF 407-E, Truman Papers; Maurice Van Hecke to Truman, 4 December 1950, PCML Records, Truman Papers.

10. HAC Hearings (1951), pp. 9–10, 13–19, 83–84; SAC Hearings (1951), pp. 5–7, 26–30; *Congressional Record,* vol. 97, pp. 4417–19, 7271; *Senate Report 214,* 82d Cong., 1st sess., 1951; *House Report 326,* 82d Cong., 1st sess., 1951.

11. *Congressional Record,* vol. 97, pp. 4979, 7277–79, 8144–46; HAC Hearings (1951), pp. 3–5, 86–88, 132–35, 145–46, 162–63; SAC Hearings (1951), pp. 3–5, 65–68, 84–85, 96–97; Coalson, "Mexican Labor," *loc. cit.*, 234–236; Michael Galvin to Frederick Lawton, July 11, 1951; White House Press Release, 13 July 1951, both in Bill File (S. 984), Truman Papers; Memorandum, David Stowe to Truman. 11 August 1951, Mexican Labor File, Stowe Papers.

12. 65 U.S., *Statutes at Large,* vol. 119; U.S. *Treaties,* vol. 2 pp. 1968–96, vol. 5, pp. 355–57, 380–85, vol. 6, pp. 6058–59, vol. 7, pp. 3427–28, vol. 10, pp. 1630, 2036–49, vol. 12, pp. 1081–82, 3130, vol. 13, pp. 2022–42.

13. HAC Hearings *Extension of Mexican Farm Labor Program, 83d Cong., 1st sess., 1953, pp. 49–50,* 63–65, 92–98; *Mexican Farm Labor,* 83d Cong., 2d sess., 1954, 106–8, 188, 216–17; *Mexican Farm Labor Program,* 84th Cong., 1st sess., 1955. pp. 159–61, 172–78; *Farm Labor,* 85th Cong., 2d sess., 1958, pp. 308–9, 437–44, 474–75, 493–99; HAC Hearings (1960), pp. 355–67, 374; U.S., *Statutes at Large,* vol. 69, p. 615; ibid., vol. 70, p. 958.

14. HAC Hearings (1953), pp. 10–14, (1955), pp. 105–6, (1958), pp. 122, 300–301, 305–9, 324. Many employers felt that the Mexicans were insisting upon excessive safeguards, and in 1954, after Mexico had stiffened her demands and allowed the existing agreement to lapse, the farm organizations did succeed in winning statutory authorization for unilateral recruiting. As it turned out, a new executive agreement soon made this unneccessary, but the employers had demonstrated their ability and determination to maintain the flow of foreign labor even if it should lead to serious international complications. HAC Hearings (1954), pp. 1–11, 31–39, 190–96; *Congressional Record,* vol. 100, pp. 2511, 2570–71; U.S., *Statutes at Large,* vol. 68, p. 28; U.S. *Treaties,* vol. 5, pp. 380–85.

15. Farm employers never approved of the postwar transfer of the Farm Placement Service from the Department of Agriculture to the Department of Labor. The latter agency, they felt, was too labor-minded and too willing to give in to Mexican demands. In 1960 they urged that the Secretary of Agriculture be given a veto over Department of Labor decisions, but this proposal collapsed when Secretary Benson refused to support it. HAC Hearings (1953), pp. 48–49, 53–55, 89, (1960), pp. 2–14, 61–69, 352–54; *Congressional Quarterly Almanac,* vol. 16 (1960), pp. 369–71; Louisa R. Shotwell, *The Harvesters* (Garden City, 1961), pp. 81–82.

16. HAC Hearings (1953), pp. 32, 40–49, 52, (1955), pp. 56–57, 64, 74–75, 104–7, 110–11, (1958), pp. 21, 201, 300–301, 303–304, 334, (1960), pp. 4, 63, 69, 84; U.S., *Statutes at Large,* vol. 67, p. 500; ibid., vol. 69, p. 615; ibid., vol. 72, p. 934; ibid., vol. 74, p. 1021.

17. U.S., *Statutes at Large,* vol. 66, p. 26.

18. HAC Hearings (1955), pp. 88–98, 110–111, (1958), pp. 21, 139, 362–63, (1960), pp. 400, 416–17; SLC Hearings (1952), pp. 44, 76; Shotwell, *Harvesters,* pp. 79–80; Richard P. Eckels, "Hungry Workers, Ripe Crops, and the Nonexistent Mexican Border," *Reporter* 13 April 1954, pp. 28–32; John G. McBride, *Vanishing Bracero* (San Antonio, 1963), pp. 6–9; *New York Times,* 16–18 August 1953, 18–20 June and 2 August 1954.

19. In 1959 there were some 305 associations with a total membership of 43,641. Only 8,150 users acted as individuals. HAC Hearings (1960), p. 386. See also *PCML Rept.*, pp. 62–63, 96–97, 106–10, 129; SLC Hearings (1952), pp. 75, 238, 261; HAC Hearings (1955), pp. 108–10 (1958), pp. 144, 334; Lloyd Fisher, *Harvest Labor Market in California* (Cambridge, Mass., 1953), pp. 97–98, 106–110; Varden Fuller, *Labor Relations in Agriculture* (Berkeley, 1955), pp. 23–29; Harry Crozier to PCML, 8 February 1951, Edward Hayes to PCML, 8 February 1951, both in PCML Records, Truman Papers.

20. Note the affiliations of the members of the Special Farm Labor Committee or those of the spokesmen for the National Farm Labor Users Committee. HAC Hearings (1955), pp. 108–10, (1960), pp. 25–36, 55–61.

21. HAC Hearings (1953), pp. 31–34, 41–45, 47, (1955), pp. 56–57, 64, 74–75, 104–5, 321, (1960), pp. 4, 67, 179, 276–78; Grant McConnell, *The Decline of Agrarian Democracy* (Berkeley, 1953), pp. 170–71; Fuller, *Labor Relations*, pp. 17–18; Noble Clark, "Captive Farms," PCML Records, Truman Papers.

22. Paul Jacobs, "The Forgotten People," *Reporter*, 22 January 1959, pp. 13–18; SLC Hearings (1952), pp. 261–64; Gordon E. Baker, *Rural versus Urban Political Power* (Garden City, 1955), pp. 11–26; Paul Taylor, "Migratory Farm Labor and the Body Politic," PCML Records, Truman Papers.

23. The jurisdiction of the agricultural committees over the farm labor program was another distinct advantage. Critics kept trying to get the program referred to the labor committees, but without success. HAC Hearings (1954), p. 79, (1960), p. 214; SLC Hearings (1952), p. 350; McConnell, *Decline of Agrarian Democracy*, p. 179: Charles M. Hardin, "Farm Political Power and the U.S. Governmental Crisis," *Journal of Farm Economics* 40 (1958): 1648–51; Louis B. Schmidt, "The Role and Techniques of Agrarian Pressure Groups," *Agricultural History* 30 (1956): 55–57; Baker, *Rural versus Urban Power*, pp. 40–49.

24. In large measure, of course, the alignment described here is only another way of noting the conservative coalition between Northern Republicans and Southern Democrats. The classifications used are those employed by the *Congressional Quarterly Almanac* with appropriate adjustments for redistricting. Urbanites are persons living in places of 2,500 or more inhabitants or in densely settled urban fringes around cities of 50,000 or more. Urban districts are those containing a city over 50,000 and in which (a) at least one-half of the population is urban or (b) the major city constitutes at least one-third of the total population. All other districts are rural or small town. *Congressional Quarterly Almanac*, vol. 7 (1951), pp. 104–5, vol. 9 (1953), pp. 126–27, vol. 12 (1956), pp. 788–91, vol. 17 (1961), pp. 648–649. The farmer-business alliance is discussed in Wesley McCune, *Who's Behind Our Farm Policy?* (New York, 1956), pp. 6–7, 15.

25. Hardin, "Politics of Agriculture," pp. 575–576; McConnell, *Decline of Agrarian Democracy*, pp. 166–72; James M. Burns, *The Deadlock of Democracy* (Englewood Cliffs, N.J., 1963), p. 252; HAC Hearings (1955), pp. 53–54, 87, (1958), pp. 234, 295; Clinton Anderson to Truman, 26 May 1949, Tom Baker to John Steelman, 10 May 1949, RLK to Matthew Connelly, 15 August 1949, all in OF 407-D, Truman Papers.

26. SLC Hearings (1952), pp. 245–47, 784, 1005–7, 1013–15; HAC Hearings (1953), p. 64, (1955), pp. 110–11, 259–61, (1958), pp. 308–9, 438–39, (1960), pp. 33–35, 62–63, 277–79; James P. Mitchell, in *Reporter*, 22 January 1959, p. 20; Report, T. N. Finney to Thomas Campbell, July 12, 1950, PCML Records, Truman Papers.

27. Varden Fuller, in *Reporter*, 5 February 1959, p. 8; Lowry Nelson, "The American Rural Heritage," *American Quarterly* 3 1949: 232–34; Schmidt, "Agrarian Pressure Groups," p. 55; Baker, *Rural versus Urban Power*. p. 1

28. The National Agricultural Workers Union claimed to speak for farm workers, but never succeeded in developing any sizable membership. Fuller, *Labor Relations*, pp. 11–13; *Commonweal*, 8 April 1960, p. 30; SLC Hearings (1952), pp. 430–432; HAC Hearings (1960), pp. 229–30, 233–34, 306.

29. HAC Hearings (1960), pp. 154, 228, 262; SAC Hearings (1951), p. 169; Senate Labor Committee, *Migratory Labor*, 86th Cong., 1st sess., 1959, pp. 600, 632, hereinafter cited as *SLC Hearings* (1959); *Congressional Record*, vol. 97, pp. 4424, 4479, 4948–49, 7161, vol. 100, p. 2497, vol. 101, p. 10011, vol. 106, pp. 14802–3, 14808–9, 14974–75.

30. McConnell, *Decline of Agrarian Democracy*, pp. 170–71. In 1953 rural representatives from the ten leading wheat states voted to extend the Mexican labor program by a count of 34 to 2, those from the ten leading corn states by a count of 31 to 5, and those from the ten leading tobacco states by a count of 43 to 9. Computed from *Congressional Quarterly Almanac*, vol. 9 (1953), pp. 126–27.

31. HAC Hearings (1954), pp. 45, 73–74, (1958), pp. 575–77, (1960), pp. 164–66, 171–72, 197, 205–6, 288–91, 375; *Congressional Record*, vol. 97, p. 4487, vol. 106, p. 14802.

32. SLC Hearings (1952), pp. 158–59, 241–42; HAC Hearings (1951), pp. 132–33, (1955), p. 228, (1960), pp. 159–60, 164–66, 228, 282–83; Hardin, "Politics of Agriculture," p. 573; Hardin, *Politics of Agriculture* (Glencoe, 1952), pp. 182–87; Schmidt, "Agrarian Pressure Groups," p. 51. The Farmers Union was strongest in the states of North and South Dakota, Nebraska, Kansas, Montana, Colorado, Oklahoma, Minnesota, and Wisconsin; yet representatives from these states voted overwhelmingly for the Mexican labor program. *Congressional Quarterly Almanac*, vol. 7 (1951), pp. 104–5, vol. 9 (1953), pp. 126–27.

33. HAC Hearings (1950), pp. 190–91, (1955), pp. 79, 319; (1960), pp. 9–10, 188, 269, 271; *Congressional Record*, vol. 106, pp. 14978, 14988; SLC Hearings (1952), pp. 665–66, 673–76, 882–83, (1960), pp. 799, 838–40, 864.

34. SLC Hearings (1952), pp. 154–55, 216–17, 250–54, 466–67, (1959), pp. 100–02, 448; SAC Hearings (1951), pp. 181–82; HAC Hearings (1958), pp. 392–94; *Congressional Record*, vol. 106, pp. 14802–3.

35. HAC Hearings (1954), pp. 176–77, (1960), pp. 57–58, 69–70; SLC Hearings (1952), pp. 137–38, 663–64, (1959), 395–96, (1960), pp. 836–37, 1043–45; *Congressional Record*, vol. 97, p. 7260, vol. 106, p. 14983; Mary H. Vorse, "America's Submerged Class," *Harper's*, February 1953, 92–93; Fisher, *Harvest Labor Market*, pp. 16–18.

36. *Congressional Record*, vol. 97, p. 4679, vol. 99, pp. 3144–45, 3148, vol. 100, pp. 2425, 2501–2, vol. 101, pp. 10007–8, vol. 106, pp. 14804, 14810: SLC Hearings (1952), pp. 250–51, 349; HAC Hearings (1951), pp. 16–17, 103–7, (1954), pp. 24, 28, 62–5, 157–59, 165–66, (1955), pp. 120–23, (1958), pp. 146, 318–19, 360, 438, 460–61, 502–4, 576, (1960), pp. 167, 210, 223–25, 246–47, 327–30, 343.

37. HAC Hearings (1951), pp. 99, 139–40, (1953), p. 93, (1954), pp. 45, 77, (1955), p. 234, (1960), p. 282; *Congressional Record*, vol. 98, pp. 4487, 4979, 7154, 7268, vol. 99, p. 3155, vol. 100, p. 2558, vol. 106, pp. 14803–4, 14984.

38. HAC Hearings (1958), pp. 21–22, 185–86, (1960), p. 14; *Congressional Record*, vol. 99, p. 3146, vol. 101, pp. 10007–8, 10014–17, vol. 104, p. 17654, vol. 106, pp. 14976–77, 14986.

39. The real effect on Mexico was another hotly debated point. While the defenders of the program emphasized the beneficial effects on the Mexican economy, the critics stressed such things as the ill treatment of braceros, the demoralizing effect on Mexican families, and the immorality of allowing a few large farmers to capitalize on the misery of Mexico. If real aid to Mexico was the goal, they argued, a foreign aid program to facilitate industrialization would be a much better way of providing it. HAC Hearings (1953), p. 32, (1955), pp. 217–18, 261–63, (1958), pp. 34, 42, 185–186, 413–14, 444, 460, (1960), pp. 14, 91, 198; SAC Hearings (1951), p. 91; Richard H. Hancock, *The Role of the Bracero in the Economic and Cultural Dynamics of Mexico* (Stanford, 1959), pp. 36–39, 121–29.

40. Critics denied that decent farm wages would necessitate any great increase in food prices; and even if some increase was necessary, they felt, most consumers would gladly pay it. In fact, said Senator Humphrey, they had a "moral obligation" to do so, and the "God-given food which we have to eat" would "taste all the better" when the migrant

laborers had an adequate standard of living. HAC Hearings (1953), p. 32, (1958), pp. 361, 397–98, 460, (1960), pp. 14, 90; SLC Hearings (1952), p. 885, (1959), p. 415, (1960), pp. 820–21; *Congressional Record*, vol. 97, p. 7156, vol. 99, p. 3151, vol. 101, p. 10011; *House Report 1642*, 86th Cong., 2d sess., (1960), pp. 3–4, 21–22; Hancock, *Bracero*, pp. 36–38.

41. HAC Hearings (1955), p. 285, (1960), p. 14; SLC Hearings (1960), pp. 851–52.

42. Hancock, *Bracero*, pp. 127, 129; HAC Hearings (1960), pp. 171, 193, 298; *Commonweal*, 8 April 1960, p. 30.

43. *Congressional Record*, vol. 97, pp. 7872, 18902, 18906, 19801–3, 20963, 20972, 21552; U.S., *Statutes at Large*, vol. 75, p. 761; *Congressional Quarterly Almanac*, vol. 17, (1961), pp. 133–38.

44. President's Committee on Migratory Labor, *Report* (1960), pp. 5–6, 31–33; Western Interstate Conference on Migratory Labor, *Proceedings* (1960), pp. 47–48; HAC Hearings (1960), pp. 306–9; Shotwell, *Harvesters*, pp. 108–10; SLC Hearings (1959), pp. 1–3, (1960), pp. 763–64.

45. "Mexican Farm Labor Program Consultants' Report," in SLC Hearings (1959), pp. 741–50. The consultants were Edward J. Thye, a former senator from Minnesota, George C. Higgins of the National Catholic Welfare Conference, Glenn E. Garrett of the Good Neighbor Commission, and Rufus B. von Kleinsmid of the University of Southern California, HAC Hearings (1960), pp. 166–67.

46. HAC Hearings (1960), pp. 3–4, 72–79, 141–42, 166–67, 195–96; House Agriculture Committee, *Mexican Farm Labor Program*, 87th Cong., 1st sess., 1961, pp. 70–71, 127, 318–21, hereinafter cited as HAC Hearings (1961); *Congressional Record*, vol. 106, pp. 14973, 14988, 18625–30; *Congressional Quarterly Almanac*, vol. 16 (1960), pp. 369–71, vol. 17 (1961), pp. 133–38; Sue Keisker, "Harvest of Shame," *Commonweal*, vol. 74 (19 May 1961), pp. 202–3.

47. HAC Hearings (1961), pp. 56–58, 72–75, 200–207; House Agriculture Committee, *Mexican Farm Labor Program*, 88th Cong., 1st sess., 1963, pp. 89–91, 143–46, 193–98, 262–65, 293–305, hereinafter cited as *HAC Hearings* (1963); *Congressional Record*, vol. 109, pp. 9820–21, 13793, 20694, 20699–700; *Commonweal*, 14 June 1963, p. 316.

48. HAC Hearings (1961), pp. 14, 28–29, 246, (1963), pp. 29–35, 96–100, 180–81, 189–90, 232–34; *Congressional Quarterly Almanac*, vol. 19 (1963), pp. 113–18, 724–25, 740–42; McBride, *Vanishing Bracero*, pp. 64–67; *Congressional Record*, vol. 107, pp. 7871–72; *Commonweal*, 14 June 1963, p. 316.

49. Computed from *Congressional Quarterly Almanac*, vol. 17 (1961), pp. 520–21, vol. 19 (1963), pp. 640–41; and *CQ Weekly Report*, vol. 20 (2 February 1962), pp. 158–69, with appropriate adjustments for redistricting.

50. House Agriculture Committee, *Mexican Farm Labor Program*, 87th Cong., 2d sess., 1962, pp. 2–22, 40–45; HAC Hearings (1963), pp. 3–7, 29–35, 98–100, 189–90; *Congressional Record*, vol. 109, p. 15185; *Congressional Quarterly Almanac*, vol. 18 (1962), p. 124, vol. 19 (1963), pp. 114–15: U.S. *Treaties*, vol. 13, pp. 2030–31.

51. HAC Hearings (1963), 102–3, 327–31; *Congressional Record*, vol. 109, pp. 9818–23, 9833–34, 15186–87, 15201–2, 15219, 20691, 20695, 20704, 20707–8, 20731, 23155, 23174, 23223; *Congressional Quarterly Almanac*, vol. 19 (1963), pp. 113–18; U.S., *Statutes at Large*, vol. 77, p. 363.

52. Section 214 of the Walter-McCarran Immigration Act provided that in case of need the Attorney General might grant temporary entry to otherwise inadmissible aliens. This provision had also appeared in previous immigration laws, and it was under it that workers were admitted from Canada, Jamaica, and the British West Indies. U.S., *Statutes at Large*, vol. 66, p. 189; HAC Hearings (1963), pp. 49–50; *New York Times*, 1 December 1964.

53. *Congressional Quarterly Almanac*, vol. 20 (1964), p. 118; *Business Week*, 16 January 1965, p. 32; *New York Times*, 1, 13, 20 December 1964.

54. *Business Week*, 16 January 1965, p. 33, 17 April 1965, pp. 45–46, 48; *New York*

Times, 29 March, 3, 4, 16, 25 April, 14 September 1965; *CQ Weekly Report*, vol. 23 (17 September 1965), p. 1906. As a concession to the growers, Wirtz did set up a special three-man panel in California to evaluate the applications for foreign labor. The panel, however, did not recommend any major change in policy.

13

"Why the Bracero Program Should Not Be Terminated"

Mexican Embassy

The Ambassador of Mexico presents his compliments to His Excellency the Secretary of State and has the honor to inform him of the position of the Government of Mexico with respect to the decision taken by the House of Representatives of the Congress of the United States on May 29 last, rejecting the bill that would have authorized the executive branch of the United States to extend the international migrant labor agreement that expires on December 31 of this year.

The Government of Mexico considers that there would be no call for any observation whatever concerning the aforesaid action, had the need for Mexican labor that has existed for a number of years among the farmers in various parts of the United States disappeared, or if systems other than those used so far were available to meet that need. It is not to be expected that the termination of an international agreement governing and regulating the rendering of service by Mexican workers in the United States will put an end to that type of seasonal migration. The aforesaid agreement is not the cause of that migration; it is the effect or result of the migratory phenomenon. Therefore, the absence of an agreement would not end the problem but rather would give rise to a de facto situation: The illegal introduction of Mexican workers into the United States, which would be extremely prejudicial to the illegal workers and, as ex-

---

Note from the Mexican Ambassador to the Secretary of State of the United States, June 21, 1963, Reprinted from U.S., *Congressional Record*, 88th Cong., 1st Sess., 1963, vol. 109, part 11, pp. 15203–4.

perience has shown, would also unfavorably affect American workers, which is precisely what the legislators of the United States are trying to prevent.

The Governments of Mexico and the United States have for many years been faced with the problem of the illegal entry of Mexican workers into U.S. territory in search of work. The maximum number of arrests made by the Immigration Service of the United States reached 803,618 in 1953, a year in which only 201,380 workers were contracted. Since that time the efforts of the two Governments to eliminate illegal entries, at the same time leaving the door open under the legal procedures of the international migrant labor agreement of 1951, produced the desired results, the number of arrests having been reduced to 31,106 in 1959, during which year 437,643 workers were contracted.

Despite the fact that in 1960 the number of contracted workers began to decrease markedly, the number of illegal workers did not increase, the conclusion being that the Mexican workers have understood and accepted the fact that if they cannot obtain work by contract, it is because they would not obtain it either by entering the United States illegally. Here are some pertinent data:

Year	Contracts Signed	Deportation
1960	315,846	28,492
1961	291,420	31,350
1962	194,978	19,283

In the last 3 years there has been a considerable increase in the number of Mexican farmworkers who have applied for and obtained residence visas to come to the United States, through letters issued by farmers and growers in the United States who have offered them employment. It is estimated that no less than 32,000 farmworkers obtained their documents in 1961 and possibly some 40,000 in 1962. The statistics on the contracting during the last 5 years show that there were barely 50,000 jobs for the workers during the 12 months of the year, open at various times during the year and in various States, so that in order to be able to work without interruption during the entire year, it would be necessary for the workers to move from one place to another. Since it is impossible to achieve precision and coordination even with the means available to the two Governments, it is concluded that the aforesaid increased number of resident farmworkers do not have permanent work but in fact continue in their status as seasonal workers, working for an employer for 6 or 8 weeks and then returning to Mexico in the hope of being called upon to work for another short period—an operation that is repeated two or three times a year. As may easily be seen, this situation will create problems for both Mexico and the United States, since during the jobless seasons the worker with a residence visa will burden the economy of one of the two countries, with the same consequences of accepting ill-paid work, obtaining official assistance, etc.

There is good reason to believe that the absence of an international agreement governing temporary employment of farmworkers will lead to an increase in the types of migration pointed out above.

Finally, it should be considered that on various occasions when at international meetings on migrant worker problems representatives of the Government of the United States have indicated their purpose of decreasing the contracting until the elimination point is reached, the Mexican representatives have requested that an attempt be made to make the decrease gradually, in order to give Mexico an opportunity to reabsorb the workers who have habitually been working in the United States and thus to stave off the sudden crisis that would come from an increase in national employment. The stoppage of the contracts at the start of 1964 would have approximately 200,000 persons out of work.

It is not considered that the contracting of Mexican workers under the international agreement has produced unfavorable effects on American workers. Quite the contrary. The benefits granted the contracted braceros, in the matter of insurance covering occupational accidents and illness, the extremely careful regulations on lodgings and transportation, and the constant inspection of food have provided a pattern that can be followed for domestic workers who lack such protection. And with regard to the wage increase obtained for Mexican workers on various occasions, chiefly in the year 1962, what was obtained through the effort of the Mexican Government and the cooperation of the Department of Labor of the United States, to such an extent that in some localities the wages are higher than those paid to domestic workers, represents the reason why this type of work is now looked upon as acceptable by the American workers.

It was precisely the presence of the "wetbacks" in the fields of the United States that created a situation undesirable from every standpoint, since those persons have not even the most elementary kind of protection and were the victims of exploitation with respect to wages, because they were forced to accept whatever pay was offered to them, and domestic workers were unable to compete and found themselves compelled to move to other areas. The lack of an agreement to facilitate contracting as long as there is a shortage of farm labor, which the Mexican workers have been covering, would tend to bring about a return to that situation. And although Mexico would make efforts to prevent it, as was indicated by the Secretary of Foreign Affairs of Mexico at a press conference on June 5, the willingness of American employers to give work to the wetbacks explains why in many cases the Mexican workers violate the law of the United States, and it is very important for the Government of this country to solve this problem.

The virtual extinction of discrimination against and segregation of persons of Mexican nationality in areas of the United States where such practices once existed can decisively be attributed to the contracting of Mexican workers under international agreements. The need for labor which only the Mexican could supply but which was not authorized for localities where special schools were maintained for Mexicans, or where they were segregated in restaurants, theaters, etc., and discriminated against in respect of wages, etc., led the authorities concerned to put an end to that situation.

There is no doubt that this has been a firm foundation for the good relations between the peoples of the two countries.

In this connection, it is appropriate to note that in September 1954, the President of Mexico stated in his annual message to the Congress that efforts were being made to solve the difficult problem caused by the exodus of Mexican farmworkers, "acting in full and friendly cooperation with the Government of the United States in this task, in order that those who go to work may do so under the protection of existing agreements." And if indeed the contracting should come to an end, it is hoped, as the Secretary of Foreign Affairs said during the press conference mentioned above, that the two Governments will act vigorously and determinedly to prevent the illegal traffic of workers, which benefits neither Mexico nor the United States and is a constant point of discussion between the two Governments and the communities where the braceros who enter illegally work.

Washington, D.C., June 21, 1963

14

"Mexico's Recent Position On Workers For the United States"

Luis Echeverría

In July 1973, an agreement was signed between the Governments of Mexico and Canada that ensures that Mexican migrant farm laborers will have legal entry to that country as well as lodging and wages equal to those received by Canadians who perform the same type of work. They are guaranteed seasonal work for periods of from six weeks to eight months with a possibility of being contracted again; the employer is obligated to pay all costs of round-trip air transportation that are in excess of a small contribution to be made by the worker, and wages are to be paid at the work site at a minimum rate of 80 dollars per week. In case of illness or accident the workers are to receive medical care and the corresponding workman's compensation, and in cases not covered by such compensation the employer is obligated to take out an insurance policy that covers these work risks to the entire satisfaction of the Government of Mexico.

In accordance with this agreement, Mexican migrant workers have already been contracted and have begun leaving for Canada. On the other hand, negotiations for a similar agreement with the United States Government have so far proved unsuccessful.

We know that this problem can only be radically solved as a result of our own economic evolution, and that it will only be ended when none of our fellow citizens need leave this country in order to earn a living. Nevertheless, for as long as this migrant phenomenon continues to exist we shall go on making every effort necessary to ensure that Mexicans residing abroad, whatever their legal status may be, will enjoy the security and be treated with the respect they deserve.

Excerpts from translated copies of President Luis Echeverría's State of the Union addresses delivered to Mexico's Congress in 1974 (*Mexican Newsletter*, no. 24, 1 September 1974, p. 33), 1975 (*Mexican Newsletter*, no. 33, 1 September 1975, p. 35) and 1976 (excerpts provided by the American Embassy in Mexico City).

. . . .

The painful problem of farm workers who cross the northern border in search of employment because of the lack of opportunities in the rural areas in Mexico persists. The great majority of them are in danger of falling prey to exploitation and insecurity, and in addition receive discriminatory wages.

Fundamentally, this phenomenon, like many other problems faced by our country, is the result of neglect of rural areas. As we have stated before, we are determined to correct this situation as an essential part of this Administration's program.

The solution to the migrant farm worker problem is dependent upon our own efforts. Farm workers must have access to a decent life in their own country. As we achieve this, the lure of immigration will diminish. But while this phenomenon persists, we will continue our struggle to ensure that our fellow-citizens are not subjected to abuses which violate the most elementary human rights.

We did not sign a new migrant labor agreement with the Government of the United States because the conditions proposed were not compatible with the interests of Mexico.

I expressed this opinion to the President of that great neighboring nation, Mr. Gerald Ford, during the interview we had on both Mexican and United States soil last October.

Cordiality and frankness prevailed in these conversations during which we confirmed our determination to deal with matters that affect us according to the standards of law and mutual respect. Based on these principles, our relations will be increasingly fruitful.

. . . .

. . . Concern for the dignity of man has impelled us to take a decided stand on the serious problem of migratory Mexican workers without papers.

We have recognized the necessity for solving this problem at its source through the accelerated creation of jobs in agriculture and industry. Our entire governmental development policy embodies this aim. But at the same time we must give immediate attention to this phenomenon arising from a complex of factors operative on both—and I emphasize the word "both"—sides of the border.

Today, in the highest tribunal of Mexico, we protest strongly against the flagrant violation of human rights and the attempts against the life and dignity of our compatriots, who deserve the respect accorded to human beings by every civilized society, regardless of such formal considerations as those involved in their immigration status.

We reject the idea of a new migrant worker agreement, for such agreements have never succeeded in preventing undocumented emigration in the past. The history of such agreements since the time of the Second World War shows us that quotas, far from solving the problem, have aggravated it.

The position we have taken with regard to human rights and our worldwide defense of the dignity of man have been unwavering. Our fellow countrymen well know that the attitude we have maintained toward the North American government has been and will continue to be uncompromising. The nation may be sure that we will do everything necessary to safeguard our rights with indomitable firmness.

IV

Illegal Mexican Workers[1]

Americans who employ illegal Mexicans have suggested a host of reasons for doing so. They have claimed that many of them are hired quite unintentionally because it is next to impossible for the employer to distinguish them from Chicanos and Mexican nationals who have entered the United States legally. Nor, the argument goes, should employers be expected to do this screening for it is properly the job of the immigration authorities.

Many employers have freely admitted their willing and knowing use of illegal labor. Some have explained their motivation in terms of humanitarian sympathies for the unfortunate Mexican migrants. But perhaps the most pervasive theme of all has been the claim that they were simply unable to hire enough legal labor, domestic and Mexican combined, to fill available jobs. Thus, it was supposedly a matter of using illegals or not filling the jobs at all.

Interests opposed to the use of illegal Mexican labor have also attempted to fathom employer motivation, and in doing so they have given little credence to the common claims of humanitarianism, poor screening ability, and the difficulty of hiring legal labor. What they see instead are employers who seek a labor force on their own terms. This means people who will work for rock-bottom wages and who will tolerate horrible working conditions without complaining. According to this perspective, the illegal Mexican fits the bill perfectly. Accustomed to a much lower standard of living, very low wages, and frequent unemployment in Mexico, he will work for less than his legal competitors. And if he ever questions the paternalistic terms under which he is hired, the immigration authorities are never more than a phone call away. According to this viewpoint, illegals are not the only victims of this system. Even many legal workers will be more docile because of the danger that if they become too assertive, their employers will decide to replace them with illegals.

The long history of illegal Mexican labor in this country cannot be understood without regard to the Janus-faced role long played by the United States government. On the one hand, it has played a law-enforcement role as evidenced by apprehensions, deportations, voluntary departures, and so forth. Yet, it has simultaneously pursued other policies which have encouraged employers to hire illegal workers. Most obvious among these practices is the long tradition of lax enforcement of the immigration laws at the Mexican border, particularly during the growing season.

Reformers have sometimes given the impression that quite limited reforms could finally bring an end to the use of illegal Mexican labor in the United States. However, any possibility of such a development is fraught with enormous difficulties. The very longevity of this migratory stream suggests that it is supported by powerful and firmly entrenched forces. For instance, we have already noted the political clout of the employers of illegal workers and there is no reason to believe that it is declining. Moreover, the number and variety of employers who have a direct interest in maintaining this labor supply have increased enormously. At one time they were limited primarily to farming and to a few other occupations within the southwestern United States. Now they are nationwide and represent literally hundreds of segments of the economy.

Several times since 1964, public officials have suggested that inauguration of a third bracero program would be an important step toward solving the illegal worker problem. The assumption has been that Mexican nationals now enter the United States illegally in such large numbers because they can no longer come as braceros. However, the historical evidence suggests that bracero programs actually stimulate rather than retard the entry of illegal Mexican workers. For example, while the bracero programs of both world wars were in existence, unprecedented numbers of illegal workers were also entering the United States. It has been suggested that this linkage may be explained by the fact that bracero programs themselves stimulate far more migration than they can accommodate.

Selection 15 is a classic study of illegal Mexican workers in the United States. It is the chapter on illegal labor taken from the monumental report of President Truman's Commission on Migratory Labor.

In the Truman era, as now, the Mexican labor debate centered around the illegal worker issue. During the late 1940s, illegal entry into the United States of Mexican nationals reached unprecedented levels and the

American government came under severe pressure to do something about it. What President Truman did was to establish the Commission on Migratory Labor. Although the commission's report is dated and has long been out-of-print, it remains one of the most thorough and scholarly studies of the Mexican labor issue ever produced. It should be noted that President Truman largely ignored the proposals made by the commission.

Selections 16 and 17 deal with the famous "El Paso Incident" of 1948. As indicated in Section III, widespread discrimination against persons of Mexican ancestry in Texas had led Mexico to ban the use of braceros in that state. Consequently, there was bitter reaction in Mexico when American immigration officials at El Paso permitted large numbers of Mexican workers to enter illegally and then "paroled" them to Texas growers. The selections reprinted here are two of the notes exchanged between the two countries. The first one is the United States's apology for the "El Paso Incident;" the second is Mexico's acceptance of the apology.

By 1951, President Truman had become convinced that there was serious danger that Mexico would terminate the bracero program altogether if the United States failed to take steps to cope with the illegal worker problem. Although Congress solidly supported the bracero program, it appeared to be in no mood to tackle the problem of the illegals. So, in an effort to save the legal Mexican labor system, President Truman sought to pressure Congress to cope with the illegal-entry problem. The exchange of letters between Truman and President Miguel Alemán indicates some interesting strategy that Truman developed for dealing with Congress. He proposed that Mexico refuse to agree to a long-term extension of the bracero agreement until Congress had taken action on the problem of illegal entry. In his reply, the Mexican president agreed to cooperate.

During 1951 and 1952, the Mexican government announced a number of measures it was taking to curtail the flow of illegals into the United States. The article from *Excélsior* and a press release from the Mexican Foreign Office discuss several of them.

The scholarly literature has devoted little attention to officials of the United States and of Mexico who are involved directly in apprehending or returning illegals to Mexico. The selection by Castaneda, a Mexican official, consists of a hard-hitting speech he delivered to a group of illegals apprehended in Texas. The reading by American immigration officer Fitch discusses some of the practical difficulties he encountered in searching a Texas farm for illegal workers.

The selection by Julian Samora reports the findings of an outstanding participant-observation study conducted by Mexican scholar Jorge Bustamante. Posing as an illegal, Bustamante entered the United States along with several illegal Mexican nationals only to be apprehended and returned to Mexico. The story is told from a very human perspective, and it gives us some appreciation of the hardships and fears experienced by these people.

The article by Joe Ortega examines illegals from a legal perspective and discusses a variety of ways in which their unlawful status deprives them of meaningful legal protection. It devotes attention to their extreme vulnerability in relations with employers and merchants and to their inability to fully use certain common government services. The article argues that "deportation" proceedings involving Mexican nationals typically fall short of even minimal standards of due process.

The brief selection from President Luis Echeverría's 1972 "State of the Nation" address notes Mexico's concern about the continuing movement of her workers into the United States and the hardships they face. As a solution he suggests continued economic development of his country.

It has sometimes been maintained that Mexican nationals have a right to live and work in the United States regardless of the immigration laws. This argument generally stresses the fact that much of the American Southwest once was part of the Republic of Mexico. The selection by Obed Lopez, a Mexican citizen living in the United States, is included because it illustrates this viewpoint.

The recent article from *Hispanoamericano,* a periodical published in Mexico, places much of the blame for the illegal entry problem on the United States. It develops the theme that illegal Mexican immigration should be seen as part of a much broader pattern that includes a simultaneous invasion of Mexico by American corporate interests.

The final selection is President Jimmy Carter's recent proposal for coping with the illegal worker problem. Among his suggestions are making unlawful the hiring of illegal aliens, increasing vigilance along the border with Mexico, strengthening Mexico's economy as a means of reducing the flow of labor into the United States, and adjusting the status of many of the illegals so that they may become lawful residents of the United States.

NOTES

1. On the subject of illegal Mexican labor in the United States, see: Jorge A. Bustamante, "The Historical Context of Undocumented Mexican Immigration to the United States," *Aztlán* 3 (1973): 257–81; Nelson G. Copp, *Wetbacks and Braceros* (San Francisco: R and E Research Associates, 1971); Sheldon L. Greene, "Immigration Law and Rural Poverty—The Problems of the Illegal Immigrant," *Duke Law Journal* 3 (1969): 475–94; Carol Norquest, *Rio Grande Wetbacks: Mexican Migrant Workers* (Albuquerque: University of New Mexico

Press, 1972); Julian Samora, *Los Mojados: The Wetback Story* (Notre Dame: University of Notre Dame Press, 1971); U.S., Congress, House, Committee on the Judiciary, *Illegal Aliens, Hearings Before Subcommittee No. 1, 92d Cong., 1st sess.*, (Washington, D.C.: Government Printing Office, 1971).

15

"The Wetback Invasion—Illegal Alien Labor in American Agriculture"

President's Commission on Migratory Labor

We were directed to investigate:

> . . . the extent of illegal migration of foreign workers into the United States and the problems created thereby, and whether, and in what respect, current law enforcement measures and the authority and means possessed by Federal, State, and local governments may be strengthened and improved to eliminate such illegal migration.

In recent years, literally hundreds of thousands of Mexican agricultural workers, known as wetbacks, have illegally entered the United States in search of employment. The wetback is a Mexican national who, figuratively, if not literally, wades or swims the Rio Grande. Whether he enters by wading or swimming, crawls through a hole in a fence, or just walks over a momentarily unguarded section of the long land border, he is a wetback. Since he enters by evading the immigration officers, he is, in any event, an illegally entered alien. The term wetback is widely accepted and is used without derision; hence for convenience it is used here.

Before 1944 the illegal traffic on the Mexican border, though always going on, was never overwhelming in numbers. Apprehensions by immigration officials leading to deportations or voluntary departures before 1944 were fairly stable and under ten thousand per year. Although the exact size of the wetback traffic is virtually impossible to determine, the

---

Reprinted from: Report of the President's Commission on Migratory Labor, *Migratory Labor in American Agriculture* (Washington, D.C.: Government Printing Office, 1951), pp. 69–88.

number of apprehensions by immigration officers is a general indicator but far from a precise means of measurement. The same individual may be apprehended several times during the season and therefore would be duplicated in the apprehension count. On the other hand, large numbers enter and leave without being apprehended and hence would not be in the deportation or departure figures at all.

The magnitude of the wetback traffic has reached entirely new levels in the past seven years. The number of deportations and voluntary departures has continuously mounted each year, from 29,000 in 1944 to 565,000 in 1950. In its newly achieved proportions, it is virtually an invasion. It is estimated that at least 400,000 of our migratory farm labor force of 1 million in 1949 were wetbacks.

The wetback traffic formerly was limited primarily to the areas near the border. Recently, it has spread, though with diminishing intensity at greater distances from the border, to virtually all states of the Union. Before 1944 employment of wetbacks was largely at hand labor in agriculture; now they are infiltrating a wide range of nonfarm jobs and occupations.

Mexican nationals employed under contract are not permitted to bring their families with them. Wetbacks, on the other hand, often bring or acquire families. Many social complications are intensified by the presence of families. It must be noted, moreover, that a child born in the United States, though of Mexican illegal alien parents, is a citizen of the United States. The parents of such a child, if apprehended by immigration authorities, may file a petition for stay of deportation on the grounds of hardship.

A comparison of more than incidental interest is the volume of the wetback traffic as contrasted to our admissions of displaced persons from Europe. In 1949, when we admitted 119,600 displaced Europeans, our apprehended wetback traffic was almost 300,000; in 1950, when we admitted 85,600 displaced Europeans, our known wetback traffic was between 500,000 and 600,000.

The newly developed magnitudes of wetback traffic have brought their inevitable consequences. Foremost among these consequences is the severe and adverse pressure on wages in the areas nearest the border. A second consequence of the wetback is competition for employment and displacement of American workers. This is particularly aggravated in the Lower Rio Grande Valley. Furthermore, there are other developments which, although not directly and entirely consequences of the wetback influx, are nevertheless inevitably associated with it. These include the astoundingly high disease and death rates in the counties lying next to the border.

To understand the wetback traffic, it is essential to know something of its foundations and the forces that produce it. Essentially, its foundations lie in a combination of factors that "push" the Mexican national northward within his own country and "pull" him across the border in violation of immigration law.

The "Push" Forces in Mexico and Their Relations to the Wetback Traffic

Of first importance among the "push" forces in Mexico is population pressure in relation to resource development. Mexico, not yet with the economy to provide its citizens with a standard of living approaching that of the United States, is experiencing a very rapid population increase. Population grew from 16.5 million in 1930 to 19.6 million in 1940, and to 25.5 million in 1950, making a population increase in the past decade of 30 percent.

Both birth and death rates are high in Mexico. Compared with the United States birth rate of 25.3 per thousand of population, the Mexican birth rate is 45.4 (both rates as of 1949). The death rate of Mexico is 17.9 per thousand population compared with the United States death rate of 9.7 (1949). The birth rate in Mexico is declining but the death rate is falling faster, which means that net survivals are increasing.

The excess of births over deaths in Mexico, as compared with the United States, means that it has a large potential for internal population growth. The economy of Mexico is still largely agricultural. Crop land is severely restricted in amount and production methods for the most part are primitive. As a result, the pressure of population on the food supply and the developed income-yielding resources of Mexico is great and is becoming more intense. The differential in income level is reflected in the 1949 per capita income in the United States of $1,453 as compared with $114 in Mexico.

Inflation is next in importance to population pressure as a factor motivating search for employment in the United States. Since 1939, the cost of living in Mexico has risen much more than in the United States. By June 1950, the cost of living index in Mexico City based on 1939 was 354; comparatively, in the same period, the United States cost of living index was 171, or less than half as much. Inflation has meant that Mexican wages, already extremely poor, have become worse.

Farm wages in areas of Mexico near the border, in December 1947, were, in United States dollars, $1.10 a day. Through continued inflation, the wage in October 1949 was only 69 cents per day in United States money. In the interior of Mexico, the farm wage in October 1949 was the equivalent of only 38 cents per day in United States money.

Population is much less dense in the north of Mexico and wages are higher than in central and southern Mexico. As population continues its rapid increase, northward expansion is the only direction feasible in either geographic or economic terms. Moreover, the Mexican side of the Rio Grande Valley recently has undergone very marked economic expansion. For example, cotton production in the Matamoros area (Lower Rio Grande Valley) is reported to have increased from 46,000 bales in 1939 to over 300,000 bales in 1949. It is further expected that within the next two or three years irrigated acreage in the Matamoros district will more than double.

Farmers in these northern areas of Mexico require seasonal labor for the cotton harvest just as do the farmers on our side of the Rio Grande. There is, accordingly, an internal northward migration for this employment. Mexican farm employers in need of seasonal labor encourage northward migratory movements within Mexico.

This rapid economic development in the areas immediately south of the border has accelerated the wetback traffic in several ways. An official in Matamoros estimates that 25,000 transient cotton pickers were needed in the 1950 season whereas the number coming from interior Mexico was estimated at 60,000. It is to be expected that many Mexican workers coming north with the anticipation of working in northern Mexico do not find employment there and ultimately spill over the border and become wetbacks. Additionally, the resident labor force at the border is expanding by leaps and bounds.

What has been happening generally in the areas of Mexico immediately south of the border is reflected by the phenomenal increase in population in the principal Mexican border towns and cities. This increase is shown in the following table:

	1950	1940	Percentage increase 1940 to 1950
			Percent
Mexicali	63,830	18,775	240
Tijuana	59,117	16,486	259
C. Juárez	121,903	48,881	149
Nogales	24,692	13,966	78
Nuevo Laredo	57,488	28,872	99
Matamoros	43,830	15,699	179

Thus, large reservoirs of potential wetbacks are accumulating at the border. It is difficult for the farm employer in the north of Mexico to get the labor supply he needs without contributing to the wetback traffic. Active seasonal employment in the Mexican areas near the border is about the same as in areas of the United States above the border. Consequently, laborers brought north to work for Mexican farmers discover that work is available at better wages on the other side of the border and they slip over.

This involves an ever-widening and self-accelerating cycle. Mexican farm employers close to the border have to recruit more workers than they need because it can be expected that many of their recruits will be lost to the wetback traffic. By recruiting on this basis, they aggravate the wetback traffic because they get too many workers.

The "Pull" Forces in the United States and Their Relation to the Wetback Traffic

Complementing the northward "push" forces within Mexico has been the expansion in unskilled hand labor requirements in the United States' Southwest. Much new land has been cleared and brought under cultivation in recent years and, at the same time, irrigation has expanded. In the Lower Rio Grande Valley, there were less than 250,000 acres of cotton in 1945, but cotton acreage had expanded to over 600,000 in 1949. Through the expansion of cotton acreage and also greater specialization in fruit and vegetable production, seasonal labor requirements have become more intensive and concentrated in shorter periods of time. Farm employers of the Southwest have encountered difficulty in meeting their short-term seasonal labor requirements from the domestic labor force on the terms offered.

Perhaps of greater importance than expansion in employment opportunities is the increasing attitude of many farm employers near the border that they are entitled to Mexican workers. Although farm employers testified they preferred legal to illegal labor, their position comes to this: If Mexican labor cannot be obtained legally on terms satisfactory to the employers, they will obtain Mexican labor illegally. The manager of the Agricultural Producers Labor Committee said as much in his testimony at Los Angeles:

> If Government red tape and the inability of the two Governments involved prevent us from putting under contract the help we need

> during the peak harvest seasons, we will use wetbacks, because we are going to harvest our crops. We have wetbacks in our employ today. In fact, one of our association's representatives is in El Centro and Calexico today legalizing wetbacks.

Farm employers near the border repeatedly testified they had used Mexican labor for years and hence implied they had a peculiar right to get Mexican workers. One of the members of this Commission asked this question of a Texas farm employer spokesman who had submitted a statement which was said to have the approval of several farm organizations:

> I would be interested in learning whether the farm organizations which have approved your statement are recommending this policy of easy entry of Mexican workers so as to provide plentiful and inexpensive labor for farmers throughout the United States, or is there a desire that these Mexican Nationals be encouraged to avoid going more than a few hundred miles from the Mexican border?

The reply to the question was this:

> . . . it is reasonable to assume that the farmers along the border would not object if the movement of Mexican Nationals were limited to a few hundred miles from the border, but I expect that those outside such areas would object. Some special requirements might have to be made for those going beyond strictly border States. I really don't know enough about the need in Northern States to discuss it at this time, but it seems to me that something could be worked out. I think that perhaps the border States need special consideration in this matter because their agricultural economy was largely developed by Mexican labor—a policy that was partly illegal, but yet condoned by our Government officials for many years.

Not to be neglected in considering the "pull" forces of the United States is the encouragement to the wetback traffic that is inherent in the legalization of wetbacks under the Mexican-United States International Agreement. This was described in the previous chapter. As we noted, Mexico has opposed recruitment of contract workers from the interior of the country when large numbers of its nationals were already illegally in the United States. To meet this position on the part of the Mexican government, we agreed to legalize wetbacks in 1947, 1949, and 1950. In fact, legalization of wetbacks has constituted the bulk of contracting activities since 1947.

For infraction of our immigration laws, some wetbacks have been prosecuted in the courts and sent to prison, but most of those who were apprehended were simply allowed to make a voluntary departure. Others, of no different offense and no less guilt, in numbers sufficient to meet all, or the majority of, legal recruiting needs have been given contracts after a token deportation to Mexico in lieu of a conventional deportation or voluntary departure. Such wetbacks were given identification slips in the United States by the Immigration and Naturalization Service which entitled them, within a few minutes, to step back across the border and become contract workers. There was no way to obtain the indispensable slip of paper except to be found illegally in the United States. Thus violators of law were rewarded by receiving legal contracts while the same opportunities were denied law-abiding citizens of Mexico. The United States, having engaged in a program giving preference in contracting to those who had broken the law, has encouraged violation of the immigration laws. Our Government thus has become a contributor to the growth of an illegal traffic which it has responsibility to prevent.

Pressures and Deals Not To Enforce the Law

We find that there have been times when pressure has been successfully exerted upon Washington to have the Immigration and Naturalization Service issue orders to field officers to go easy on deportations until crops have been harvested. The district director at El Paso testified as follows:

> . . . Over the years, from the time I came on the job as district director in March 1926, nearly every year at cotton-chopping or cotton-picking time, the farmers would send a complaint to the Secretary of Labor—we were in the Labor Department at that time—or to the Commissioner of Immigration, I am certain for no other purpose than to cause an investigation that would result in one of two things: Either I get word from some higher official to go easy until cotton-chopping time was over, or cotton-picking time was over; or the men who were doing the work would be so upset by the investigation that they would go easy on their own.
>
> Now, in 1937, one of those complaints went to Washington, and Commissioner Houghteling sent it to me and said, "I want you to

> personally investigate this and make a report to me." I did make the investigation and I submitted the report. . . . The Commissioner's answer to the complainants, . . . was in substance this: "I find that our officers are doing their duty and I hope they will continue to do their duty." That was the first time since I went on the job in 1926, that we had ever had any definite statement from any high-ranking official that they were going to stand behind us in our work of keeping "wetbacks" off of the farms, and from that time until about a year after we got in the war, we bored into them more and more, and kept it just as clean as we possibly could. And it was, at that time, a small percentage.

Another Immigration and Naturalization officer explained the source of this pressure upon Washington in these terms:

> This pressure group is truck farmers and ranchers all over the country that have plenty of money, they are able to make a trip to Washington and to apply that pressure. The man that wants to apply it (immigration law) is the little man. He is the man who gets out there and does the work. He is the one that the wetbacks are taking the job away from. He doesn't have money to go to Washington. He can write a letter to his Representative or Congressman. On the other hand, your farmer or rancher goes up there, and he can call him by his first name. So I think that is the reason that the pressure group, even though it is a minority group, is so effective.

Not only did we receive testimony that the Immigration and Naturalization Service was susceptible to political pressure such as the foregoing excerpts indicate, we found instances of deals between Government agencies. The 1949 Idaho State Employment Service Report reads:

> The United States Immigration and Naturalization Service recognizes the need for farm workers in Idaho, and, through cooperation with the State employment service, withholds its search and deportation until such times as there is not a shortage of farm workers.

The immigration officer for the Northwest district explained at our Portland hearing:

> I might state that in 1949 representatives of the Federal Employment Service asked us not to send our inspectors into the field to apprehend "wet" Mexicans, for the purpose of deporting them, until after the emergency of harvesting the crops had been met. In that

> particular instance, we did not send the officers into the field as early as we would have otherwise.

In Washington, D. C., in October 1950, we questioned the Assistant Commissioner of the Immigration and Naturalization Service on enforcement of the immigration law on the Mexican border. Without denying that instructions not to enforce the law had gone out in earlier years, he replied as follows:

> I may say that the pressure here is considerable. I think I can answer your question very briefly by saying, during the past year, there has been no instruction issued to our field offices to refrain in any way from enforcing the law.

Thirty years ago, nonfarm employers disliked the immigration law and wanted it changed. Congress and the Immigration Service both withstood that pressure. The Commissioner of Immigration of that day stated his position to be: "The immigration laws, as they now stand, seem to me to express the thought of the country at large in favor of a high-wage scale, as being an accompaniment, I may say almost a requisite, to better citizenship."

Mechanics of the Wetback Traffic

The hub of the wetback traffic is in the plazas of the Mexican towns and cities immediately below the border. Here, or in sections around the railroad which serve the same purpose, the wetback seeks information about jobs in the United States and how to get them. It is here that he encounters the first of many exploiters he will come to know well before he is once again in his homeland. The principal topic of conversation in the plazas of the Mexican border towns for several months of the year is how to get into the United States and what crops and jobs promise employment once there. His urgent need of food and money makes him an easy mark for the smuggler, the labor contractor, or the agent of the farm employer. He is eager when any of these approach him and whisper that there is a way to get out of the vast mob, all looking for a job and a chance to get into the United States where jobs seem plentiful and wages seem high.

Although smuggling of wetbacks is widespread, the majority of wetbacks apparently enter alone or in small groups without a smuggler's assistance. In a group moving without the aid of a smuggler there usually is one who has made the trip before and who is willing to show the way. Not infrequently the same individual knows the farm to which the group intends to go and sometimes he has made advance arrangements with the farm employer to return at an appointed date with his group. Such wetbacks stream into the United States by the thousands through the deserts near El Paso and Calexico or across the Rio Grande between Rio Grande City and Brownsville. When employment on the farms adjacent to the border is filled, the wetbacks push northward into new areas following rumor or promise of employment.

Often the wetbacks entering alone or in small groups have written to farm employers or friends in the United States and have made arrangements to be met at some cross road, gate, or other well-known place within a night's walk of the border. Some make two or three separate entries within a season, after having been apprehended, and head for the place where they were formerly employed.

If the wetback makes a deal to be guided or escorted across the Rio Grande or some section of the land border, everything he is able to pay is usually extracted in return for the service which may be no more than being guided around the fence or being given a boat ride across the Rio Grande. Wetbacks who are without funds to pay the smuggler for bringing them in or to pay the trucker-contractor who furnishes transportation and direction from the boundary to the farm are frequently "sold" from one exploiter to the next. For example, the smuggler will offer to bring a specified number of wetbacks across the river for such an amount as $10 or $15 per man. The smuggler or boatman with his party in tow will be met by the trucker-contractor who will then "buy" the wetback party by paying off the smuggler. This trucker-contractor, in turn, will have a deal to deliver workers to farm employers at an agreed-upon price per head.

There are other well-known and well-established practices to facilitate and encourage the entrance of wetbacks. They range from spreading news of employment in the plazas and over the radio to the withholding from wages of what is called a "deposit" which is intended to urge, if not guarantee, the return to the same farm as quickly as possible of a wetback employee who may be apprehended and taken back to Mexico.

The term "deposit" requires some explanation. Members of this Commission personally interviewed wetback workers apprehended by immigration officers in the Lower Rio Grande Valley. These workers had been paid for the cotton they had picked during the preceding two or three weeks. However, their employers had withheld $10 to $15 from their pay.

Such sums, we discovered, are known as "deposits." To redeem this deposit, the wetback was required to reenter illegally and to reappear on the farm employer's premises within ten days.

Once on the United States side of the border and on the farm, numerous devices are employed to keep the wetback on the job. Basic to all these devices is the fact that the wetback is a person of legal disability who is under jeopardy of immediate deportation if caught. He is told that if he leaves the farm, he will be reported to the Immigration Service or that, equally unfortunate to him, the Immigration Service will surely find him if he ventures into town or out onto the roads. To assure that he will stay until his services are no longer needed, his pay, or some portion thereof, frequently is held back. Sometimes, he is deliberately kept indebted to the farmer's store or commissary until the end of the season, at which time he may be given enough to buy shoes or clothing and encouraged to return the following season.

When the work is done, neither the farmer nor the community wants the wetback around. The number of apprehensions and deportations tends to rise very rapidly at the close of a seasonal work period. This can be interpreted not alone to mean that the immigration officer suddenly goes about his work with renewed zeal and vigor, but rather that at this time of the year "cooperation" in law enforcement by farm employers and townspeople rapidly undergoes considerable improvement.

Consequences of the Wetback Traffic: Wages

The wetback is a hungry human being. His need of food and clothing is immediate and pressing. He is a fugitive and it is as a fugitive that he lives. Under the constant threat of apprehension and deportation, he cannot protest or appeal no matter how unjustly he is treated. Law operates against him but not for him. Those who capitalize on the legal disability of the wetbacks are numerous and their devices are many and various.

Wage rates reflect graphically and dramatically the impact and consequences of the wetback traffic. In 1947, when daily wages for chopping cotton (thinning the rows of cotton plants) in the Lower Rio Grande Valley were $2.25 (10 hours), wages were continuously higher at points northward from the border: in the Sandy Lands of Texas, $3; in the Corpus Christi and Coast Prairie Areas, $4; in the Rolling Plains, $5; in the High Plains, $5.25.

When the Commission held hearings in Texas in August 1950, wage rates for picking short staple cotton in the Lower Rio Grande Valley were reported as low as 50 cents per hundredweight and as high as $1.75 per hundredweight. From the evidence presented, we conclude that the bulk of the cotton in this area was picked in 1950 for approximately $1.25 per hundredweight. Comparative wage rates for picking cotton elsewhere in Texas were not obtained in the hearings because no other area had yet commenced its cotton harvest. However, the Statewide average 1950 rate for Texas is now reported officially by the United States Department of Agriculture to have been $2.45 per hundredweight. Thus, the Lower Rio Grande Valley cotton growers got their cotton picked for approximately one-half the wages paid by the average cotton grower of Texas.

Wages for common hand labor in the Lower Rio Grande Valley, according to the testimony, were as low as 15 to 25 cents per hour. To the north and the west through El Paso Valley, we found a marked tendency for wages for similar work to rise. In southern New Mexico, the prevailing wages for the same type of work were reported to be 40 to 50 cents per hour. Thus, New Mexico was paying twice as much to get its hand labor work done as was being paid in the Lower Rio Grande Valley.

Further west in Arizona, wages are still better. In 1950, the statewide average for picking of short staple cotton in Arizona was officially reported to be $3.10 per hundredweight. Cotton chopping and common farm labor wages were reported, in August 1950, to be $4 to $7 per ten-hour day.

The fact that wages in areas near the border tend to rise to the westward conforms to the general pattern in which state-wide average farm wages also rise to the westward. This is evident in the state average wages for all farm work as reported by the United States Department of Agriculture, which for 1950 were:

	Cents per hour
Texas	54
New Mexico	54
Arizona	64
California	88

Notwithstanding the strong and clear tendency for wages to rise as one moves westward, with California the highest of the group, we found wages in the Imperial Valley on the Mexican border to represent a complete reversal of this pattern. The going wage rate for common and hand labor in the Imperial Valley was 50 cents per hour. Thus Imperial Valley farm employers pay no more to get their farm work done tha do farm employers in southern New Mexico, and probably less than do Arizona farm employers. Direct comparisons in wages paid in cotton cannot be made since Imperial Valley has no cotton, but the comparison in terms of wages paid to hand labor for other types of work leads to this conclusion.

It is thus clear that the Imperial Valley, with its large wetback traffic, represents a substantial contradiction to an otherwise consistent general tendency for farm wages to improve toward the west. The force of the Imperial Valley wetback traffic is strong enough to upset this well-established east-west wage pattern; at the same time, it is strong enough to institute in one of the high farm wage states of the nation, the same type of wage differential that is found on the Texas border. While common farm labor wages in 1950 in the Imperial Valley were 50 cents per hour, the going rate in the San Joaquin Valley was 85 cents per hour.

That the wetback traffic has severely depressed farm wages is unquestionable. We further inquired if the wetback, as an individual among others doing similar work, was paid a discriminatory, low wage. The testimony on this point was conflicting. In some cases, it was said that the wetback was paid the same rate as everyone else; in other cases, it was claimed that the wetback was paid less. Apparently, the answer to this question is determined by the proportion which wetbacks are of the local labor force. In the Lower Rio Grande Valley, the wetback proportion is so high that the wages paid them largely determine the wages paid to everyone there. The wetback wage tends to become the prevailing wage. In comparison, the wetback appears to be proportionally less important in the Imperial Valley and, accordingly, there is a chance for discrimination to occur. This is reflected by the testimony of a Deputy Labor Commissioner of California:

> The Mexican wetbacks work for 40 cents an hour and a few of them work for between 25 and 30 cents an hour. In many of our complaints the employer will bring in records showing that the wetbacks didn't work the number of hours claimed, and I would say that, in the majority of cases, they finally settled for anywhere from 25 percent to 75 percent of the original claim, which gives the farmer an opportunity to make a little additional saving in his labor bill by just cutting it down.

Consequences of the Wetback Traffic: Labor Competition and Displacement

South Texas with its large Spanish-American and Mexican-American population has long been a home base or winter quarters for migratory agricultural workers who in the summer season move northward principally into the Rocky Mountain States or the Great Lakes States. These people are citizens, some of two or three generations in the Southwest. Out of Texas, they are commonly referred to as Texas-Mexicans. Parallel with the increase in the wetback traffic, the number of Texas-Mexican residents entering the migratory labor stream has greatly increased. An authority on Mexican-American affairs explained this phenomenon to the Commission in the following words:

> The free and easy dipping into the cheap-labor reservoir that is Mexico, has made it virtually impossible for the citizens of Mexican descent in this area to make a satisfactory living. They are pushed farther north by the competition of 15 and 20 cents an hour labor, and as they move north they complicate the economic-social situation all up the line. . . . We have detailed statistics on the migration of the residents of Hidalgo County, in the period of two years. . . . Of 16,000 persons included in the survey, 8,000 migrated from Hidalgo County. Those 8,000 migrants went to every single State in the United States in that migration during that period. They went out to do, primarily, agricultural labor, stoop labor, that they were prohibited from doing in their home county because of the competition of contraband labor that can be employed at 15, 20, and 25 cents an hour.

Nelson and Meyers, of the University of Texas, commenting on the same subject report that:

> The living standards which Mexican nationals are willing to tolerate, and the fact that so many of them are only temporary residents, have made it unneccessary for Valley farmers to provide housing, sanitary facilities, and other non-wage prerequisites adequate to retain a permanent resident farm population familiar with or educated to normal American standards. These two factors—low wages and poor living conditions—undoubtedly provide the incentive to movement from the Valley, about which so many Valley farmers complain, and upon which they rely in their argument for the necessity of continued unrestricted entry of Mexican nationals.

In contrast to the observations of objective investigators and the experience of workers who earlier had made their livelihood in south Texas, Texas farm employers repeatedly told the Commission that their local resident labor supply had become unreliable and was no longer willing to do hard hand work in the fields. Most farm employers testified that the problem was not one of wages—that domestic labor could not be induced to work at any price. However, one farm employer spokesman from the Lower Rio Grande Valley testified that the wage rate was a factor in the availability of local labor, for he said:

> Q. You say that a citizen worker doesn't want to go out on a farm. In Illinois they work on the farm and it is stoop labor too.
>
> A. That is because they have a higher wage.
>
> Q. You think they will work on farms but they won't work for 40 cents? Is that it?
>
> A. That is right, I think we could get them to work for 75 cents.

The displaced Texas-Mexican, who has come to be considered unreliable by farm employers in his home territory, is well regarded and welcomed elsewhere. Note the testimony of a cotton grower in Arizona:

> Q. You spoke mainly of Mexican workers and others? What is the race of the other workers that you employ?
>
> A. They are Mexicans. They are good Mexicans. Since the Cotton Growers Association went into a recruiting program here a couple of years ago, . . . they had never been around before, just been around I think it was Houston or San Antonio, and they are very good Mexicans. They send their money home and save their money. We have no trouble.
>
> Q. Are those American citizens?
>
> A. Yes, all American citizens.

Let the testimony of a Texas-Mexican worker who came to our hearing at Phoenix, Ariz., speak for itself:

> Q. Where is your home in Texas?
>
> A. Weslaco, Tex. (Lower Rio Grande Valley.)
>
> Q. Why don't you stay down around Weslaco and work down there?
>
> A. Well, I don't stay there because I can't make any money over there in that town.
>
> Q. What is the reason you can't make any money there?
>
> A. Well, because there is a lot of laborers in that town and they can't get any work. This year they promised us to pay 75 cents an hour. You can go anywhere to look for a job and you can't find any job. . .

Q. Who promised you 75 cents?

A. Well, on the radio, I listen to the radio, and they took all the Nationals back to Mexico and so want to raise the price for us, but I and my brothers, my two brothers, was looking for a job all the way around the town and they couldn't find any, and myself started to work about 20 days after I got there, and I got started to get some people to get ready to come to Montana with me.

Q. I wanted to ask Mr. F—— about these Mexican Nationals in Texas. You say that you couldn't make any money there and wages were too low, there weren't any jobs because there was an abundance of other workers?

A. Yes.

Q. Were those other workers Mexican Nationals that came across the river?

A. Yes, sir; they crossed the river, and they worked for 3 or 4 days, dollar a day, two dollars and a half, and that is the reason we can't get jobs.

Q. You mean they paid them two dollars or two and a half?

A. Two and a half or three dollars.

Q. For how many hours?

A. Ten hours.

Q. They are getting about 25 cents an hour?

A. Yes.

Q. You spoke about the Mexican Nationals. Do you happen to know whether those are wetback Mexicans, or were those contract Mexicans that were brought in under the Government program? Which of those two was it that took most of the work around Weslaco?

A. Well, it is Mexicans that is from Mexico. They just crossed the river, and that is the reason they got a lot of laborers there in that town, and they don't get any jobs for us on farm labor.

Labor competition and displacement by the wetback is not limited to farm work. Labor union representatives of several crafts testified that wetback workers were being widely employed in many nonfarm occupations. Immigration officers have apprehended wetback Mexicans engaged in nonagricultural occupations in many states.

The representative of the Operating Engineers Union testified that, around the Brownsville area, it was universal practice for construction contractors to employ illegal alien labor. Wetback labor is also penetrating into the highly skilled trades according to the testimony of the Iron Workers Union:

> We have been having here . . . a number of cases of I guess they call them the "wetbacks", migratory labor, taking over, I'll say a very high craftman's job, which is the iron worker of construction work. . . . I will say it makes it awfully hard on my organization, men that have spent their time in their apprenticeship and serving their time to do their work, of which we have spent so much time in negotiating agreements and making working conditions for our members, and to have our working conditions broken down in this manner of using "wetback" labor.

Border State Farm Employers Who Do Not Get Wetbacks Protest Discrimination

The intensity of the wetback traffic is not uniform along the border. Most intense in the Lower Rio Grande Valley, it lessens to the north and the west of Texas. The traffic is much more intense in the Imperial Valley than in Arizona or New Mexico. Of all the states offering the kind of employment in which wetbacks are found, Arizona evidently has the least wetback traffic. This unequal access to wetback labor causes resentment, as is well expressed in the testimony of the manager of the Arizona Cooperative Cotton Growers' Association:

> Our farmers for several years have had a continuous and loud complaint that their friends and acquaintances in other bordering States have a comparatively large supply of wetback labor, while in Arizona the border patrol very successfully and carefully enforces the law against illegal aliens on the ranches. We have never tried to exert pressure to have this enforcement relieved, but we do want to call the attention of high figures (officials) to the fact that the other States should be treated alike; that if enforcement is being relaxed in other States, it should be relaxed in Arizona; that if enforcement is going to be strict in Arizona, we want it strict in other States.

Death and Disease

In the areas of wetback traffic, death and disease assume far more the characteristics of Mexico than of the United States. The foundations of these phenomena unquestionably predate the last few years in which the wetback traffic has achieved its present proportions. Consequently, the problems of death and disease cannot be exclusively attributed to the wetback traffic. Public health, sanitation, death, and disease in the border counties have long demanded attention. The wetback traffic inescapably postpones effective remedial measures and aggravates these problems. The wetback undergoes no health or physical examination as he illicitly enters the United States. The bringing in of disease and contagion cannot, therefore, be avoided. Moreover, while he is here as an illegal alien, the wetback will not ordinarily risk the chance of apprehension by seeking medical or health assistance. Reciprocally, the health and medical service agencies that might otherwise be ready to provide assistance for residents will ordinarily be foreclosed to the wetback, even if he were to seek aid, because of residence ineligibility. This circumstance does not arise with legal foreigners for whom provision is made.

One of the most sensitive indicators of the state of public health in any population is the rate of infant mortality. This is defined as the number of deaths under 1 year of age per 1,000 live births. For the United States at large, this rate in 1948 was 32. The state-wide average for Texas was 46.2; for the 28 counties of Texas on or immediately adjacent to the border, the average rate was 79.5. In the three counties commonly regarded as constituting the Lower Rio Grande Valley, the infant mortality rates were as follows:

Cameron	82.5
Hidalgo	107.2
Willacy	127.6

The only other counties in Texas with infant mortality rates higher than the lowest of the above are Brewster (86.4); Dimmit (93.0); Maverick (83.1); and Reeves (96.3). All of these counties are on the Mexican border or immediately adjacent except Reeves which is in Pecos Valley, lying in the narrow strip of Texas between Mexico and New Mexico.

New Mexico and Arizona both have high rates of infant mortality, 70.1 and 56.4, respectively, but the infant death problem in these areas is associated with large Indian populations rather than with Mexican-American people or with wetback traffic. In California, the state-wide infant mortality rate is 28.6 but the rate of 56.2 for the Imperial Valley is almost double.

Dysentery, diarrhea, and enteritis loom disproportionately large in the picture of infant deaths. These are the diseases of filth and insanitation. In California, the state-wide average infant death rate from diarrhea, enteritis, and dysentery is 1.8; for Imperial County, it is 12.9. In both Texas and California an overwhelming proportion of infant deaths from these causes is known to be in families of Mexican origin.

Disproportionate rates of death and disease are not confined to children alone. Reported diseases for the entire population in the areas of wetback traffic in Texas are unfavorably high as may be noted in the following comparison where the extent of those diseases listed is shown as a rate per 100 thousand population:

Disease	Texas— State-wide average	Texas— 28 border counties
Tuberculosis	76.4	122.9
Dysentery	312.0	1,554.1
Syphilis	199.8	332.3
Malaria	37.4	126.1
Typhoid	3.7	6.5

Housing

A wetback is in no position when offered work to ask whether there is satisfactory housing or indeed whether there is any housing at all. Members of this Commission personally inspected wetback camps in the Lower Rio Grande Valley, in the El Paso Valley, and in the Imperial Valley. Where the wetback makes up the major proportion of the seasonal and migratory work force, virtually no housing, sanitary facilities, or other conditions of civilized living are supplied. Where the wetback concentration is proportionately less, housing conditions tend to improve but even so, remain far below the level of decency. A witness testifying at Brownsville did not overstate the squalor of the housing and living conditions that are much too common in the Lower Rio Grande Valley when he said, "I have seen, with my own eyes, people living in these shacks and sheds, getting their water to use, drink, and cook with, out of irrigation ditches, no type of sanitary facilities, bathing or toilet facilities of any kind within sight; living in shacks that I wouldn't put a horse in."

Speaking of the Imperial Valley, a Deputy Labor Commissioner of the State of California told us:

> The plight of the wetbacks I consider very serious there because the majority of them live on the ditch banks or in shed housing

which is very, very poor. I would say that this is true mostly with the small farmers rather than the large growers as most of the large growers have facilities, but the small growers or the small operators get them to live on the ditch banks or a chicken house. I have seen lots cleaner and better chicken houses for chickens than I have seen for human beings in the Imperial Valley.

Problems Encountered in Enforcing Immigration Law

The problem of immigration-law enforcement includes the Mexican national who secures employment and wages through unlawful entry, the smuggler who gains from conspiring in the unlawful entry, the farm employer who gains from the employment of the illegal alien at low wages, and finally the governments of both countries. In illegally crossing the border, the wetback violates the laws of Mexico just as much as he does those of the United States. If Mexican farm workers are to be permitted temporary legal employment in the United States, one of the urgent problems faced by both governments is to devise a legal farm-labor program that will be a decent and orderly substitute for the wetback traffic and not a means of accelerating it. Beyond this first obvious step, which must be principally a matter of intergovernmental negotiation, the problems involved in taking affirmative measures against the respective participating parties require appropriate action by the United States.

When legal action is taken against the wetback, which is done only in very few cases and principally with repeated violators, there is little difficulty of prosecution and conviction. Here the problem is that great numbers make it impossible to proceed against each individual. While there is little difficulty of convicting the wetback, similar actions against those who assist illegal entry are not equally successful. Given the climate of local opinion in the areas of wetback traffic, it is extremely difficult and frequently impossible to prosecute and convict those who conspire to violate the immigration law. Here, as far as the smuggler is concerned, the problem is the enforcement of national law in an area which is unsympathetic to that law. The law against the introduction of excluded aliens is adequate; the problem is enforcement. Against those who harbor and conceal an illegal alien, the law is not adequate. The Supreme Court (*U.S. v. Evans*, 333 U.S. 483, Mar. 15, 1948) held that, because of lack of a penalty in the statute, the Immigration Act does not make it a punishable offense to conceal or harbor aliens not entitled to enter the United States.

New legislation is needed which will penalize the acts of transporting, harboring, and concealing of illegal aliens.

Another obstacle in immigration law enforcement is the limited right of immigration officers to enter private property to search for illegal aliens. Many farm employers contest this and some have used arms and threats of bodily harm to resist inspection. Farm employers' objection to inspection of farm properties in search of illegal aliens was reported to us by the president of the New Mexico Farm and Livestock Bureau as follows:

> Another point that we would like to bring out is that farmers in New Mexico do not like the system now being used by the Immigration and Naturalization Service under which immigration officers overrun our farms indiscriminately, and fly their planes at housetop level over our farms and homes looking for illegal Mexican workers. It may or may not be legal, but it is not democratic procedure. It is a violation of the rights of citizens and private property. No farmer, nor any decent citizen, approves of such tactics, and there is nothing the farmer would like better than to cooperate with Federal agencies in enforcing a legal system of obtaining alien labor.

The authority is clear for an immigration officer to enter private property if he has a warrant; without a warrant he may enter if a deportable alien is known to be on the property who is likely to escape. The authority is not clear, however, for immigration officers to enter upon farms, ranches, or other enclosed lands to inspect or search for illegal aliens.

It must be noted that farms employing workers in significant numbers are places of employment and therefore affected with a public interest. Should they not be open to inspection for the enforcement of law? Under safety and accident prevention laws, it was long ago acknowledged that factory inspectors had the right to enter places of employment. Likewise, government officials inspect places of employment to administer child labor, minimum wage, maximum hours, sanitation and other laws. The farmer's home, whether on his farm or elsewhere, is a different thing from the farm property on which employment occurs. Perhaps it is time we modernize our concept of the farm employing several workers, recognizing it (apart from the farmer's home) as not a personal castle but rather a place of employment affected with a public interest and on which inspections may be made in the enforcement of law.

Statutory clarification on the above points will aid in taking action against the conveyors and receivers of the wetback. These clarifications of the statute, together with increased funds and personnel for enforcement, are possibly all that are needed to deal effectively with the smuggler and the intermediary. But this will not be enough. Something more needs to be done to discourage the employment of wetbacks and to take the profit out of it. It was repeatedly suggested to the Commission that it recommend making the employment of a wetback a crime. This suggestion has merit since, if the risk involved in employing wetbacks were increased, the traffic would soon diminish. In addition to making employment of an illegal alien unlawful, much would be accomplished by taking the profit out of such employment. It seems likely that if farm employers had to maintain a decent standard of minimum wages, irrespective of the nationality of the worker to whom the wages are paid, the advantages of wetback employment would disappear.

The attack on the problem will have to be manifold. The wetback traffic has reached such proportions in volume and in consequent chaos, it should not be neglected any longer. The techniques to be employed may be of various types but we believe the basic approaches are encompassed in our recommendations.

Recommendations

We recommend that:

(1) The Immigration and Naturalization Service be strengthened by (a) clear statutory authority to enter places of employment to determine if illegal aliens are employed, (b) clear statutory penalties for harboring, concealing, or transporting illegal aliens, and (c) increased appropriations for personnel and equipment.

(2) Legislation be enacted making it unlawful to employ aliens illegally in the United States, the sanctions to be: (a) removal by the Immigration and Naturalization Service of all legally imported labor from any place of employment on which any illegal alien is found employed; (b) fine and imprisonment; (c) restraining orders and injunctions; and (d) prohibiting the shipment in interstate commerce of any product on which illegal alien labor has worked.

(3) Legalization for employment purposes of aliens illegally in the United States be discontinued and forbidden. This is not intended to interfere with handling of hardship cases as authorized by present immigration laws.

(4) The Department of State seek the active cooperation of the Government of Mexico in a program for eliminating the illegal migration of

Mexican workers into the United States, by (a) the strict enforcement of the Mexican emigration laws, (b) preventing the concentration, in areas close to the border, of surplus supplies of Mexican labor, and (c) refraining from attempts to obtain legalization for employment in the United States of Mexican workers illegally in this country.

16

"United States Apologizes for El Paso Incident"

Robert A. Lovett

I refer further to your attentive note of October 18, 1948, concerning irregularities which have occurred in the vicinity of El Paso in connection with the entry of certain Mexican farm workers under conditions other than those established by the exchange of notes of February 11, 1948.

An investigation of the circumstances of this case confirms that the entry of these Mexican nationals was indeed illegal and that they were not, as required by Article 29 of the agreement, immediately deported to Mexico. I deeply regret that these irregularities have occurred.

I am happy to inform you at this time, however, that orders have been issued that the Mexican nationals who entered illegally be promptly returned to Ciudad Juárez. Repatriation of these workers has already commenced.

Orders have already been issued to stop all further illegal or clandestine immigration along the border.

Nothing which has happened, of course, will in any way affect the rights and privileges of the Mexican nationals who are now legally in the United States in fulfillment of contracts entered into under the agreement. They will continue to enjoy the immunities and prerogatives set forth in the agreement and individual work contracts and the existing

---

Letter from Robert A. Lovett (Acting Secretary of State) to Don Rafael de la Colina (Minister Plenipotentiary, Chargé d'Affaires ad interim of Mexico), Ocotber 22, 1948, Papers of David H. Stowe, Folder marked "Mexican Farm Labor 1949–50," Harry S. Truman Library.

satisfactory arrangements for participation of Mexican consuls in discussions of any misunderstandings which may arise will continue as in the past. It is my sincere hope that the corrective measures which have been described above and which will be carried out to the best of my Government's ability, will be found satisfactory to your Government.

With sincere expressions of profound regret for the serious instance of noncompliance which has occurred, I take this opportunity to express my Government's appreciation for the cooperation Mexico has given in the past and which I hope will continue in the future.

I avail myself of this opportunity to renew the assurances of my high consideration.

17

"Mexico Accepts United States Apology For El Paso Incident"

Rafael de la Colina

I have the honor to acknowledge receipt of Your Excellency's note of October 22 relative to the irregularities which occurred in the vicinity of El Paso in connection with the entry into the United States of Mexican agricultural workers under conditions other than those expressed in the exchange of notes of February 21, 1948.

Upon instructions from my Government, I am pleased to inform Your Excellency that it has found satisfactory the statements made by the Department of State, as well as the measures adopted by the American authorities, measures the realization of which, already commenced, brings an end to this lamentable incident, which has been resolved, as was to be expected, in the spirit of justice, good neighborliness and friendly cooperation which has always governed relations between Mexico and the United States.

Letter from Rafael de la Colina (Mexican Chargé d'Affaires ad interim) to Robert A. Lovett (Acting Secretary of State), October 23, 1948, Papers of David H. Stowe, Folder labeled "Mexican Farm Labor 1949–50," Harry S. Truman Library.

I avail myself of this opportunity to renew to Your Excellency the testimony of my highest and most distinguished consideration.

18

"Truman Writes Mexico's President About The Wetback Problem"

Harry S. Truman

As you know, the United States Congress has passed a bill authorizing this government to transport contract farm workers from within Mexico into this country, to provide reception centers for them, to help them make arrangements for contract work with employers here and finally, to guarantee that the workers will in fact obtain the wage and transportation terms of these contracts.

I have approved this bill and it has thus become law. With the authority granted by this law I feel confident that we can now give the assurances which your government regarded as essential to a new agreement permitting United States importation of contract workers from Mexico. I believe that the difficulties which led your government to terminate the present agreement can now be overcome.

In consequence, representatives of this government are in Mexico City to negotiate a new agreement. I feel sure that mutually satisfactory terms can now be worked out.

There is, however, one aspect of the matter which causes me great concern. It is on that account that I am writing directly to you. I have asked one of my personal assistants, Mr. David H. Stowe, to accompany our delegation so that he might bring this letter to you and give you whatever further information you may desire.

The problem which concerns me is expressed in the message I have sent to the Congress in connection with my approval of the new law. Mr. Stowe has a copy of this message for you.

Letter from Harry S. Truman to Miguel Alemán (President of the United Mexican States), July 14, 1951, Papers of David H. Stowe, Folder labeled "Mexican Labor 1951, Folder 2," Harry S. Truman Library

I have pointed out to the Congress that this law, taken by itself, cannot cure the social and economic difficulties which we face in dealing with the farm labor situation in the southwestern United States. I am anxious to see progress made toward improving working conditions and living standards for our own citizens and for the contract workers from Mexico who are employed on our farms. That will be of great benefit to the individuals concerned and to the stability of our agricultural production. But if these things are to occur the governments of the United States and Mexico must take steps to shut off the stream of Mexican citizens immigrating illegally into the United States.

The low wages paid to these people and the poor conditions under which they are forced to live have had the effect of lowering living and working standards for our own citizens and for Mexican citizens legally employed in this country. Other undesirable social consequences have followed the flow of illegal immigrants, consequences which bear most heavily on our citizens and resident aliens of Mexican nationality.

The experts in this government and those in private life who have studied this problem are convinced that to improve economic and social conditions in the farm lands of the southwest, we must first curtail illegal immigration from Mexico. This will require the Congress of the United States to pass new legislation and to appropriate additional funds.

I have asked in my Message that the Congress take this needed action at once. I have indicated that my approval of the new law on Mexican contract labor was given only because of assurances that the Congress would consider the other needed measures. I am concerned, however, that once the two governments reach a new agreement for the continued importation of contract workers from Mexico, the Congress might not act upon the more basic problem of controlling illegal immigration.

Therefore, I would like to suggest, for your consideration, that the new agreement between Mexico and the United States, for contract workers, might well be confined to a six month period. That would allow time for further action by the United States Congress, and if this action were not forthcoming, a further renewal of the agreement could be postponed.

I make this suggestion because I feel so strongly that the people of both Mexico and the United States have much to gain if this illegal immigration can be brought to an end. The Mexican citizens who come here legally to do farm work on contract would surely benefit just as would our own citizens who are working as farm laborers.

I have asked Mr. Stowe to convey to you my warmest personal regards.

19

"Mexico's President Responds To Truman's Letter Regarding Wetbacks"

Miguel Alemán

Mr. David H. Stowe, whom, accompanied by Mr. Richard Rubottom, Jr., I had the pleasure of receiving personally, handed me your courteous letter of July 14 in which you informed me of the signing of the law, recently approved by the Congress of the United States of America, by virtue of which the contracting of Mexican agricultural workers, permitting them to work there, will be carried out. This will be done under arrangements which, based on experience, we consider indispensable in order that this collaboration which—with complete solidarity—Mexico offers to the United States, may be effected as much in behalf of the good will which unites our two peoples and our two Governments as for those who use the workers.

I have read the message which you delivered to the Congress of the United States on signing the above-mentioned law, and I am pleased to say to you that I find in it a clear reflection of the concern which my Government has felt for some time and of the plan which we have had in mind for providing an adequate solution to this problem. In effect, I believe that if we do not succeed, by combining our efforts, in putting a definite stop to the illegal movement of agricultural workers, this will not only redound to the detriment of the economies of our respective countries, but the possibilities for our cooperation will be affected in a very serious way. For that reason, I was pleased at the tone of your message and at the firm intent of your Government to collaborate with that of Mexico in this important matter. Once this problem referred to above has been completely resolved, it will be much easier to find adequate solutions with respect to the salaries, working conditions, and living conditions for those Mexicans who may be contracted under the agreement between our two Governments. Meanwhile, I have given instructions to

---

Translated copy of letter from M. Alemán to Harry S. Truman, July 27, 1951, Papers of Harry S. Truman (Official File), folder labeled "407-D, Mexican Agricultural Workers—Aug. 1951–53," Harry S. Truman Library.

the Mexican representatives in the discussions now being held with the United States that the new agreement be limited to a period of six months. This is sufficient time for the Congress of the United States to adopt additional legislation and we could observe the effect which the new agreement may have on the illegal traffic in Mexican workers and its effect on employers who, lacking a clear sense of their social responsibility, place personal interests before the well-being of the whole.

With appreciation for your kind message, I am pleased to reiterate the assurance of my most sincere friendship.

20

"Mexico Adopts Measures to Curtail Wetback Emigration"

Excélsior

Our Government considers that the most serious obstacle which has been encountered in seeking a frank collaboration between Mexico and the United States for the contracting of agricultural workers in that country, is the exodus of our braceros who, under illusions, and deceived by hookers who only seek personal gain, have illegally entered the United States.

Facing so delicate a problem, various branches of the Federal Government, including the Ministries for Foreign Relations, the Interior (*Gobernación*), Defense, and Agriculture, under express recommendations of the President of the Republic, are adopting the measures they deem necessary to avoid the illegal departure of our workers, applying the sanctions indicated by the Penal Code as well as by the General Law of Population.

The Ministries of Foreign Relations and *Gobernación*, by presidential order, last night made the following statements:

From translated copy of "Rigid Control of Emigration of Braceros," *Excélsior*, July 20, 1951, Papers of David H. Stowe, folder labeled "Mexican Labor, 1951, Folder 2," Harry S. Truman Library.

With regard to the conversations being held by representatives of Mexico and the United States of America to arrange a new agreement to permit the contracting of Mexican agricultural workers to serve temporarily in the neighboring country, the Ministries of *Gobernación* and Foreign Relations, by instruction of the President of the Republic, consider it opportune to make the following statements:

> "The most serious difficulty which has been encountered in this collaboration between the two countries has been based on the exodus of Mexican laborers who, lured by vain illusions, and deceived by hookers who seek only their own interest, have entered the United States of America illegally, and have been contracted by employers without scruples.

Disadvantages of the Adventure

> "Through the most varied channels, and by the most diverse procedures, the Government of Mexico has pointed out to our compatriots the serious disadvantages of setting out on such an adventure, since they not only expose themselves to receiving insufficient wages, to being deprived of social benefits of the most elemental nature, and to being unable to resort to the protection of our consular representatives and the American authorities, but also, their clandestine immigration brings serious damage to our economy, which is based on the principle—as stated by the President of the Republic—of permitting the contracting only of those persons whose presence in Mexico is not indispensable for our agriculture and our industry.
>
> "Together with this work of persuasion, the Ministry of *Gobernación* is constantly adopting new measures to have our border authorities keep a strict vigilance over the departure of our compatriots and prevent the departure of those who are not properly documented.
>
> "Even though the law recently approved by the Government of the United States of America constitutes a truly great step toward the solution of various aspects of this problem, among other reasons because the American Government will guarantee compliance with the individual labor contracts and because workers will not be supplied to employers who employ illegal immigrants, the problem will not be completely solved until a definite end has been made to

the clandestine exodus of workers. In order to gain this objective, the agreement now under discussion by representatives of the two countries will contain a clause by virtue of which the duration of the agreement will be short. During that time there will be opportunity to examine the effects of the agreement on the illicit flow of workers, and there will be time for the Congress of the United States of America to announce its views concerning the recommendation made to it by President Harry S. Truman, to the effect that the necessary legislation be adopted for the punishment of those who give work to clandestine immigrants.

Better System of Vigilance

"In the meantime, the Ministry of *Gobernación,* following instructions of the President of the Republic, is proceeding urgently to improve the system of vigilance to coordinate the corresponding elements of the Ministries of National Defense, Treasury and Public Credit, Health and Assistance, Agriculture and Cattleraising, with those of the border and the respective cities, with the object of carrying out the mobilization of all these elements in order more effectively to prevent the illegal departure of our compatriots from Mexican Territory. The Ministry for National Defense immediately issued orders for the reinforcement of border garrisons, supplying them light vehicles to contribute to their rapid mobilization. Lastly, the personnel of the Offices of Population, of the Ministry of *Gobernación,* has been increased and instructions have been issued for it immediately to intensify the vigilance it has been carrying out in order to apply with all severity the sanctions established by the Penal Code and Article 108 of the General Law of Population, which says: 'A penalty of 3 to 9 years in jail and a fine up to $10,000.00 will be imposed on hookers, agents, and in general all those who, for their own account, or for account of others, try to take, or take, Mexican workers abroad without previous authorization of the Ministry of *Gobernación.*' "

Predominating Criterion in the Conversations

Ample guaranties and effective assurances on the part of the American authorities for Mexican workers who go to the United States legally contracted to perform agricultural work, is the principal objective maintained and defended by the Mexican delegates in their conversations at the Ministry for Foreign Relations in the negotiations between both governments.

Formerly, the principal objective of the conversations was that the United States legally obtain the greatest number of Mexican workers as an aid in avoiding the loss of crops; but now the purpose which is discussed with most interest in these conversations is that of obtaining for the Mexican workers the most ample guaranties and compensations in their work and in everything related thereto.

It is for this reason that in the present conversations the work of our delegation has been persistent and intense to obtain complete approval of the demands already made known to the American representatives.

In any event, it was indicated yesterday by conference circles conferring at the Ministry for Foreign Relations, that the agencies of our Government, among them Foreign Relations, *Gobernación*, Labor, and Agriculture, as well as the Legislative bodies, have acted jointly in the work of presenting concrete propositions for the elaboration of a new agreement which will satisfy the objective that the Mexican workers who go to the United States legally will do so under conditions that will guarantee their wages, transportation, and other compensations.

Valuable Aid of President Truman

It was likewise indicated that it would not be correct or just to fail to recognize publicly that the most important contribution to the success of the conversations taking place among representatives of the two governments has been the valuable cooperation of President Truman and of his collaborators, who, in a spirit of understanding and good will have recognized and considered the justice of the attitude assumed by our Government with regard to the conditions for a new agreement. They have thus shown, realistically, that they will not permit Mexican workers to be the victims of abuse and exploitation in the United States. . . .

21

"Mexico Issues Statement On Wetback Problem"

Mexican Foreign Office

Due to the problem created for Mexico by the return of workers who enter the United States illegally, the Ministry of Foreign Relations and Gobernación consider it opportune to state that one of the clauses of the International Agreement reached by the Governments of Mexico and the United States for the contracting of agricultural laborers, contains the obligation of dictating effective measures to avoid the departure of Mexican workers without the guarantee to a legitimate work contract, and of taking the necessary steps for the immediate return of every Mexican worker who is found in the United States and who is not able to demonstrate his legal entry into that country. Therefore, the return of those who undertake the adventure of going to the United States illegally, is no more than the inevitable consequence of the violation that they commit, both of our own laws and the laws of the United States, paying no heed to the warnings that have been made constantly asking them to desist from entering into an adventure that can bring them only many inconveniences and numerous penalties.

Notwithstanding the foregoing, the Ministries of Foreign Relation and Gobernación, by order of the President of the Republic, are proceeding coordinately to adopt emergency measures with the object of meeting the situation created by the illegal exodus of our countrymen and their correlative return to Mexico. Among those measures are the following:

1. The Government of Mexico is already coming to an agreement with the Government of the United States so that the repatriation be made in such a way that our countrymen can be tended to, when they arrive at the border, by the Mexican migration authorities, and conducted in an orderly manner, either to the centers where hand labor is scarce and they may care to work, or else, to their place of origin.

Translated copy of press release furnished American Embassy by Mexican Foreign Office, July 24, 1952, Papers of David H. Stowe, folder labeled "Mexican Labor, 1952, Folder 2," Harry S. Truman Library.

2. The migration patrols in charge of the vigilance of our border will be provided with "jeeps" so that they may constantly patrol the various localities through which this illicit traffic is being effected with the object of stopping it.

3. The Ministry of Gobernación is already requesting the cooperation of the Federal, Local, and Municipal authorities, so that, by every means in their power, they cooperate in the vigilance of our border and avoid in every way, the illegal departure of our countrymen.

4. The Ministry of Foreign Relations is requesting, through the American Embassy, that said government intensify the vigilance of its borders and that it instruct the American Immigration authorities, in order to obtain better results, to coordinate its activities with those of the Mexican Immigration authorities.

5. Finally, the Ministry of Gobernación will continue to bring before the proper Mexican authorities all those persons who traffic with our countrymen.

The Federal Government, in making an urgent appeal to the Mexicans so that they do not, under any circumstances, abandon their homes and their work with the intention of entering the United States illegally, addresses, through the Ministry of Gobernación, the State Governors, so that, using all means of convincing the people that are in their power, they realize an extensive campaign in the respective federal entities, asking all Mexicans not to undertake an adventure in which, in the end, they will result prejudiced, with the consequent damage to the economy of Mexico.

22

"Mexican Official Blasts Apprehended Wetbacks"

Xavier Castaneda

Good afternoon. In the name of our Government and that of the United States, I have been appointed to speak a few words of orientation and advice to you in regard to this folly you are committing by violating the laws and crossing to this country without the proper permit.

It gives me deep satisfaction to know that the American officer here is giving you a better treatment than you would receive from an equal Mexican official. The American has given you many considerations, for example: they have brought you here in the shade to wait; they have given you sandwiches to eat and cool water to drink. All those courtesies you have been accorded, although without doubt you have not requested them. I do not think you would have been treated so in the jails of Mexico. On behalf of the Mexican Government, I am highly grateful for the civil treatment given to you, my Mexican compatriots, and to all members of the Mexican race who, because of a whim or lack of forethought, have crossed to this country without the proper permit.

I am charged to tell you that you have committed a great sin in coming to this country without being asked for, without being needed here. The Government of Mexico is disgusted, fed up with this clandestine business of you, its citizens, going to the United States just because of a fancy. All this for the mirage of the dollar. But now it is all finished.

The Government of the United States is very much in your favor. Why? This I am going to explain. There are the rich landowners who have sent for you, and when you come have not paid you well; they have exploited you. The Government of the United States has seen these injustices and has turned in favor of you, the laborers of Mexico, with the object of getting rid of you as wet-backs. Then, if needed, you will be contracted in Mexico by these landowners, who will have to go there

---

English-language copy of speech made to departing airlift wetbacks by Xavier Castaneda (Mexican Public Health Officer) at Rio Grande Valley International Airport, Brownsville, Texas, 1951, Papers of David H. Stowe, folder labeled "Mexican Labor, 1951, Folder 1," Harry S. Truman Library.

to hire you, if they want you to pick their cotton. With few exceptions, every Mexican laborer who comes here under contract is valued and appreciated. The exceptions among you are those undesirables who commit your crimes in Mexico and seek refuge in this country, passing yourselves off as laborers.

Inasmuch as this deportation by air is entirely just and legal, I want one of your own number to read a paragraph from a leaflet you will be given before you leave. (One of the wet-backs reads from leaflet, and English translation of which reads as follows: "Thusly, you are advised that the lucrative days for the wet-backs are over. The Immigration Service of the United States is redoubling its forces in order to put a stop to this illegal traffic, not only to enforce the law, but also in compliance with a pact which exists between the Governments of Mexico and of the United States.")

Thus, it is a pact which has been made between the Governments of Mexico and of the United States. In compliance with this pact, these air deportations are being effected. Already, between 16 and 17 thousand have been deported in airplanes. This is in addition to those who have been allowed to go across the bridge.

All of this illegal traffic from Mexico to the United States, all of this clandestine movement, is very damaging to us as Mexicans, and why is it done? Because of this ambition you have to come here and earn dollars. But it doesn't hold water; it is a lie.

We do not even know but what among you there are criminals, or vicious Communists, who come here to the detriment of Mexico and the United States.

All in all, you yourselves are witnesses and judges of your own situations. What have you gained here? Nothing. Nothing but sorrowful illusions. And why has this come to pass? Because you have been deceived by rumors.

But the government of the United States has seen fit to act, as I have said before, humanely. Note it my friends; put it down. You are hauled around in cars, not made to walk; I am sure that in no part of the United States are prisoners treated better.

You are all insured for $14,000 (sic). Thus in the case of the individual who has lied about his name, his beneficiaries have no recourse.

Now I beg you, in the name of our country, in the name of Mexico, I beg you not to return in this clandestine manner. In the name of the Mexican Immigration, in the name of these American officers, I am charged with speaking to you in clear and simple Spanish, that you abstain. Your hands are needed in Mexico, and only the man who is worth nothing there, comes here in this manner. Do not continue to make yourselves warehouses full of cheap Indians. You should be ashamed of yourselves, abandoning your homes, traitors to your Mexico. Mexico is esteemed and loved in the world, and you are making a bad example with this situation.

Perhaps it is because you have been deceived. Be that as it may, it is now all over. From now on, he who fails to listen to these supplications from our beloved Mexico, he who does not heed this request from the United States, will be drastically punished with a year in prison and a fine of $250. And if he does not have this fine of $250, it will be one more year of prison. This decision has been taken in Washington and we have already received telegrams verifying these sentences.

So I, a Mexican among the rest of you, with all my soul, as the shield of the University of Mexico says, "My spirit speaks for my race", I am speaking for my race. The wise man need not have a long beard; he who gives good advice can also be called professor. And I am telling you that they do not need you here, in this illegal manner. So I want you to tell me, boys, are you going to come back illegally? (All answer "No, no.") Louder, are you going to come back? ("No, no.") Truthfully, with all your heart? ("No.") May God help you and the Fatherland reward you.

Above all, Mexico is our country. Later, if they start contracting, everyone of you who comes here legally contracted will be received with open arms. You will bear the name of a true Mexican citizen, rather than as a wet-back, as you are now designated, a very sad thing for Mexico. You all know that by her efforts, Mexico has lifted our flag to a very high position, and you all are humiliating it. I hope to God that you do not return in this manner; that if you do return, you come legally.

Once more, I repeat, on behalf of our Governments which are now working so closely together on this problem, do not return illegally. If you can come back legally contracted you will enjoy the rights of all men living under the eye of Jesus Christ. You are not murderers, I know; you are workers, and the worker is always welcome here if he is legally documented. The man who comes otherwise is distrusted. He who comes legally is trusted; they tell him, "Come in, senor." That is what the United States is now doing: deporting you out of here so if you come back they can say to you, "Come in, good Mexicans, to work."

Finally, in the name of Mexico, I am going to repeat once more, are you going to come back without permits? (Answer: No.) We hope to God you don't. Go on back to your country. Your mothers, your daughters, the most precious treasures are awaiting you there. Viva Mexico!

23

"The Hardships of a Border Patrol Officer"

Massey L. Fitch

Arrangements were made by this officer to check the laborers on the Sam Smith* farm near Ysleta, Texas as a result of some information we had received concerning smuggled aliens being on the farm. Arrangements were made to have the Border Patrol airplane fly over the farm and spot the laborers and the officers were to use two jeeps and a patrol car. I went in the patrol car and when the plane spotted the aliens I went to the home of Mr. Sam Smith to tell him that we were checking his laborers and ask him if he wanted to go along. He readily agreed to go and went with me in the patrol car.

The Smith farm is a very difficult place to check for various reasons but the newest is that Mr. Smith has placed posts at the entrance of each road and locked a chain across the road. It is necessary to unlock and relock each chain before going down any of the roads. Mr. Smith told me that there were about twenty of these chains on the farms. We entered the main entrance and proceeded about 200 yards to where we found 5 separate roads branching off and each with a chain across it. We entered one and Mr. Smith carefully locked the chain behind us. I remarked that it must be lots of trouble to have so many chains to lock and unlock. He agreed that they were but they were necessary to keep the peddlers from going through his farm. He stressed the fact that it was not the Border Patrol he was trying to keep out. But the fact is that by the time the Border Patrol is through one chain all of the wet Mexicans have long disappeared into the tall cotton and drainage ditches.

I checked one group of laborers and then went on to where one of the jeeps was checking a field. The airplane reported that there had been 8 or 9 men working in the field when he first went over it but only 4 were visible at the time. I went out into the field and with Inspector Cartter

---

Memorandum from Massey L. Fitch (Patrol Inspector in Charge, Ysleta, Texas) to G. J. McBee (Chief Patrol Inspector, El Paso), August 2, 1950, Records of the President's Commission on Migratory Labor, folder labeled "El Paso, Texas, Aug. 4–5, 1950, Statements," Harry S. Truman Library.

*The real name of the farmer appeared in the Fitch memo but is not used here.—EDS.

managed to dig out three of the aliens who had hidden. While I was in the field Mr. and Mrs. K. S. Smith drove up but left before I came out. Sam Smith told me that his mother had jumped on Inspector Kinderknecht for going around the gate when entering the field. About this time we discovered a pair of Government binoculars had disappeared from Patrol car #212 and we spent a time looking for them. I took Mr. Smith to his home and he asked me to stop at the gate where Inspectors Kinderknecht and Cartter had entered. He got out and took pictures of the tracks of the jeep and other cars and of the patrol car. We then brought the aliens to El Paso for processing. We apprehended only seven aliens but are convinced that at least that many more had made good their escape.

24

"Through the Eyes of a Wetback— A Personal Experience"

Julian Samora

Our concern to cover all possible aspects of the wetback story kept us searching for means and methods of gathering more information and of controlling the reliability and validity of that information already obtained. We decided that the technique of participant observation could be validly used, and a Mexican researcher thoroughly familiar with literature on wetbacks as well as the research project was engaged to become a wetback. The Immigration and Naturalization Service in Washington would be advised of the general plan (but not the details) in order to protect the observer's legal status in the U.S. in the future and in case of unforeseen

---

From Julian Samora, *Los Mojados: The Wetback Story* (Notre Dame: University of Notre Dame Press, 1971), pages 107–27. Reprinted by permission of the University of Notre Dame Press.

difficulties relative to his safety. The observer was to leave all of his documentation, together with a letter from the director of the project, in the hands of a lawyer in a U.S. border city. The observer was to go to Mexico, assume the clothing and behavior of a lower-class worker from the interior, and upon reaching a Mexican border city he was to seek assistance in crossing illegally into the U.S. Upon crossing the border he would behave as a wetback along with his companions. He would try to obtain employment, be apprehended by the Border Patrol, sent to a detention center, and expelled from the country. During this period the observer would keep a diary and careful notes of his experience and send the materials to the research project in the form of letters. Below is a summary of his report.

The Participant Observer's Report*

Dressed like the type of wetback I was planning to portray, and with twenty-five dollars in my pocket, I crossed the U.S.-Mexican border at Hidalgo, Texas, and arrived at Reynosa, Tamaulipas, Mexico, where I went to the *plaza principal* and started walking around, looking for persons who were planning to cross the river into the U.S. Previous information was confirmed on the openness with which people speak about crossing the river without the benefit of the bridge.

On this morning I was able to join four groups in the main square who were discussing the details of crossing. I was interested not only in what they were talking about but also, of course, in the way I was received and accepted as any other would-be wetback. In spite of some differences in speech, through which they noticed I was not a peasant, they allowed me in their conversation without any apparent suspicion. The story I had prepared was that I was born and raised in Zamora, Michoacán; my mother was a maid for a wealthy family for whom I was working as a servant (houseboy). I went to school, finishing *secundaria* (junior high school), and four years ago I went to Mexico City to work in construction, where I learned how to operate construction machinery. I was out of a job and that was the first time I was going to cross as a wetback. This story fitted a type which is not uncommon among wetbacks, according to our information, although the urban type of wetback is more likely to cross at El Paso, Texas, or California—where jobs in services may be available—

*This chapter was originally written by Jorge A. Bustamante F.

than in the lower Rio Grande valley, where I was. For those who live in the central states of Mexico, this valley is the closest and the least expensive point to reach; it is also the region where the poor peasant is more likely to cross as a wetback.

When a person arrives in a Mexican border town wanting to cross the river illegally for the first time he goes around asking questions on how to do it. Group discussions about crossing without proper documents are so open that a person who arrives in Reynosa in the morning will have found a group the same day and will cross that evening. The one who seems to have the most experience will lead a group of two to five persons, without any apparent concern about who they are. These groups are frequently approached by smugglers recruiting clients and offering, at varying prices, the safest way to get across the border or beyond the checking points of the Border Patrol. What they offer is not only their knowledge of the terrain but very often contacts for jobs in a great variety of places, from just across the river, to Kansas or the Midwest. Where I was the prices ranged from fifty dollars for being smuggled to the first highway going to McAllen, to $400 for being smuggled to Chicago. Four "coyotes" (smugglers) that I found were green card bearers.

I was looking for a local "veteran wetback" who was planning to cross that day and with whom I could join without having to pay for his assistance. The type I had in mind was one who lives in Reynosa and goes frequently to the U.S. without inspection. So I walked along the river and after several inquiries I found a group of people, all of them residents of El Ejido Longoria, which is located two miles from Reynosa. After I gave them my story, they began to advise me as to how to behave in order to avoid being caught by *la migra* (the Border Patrol). Two men, about forty-five or fifty, were speaking enthusiastically about the bracero epoch during the Second World War. One said. "That was a time when it didn't matter if you were kicked by the gringo because you could make good money." The other added, "After the war everything changed and *echársela de mojado* [to go as a wetback] *valió madre* [wasn't worth a damn]. The farmers were paying less and less; I think that happened because it seemed like all the Mexicans were crossing the Rio Grande after the war, and particularly during the fifties." Another who seemed to be younger and more educated said, "Where it is worth going nowadays is to Chicago to work in the factories. You make good money. But the problem is the damn weather up there—that cold is not for Christians." A fourth one added, "I am not going anymore because *la migra me la tiene sentenciada* [those of the Border Patrol have a sentence pending on my head] and if they catch me again they will bury me in 'La Tuna' [a federal prison near El Paso] for a long time, and I cannot afford that now."

The owner of the place where we were gathered told me that his nephew was planning to go across that night and he would ask him if I could go along. His nephew, whom we shall call Juan, was twenty-five years old and a "veteran wetback." He was going to San Antonio where he knew someone who could hire him. He accepted my company and everything was settled to leave by sunset. Another "veteran wetback" from the neighborhood came to join us, and although he clearly did not like the idea of going with a first-timer like myself, he finally went with us. We shall call him José.

At 7:30 P.M. Juan respectfully received the blessings of farewell from his father. His father was bedridden, unable to walk as a result of a tractor accident eight years ago, while working as a bracero near Weslaco, Texas. Juan, his only support, was looking for work in order to buy a long-needed medical prescription for his father. He hoped that *this time* he could stay long enough in the U.S. to make the money he needed.

Making the Crossing

We left the house and walked about two miles to the place they knew as the most convenient for crossing. The river was running straight at that place and was about 140 feet wide. They explained that we should not cross where the river curves because, there, deep holes and whirlpools make it dangerous. As we got closer to the crossing point they lowered their voices and tried to walk noiselessly. They warned me about two deeper zones on each side of the river. We were supposed to wade with the exception of the last twenty feet, where we would have to swim. We were to cross diagonally along with the current, carrying our clothes in plastic bags.

Very quietly we took off our clothes and began the crossing. They were ahead of me and I saw them sinking until the water reached two inches from their shoulders. Right then I realized I would have problems, because they were taller than I. I stepped on the bottom of the river, which was muddy on the surface but became firm an inch deeper. The water was soon over my shoulders and I could no longer stand against the stream. Juan realized my problem and told me to throw my bag to him so that I could swim freely. I drifted about twelve feet downstream from them; perhaps this was why each time I tried to touch the bottom I could not, yet I saw that they were still walking. I should mention that I have always had trouble swimming for a distance longer than a hundred feet, so in the middle of the river I began to feel tired. At this point I tried for the last time to touch the ground in order to rest. I had seen them in the middle of the river, with the water at their waist, but I was unable to keep my vertical position because where I was crossing the river was deeper. I decided not to try walking again and kept on swimming for the rest of the crossing. There was a point when I thought that I couldn't make it; I was exhausted. I heard Juan asking if I needed help. I did not answer but made the last effort to reach the U.S. edge of the river.

It took me a while to recover enough to try to climb the bank, which, at that point, was slanted more than forty degrees. I couldn't do it, so, holding onto the grass at the river's edge, I pulled myself along to the point where Juan and José were waiting for me. When I finally did reach them they were staring at me in a way that seemed to indicate I was doing things wrong. Later they explained that they had chosen that point of the river for crossing because we could wade most of the way. They said that one should stay immersed as much as possible because a naked person wading the river is very difficult to see at night but a person swimming becomes very easy to spot if he splashes while swimming. The splashing noise I made while swimming and trying to climb the bank made them fear that we might have been seen by the Border Patrol. José said, "When I saw you swimming with that *chapoteadero* [splashing], it seemed like you were making signs to call *la migra*." It was clear that I had done all the things they were trying not to do.

Once I finally stood up on the river bank, Juan motioned to me to be quiet and hide myself in the grass. We were there for more than twenty minutes just waiting, alert to any noise that would indicate that the Border Patrol had spotted us. We stayed naked so that we could cross back quickly should they approach. There was a moment, while we were waiting, when Juan and José said a prayer very quietly, just moving their lips, with their arms crossed and serious expressions on their faces.

Evading the Patrol

It was already dark, but not totally dark. The clouds did not hide the moon as Juan had anticipated. This disturbed them a little—to the extent of causing them to swear at the uncooperative wind. Finally, Juan climbed up to the top of the bank, where a dirt road went along the U.S. side of the river. He watched for a while and then came down, telling us to get dressed quickly. The plan was to move away from the river as fast as possible. Walking on the road was very dangerous, for the Border Patrol might come at any moment, and it would be easy to see a person walking across the newly planted fields. We crossed the road and decided to crawl through the fields. This distance was long and difficult for me to cover. José and Juan crawled faster than I, with almost feline movements that contrasted with the difficulties I found in crawling while carrying the bag that held my clothes and a bottle of water. After the first three fields planted with peppers, we continued through several cotton fields, which provided better hiding and made it unneccessary to crawl. We did not stop for approximately two miles until we got to a dirt road. We were crossing a third dirt road when the lights of a car appeared. We immediately ran into the bushes to hide, lying down. After the car passed by they urged me to move faster whenever the lights of a car approached. At that hour of the night we must assume that any car would be a Border Patrol car. The next time we saw the lights of a car I did exactly what they told me, but a tremendous noise made clear again who was the novice; my water bottle fell and broke. Once again I saw a couple of serious faces as we came out of our hiding places. Shaking his head, José made the only comment. "We were again very lucky that it wasn't a Border Patrol car. The noise you made was heard in McAllen." I just said, "I am sorry."

We were approaching McAllen, but we did not plan to enter the city but rather to go around it toward Edinburg, Texas. We crossed Highway 83, which is west of McAllen, and continued through orange fields, when a dog began barking. We then changed direction, and Juan said, "This is too bad, that dog was barking at people." I asked him what he meant and he said "Don't you know that dogs bark differently depending upon what they are barking at? Now the people in the house know by the barking that we are here. They might have called the police, so let's get out of here quickly. If the town police catch us it will be worse for us than if we were caught by the Border Patrol. Those *chotas* [cops] are really bad with Mexicans." We ran from that field and didn't stop until we had crossed another highway going northeast toward Edinburg.

Our First Encounter

We were crossing a farm road when Juan asked José to hold his bag while he took a stone from his shoe. He was almost through when we heard a car coming. This time I ran faster than they and got deeper in the thicket. I felt Juan behind me and I saw José stoop to pick up the things he was carrying, thus losing a few seconds. The car was making a turn when its headlights spotted us just before we had hidden ourselves. I heard the car stop and its door open, then a loud voice saying, in Spanish, "Come out immediately. We have seen you." No one moved and I decided to wait and see what Juan and José would do. The same voice repeated. "Don't play games with us because it will be worse for you. You'd better come up or we will go and get you."

Again no one made any noise, but we could hear the officers walking on the road. Then a second voice said, "Let's go and get them," and the other answered, "No, wait."

Then again the first voice said, "Don't make us angry, you bastards. Come out right now or I'll make you come out with bullets."

After twenty or thirty seconds I heard three shots.* Ten seconds later the grass moved and one of the officers said, "Here is one." Then, in an angry tone, "Don't get smart—move. Didn't you hear what I said?"

I knew by the distance of the voice that it had been José who had been discovered. There was the sound of a person standing up from the grass, and one of the officers said, "Where are the others?"

José answered quietly, "What others? I am alone."

Then, with the sound of a blow against a body, one officer said furiously, "Do you think we are stupid or blind? We saw all of you and you better tell me where they are."

José said, "They must be far away by now."

The other officer told him to get in the car and shouted, "For the last time . . . come out right away or I'll shoot you."

He then shot three times and nothing was heard after that until the other officer said loudly so that we would hear: "Let them go and let the rattlesnakes get them. It's going to be worse for them with the rattlesnakes than with us."

The mention of the snakes scared me more than the shooting but I didn't move, waiting to see what Juan would do. For some reason the officers never got to our hiding place. I heard voices speaking in English and then the car left. I stayed quiet for maybe four or five minutes more, waiting for Juan to make the first move. I had the sensation that I was

---

*James F. Greene, Associate Commissioner, U.S. Department of Justice, told us "it is definitely against Service policy to strike an alien or to use firearms except in self-defense or in defense of a third party," and he believes this case was an isolated incident.

surrounded by rattlesnakes and that at any moment I would feel one biting me. It also came to my mind that since Juan was not moving, perhaps one of the shots had killed him. Finally Juan got up and went to the road to look. I saw his silhouette coming back. He began to laugh nervously, and then louder and louder, hysterically, I shook him to make him stop. Once calmed down he said, "This is a miracle of the Virgin of Perpetuo Socorro . . . she made them leave without having them come to look for us. They never do that, they never leave when they have spotted a wetback." Then he said, "We must get out of here. They might come back now that they know we are around."

We continued walking toward Edinburg, not without regretting what had happened to José. Juan said, "Poor guy, I think he will be taken now to 'La Tuna' for sure. He has been on probation. Well, that's the way it is in this business. He wanted to make money to buy a bicycle in order to be eligible for a job as a bill collector in Reynosa. Now he won't need money for a while."

Juan anticipated a new search by the Border Patrol and we had to move fast. He asked me for a road map of Hidalgo County which I had told him a cousin of mine had given to me when he knew that I was going to come to the border. By the light of a match we looked at the map and Juan located ourselves northeast of McAllen, near Twenty-third Street which goes north. He guessed that the Border Patrol would look for us thinking that we would follow Twenty-third Street or a drainage ditch to Edinburg. Juan decided to take neither of these logical alternatives but to go east and stop at some point near Tenth Street, where we would sleep until there was enough traffic to hitchhike to Starr County. We would not enter Edinburg but turn north, taking Jackson Road to Monte Cristo Road. When we arrived at a place where we could get food and water, we would decide whether to continue toward Lake Edinburg.

Our next problem was the lack of water. I had broken my bottle and José had been caught with Juan's bag and his bottle of water. Very soon our thirst became our main concern and we changed directions toward a place where Juan knew there was a pond used for irrigation. I was impressed with Juan's knowledge of the terrain. It was very dark but he was walking with apparent certainty, checking our location with signs that he had anticipated. Finally we arrived at the pond. We had to hang down from the side of the pond, without being able to see the level of the water because of the darkness. It had a very stagnant smell, but at that moment I couldn't have cared less. Since we had no way to carry water, we wouldn't be able to drink again for eight to ten hours.

An hour and a half later we reached Tenth Street and Juan found a spot where the grass was high enough to provide a good hiding place for us to sleep. I was extremely tried, but I had not forgotten the officer's threat about the rattlesnakes. Juan did not sound very convincing to me when he said, "Don't worry, *hombre*, remember that we had a sign already that the Virgin is taking care of us. She will keep the snakes away from us." The advantage of Juan's great faith was evident two minutes later when Juan was snoring and I was awake waiting to be bitten.

The next morning Juan awakened me, saying that it was past eight o'clock and we must continue. We hitchhiked from that point to the crossing of Sugar Road and SH 107, which is closer to Edinburg than the point that Juan had in mind the day before. Juan said he knew a place where we could find a job for the day, but I was not in any physical condition to work. I told him to go ahead without me and that I would go into Edinburg to look for some medicine for my feet. The long walk of the night before had been too much for my feet, which were accustomed to being beneath a desk. Dark stains of coagulated blood were showing over the broken leather of my shoes and I feared an infection. Juan did not want to go into the town, so we decided to meet at the same place between five and six o'clock that evening.

I went into Edinburg and spent the day taking care of my feet and writing notes. While in Edinburg I spoke English all the time in order to lessen the possibilities of being turned in to the Border Patrol. I went to a hotel and rented a room for two dollars, then to a pharmacy and to the public library. About four o'clock I had finished my notes and sent the original copy to Mexico City and one to South Bend, Indiana.

Late in the afternoon I went to the place where Juan and I were to meet, but he did not show up. I returned to Edinburg quite confused about how to carry out my plans. I realized how much I was depending upon him for what I was doing. I thought I wouldn't be able to continue north without somebody's guidance and I was not in good enough physical condition to continue walking; so I went to the bus station in Edinburg, where I thought I could find an Immigration official who would apprehend me. I opened the door and the first person I saw was an officer checking the documents of another man. He was looking at an I.D. against the light and stared at me for a second as I was entering. I thought he was going to stop me but he continued what he was doing, and finally I heard him say that the document was false and he would take the individual to the Border Patrol station.

The official then took the man by the arm and walked out, passing very close to where I was sitting.

I left the place five minutes later with the idea of sending a note to my lawyer telling him about my plans. Two blocks from the bus station I heard "psst . . . psst." Turning, I saw Juan hidden in a thicket of a vacant lot. He made a sign with his hand asking me to come close, and it took me two minutes to express to him how happy I was to see him again. He told me he couldn't make it at our appointed time because he was delayed arguing with the foreman where he had worked all day. The foreman refused to pay him as he had promised to do at the end of the day. He said that Juan must stay until the weekend. Juan insisted on the terms he had made when he was hired, but he had to run away after the foreman threatened to call the Border Patrol. I was moved by the fact that Juan was looking for me in Edinburg in spite of his determination not to enter any town until after passing the immigration checking points further north of the border.

I convinced him to accompany me to a hotel instead of sleeping outside as we had the night before. Very reluctantly he accepted and we went to the same hotel where I had been earlier. The next morning we had breakfast and bought some cans of food and juices for our journey.

Under Juan's assumption that the checking point was located approximately ten miles south of Falfurrias, Texas, on U.S. 281, we planned to hitchhike and get off before that point. Then we would walk north through the countryside east of the highway, skipping the checking point and going back to the highway near Falfurrias, where we should arrive before dark.

This time it took us longer to get a ride; traffic was heavy but the cars did not stop. We were finally picked up by a person who looked Mexican and who spoke to us in Spanish. His first question was, "Are you wetbacks?" Juan and I answered at the same time. He said "no" and I said "yes." The driver smiled and told us that it did not matter to him. He said that the Border Patrol had moved north two days ago, so we could get off further north than the point we had told him, but Juan insisted that we get off where he had planned. He then told me, "That guy was very suspicious. I think he wanted to turn us in to the Border Patrol himself." I said that my impression had been the opposite and that it seemed to me he was trying to help us. Juan then said, "You will learn very soon that you cannot trust a person who wears a tie; rich people hate us in this country even if they are of our race." I thought that was a very interesting definition of the situation.

An Episode of Snakes

It was perhaps 10:30 when we jumped over a fence which ran along the highway. We passed the first three hours without incident to speak of. Juan was leading with the same apparent self-confidence that he had shown previously. He was walking ahead of me and we were going up a little hill when Juan suddenly stopped and raised his arm in order to make me stop behind him. I asked him what happened, but a noise, one that I had been fearing to hear since the night when José was caught, gave me the answer. I thought I was seeing the longest rattlesnake I had ever seen, but it turned out to be two snakes together. Juan just said, "You see why we should not walk through here by night?" We went around the snakes and Juan said, as though talking to himself, "Yes, I think those bodies we found were of guys who were bitten by snakes." I was shaken by the comment and by the way he was taking the fact of having found two bodies earlier in the year on the same route we were following.

I asked him how he had found those corpses. He said that he was walking with two others approximately two miles north of where we were when they found a corpse with part of the skeleton showing, which made them believe that he had died perhaps a month before. The corpse still had some clothes on but they couldn't ascertain either his age or any physical features for identification. They made a cross and put it over him. Later in the same day they found another body. This one apparently had died more recently, judging from the state of the clothes. Juan found a letter in one of his pockets, but the writing was almost totally erased. He took the letter with him with the idea of looking at it more carefully later on to see if he could find any clue to his name or the name of a relative whom he could notify. Juan was thinking of doing this because he was very much concerned about the soul of the person they found dead. He said, "If no one knows that guy died, no one is praying for his soul. And if no one is praying for him, his soul will be wandering around suffering."*

I insisted on knowing more details about those encounters but Juan said, "What's the matter with you? What more can one tell about death? They were dead, that's all . . . everybody takes that chance in this business and when the time comes for you you've got what God's will has

---

*Juan was never able to identify the body because he was apprehended and the letter seized by the Border Patrol.

determined and that's all." I think he meant that finding a person dead in that area should be considered normal or expected. Juan's calm while speaking about the two bodies was impressive. He laconically summarized what he meant by saying, "They just didn't make it." Obviously, I couldn't see the situation from that perspective. I was shocked. I felt a profound sadness that immediately evolved into a bitter feeling of frustration. For me those bodies represented cases of murder: two human beings killed by a social system, by creating and maintaining the circumstances in which people find death while looking for the scarce avenues to escape from misery, a misery for which the social system where they lived or died is responsible.

Juan spoke about the bodies with a mixture of sadness and fatalism, shaking his head slowly while looking at the ground and distractedly hitting one of his shoes with a twig. He made me think that if we hadn't had that encounter with the rattlesnakes he wouldn't have told me about something that for him was not unusual enough to be mentioned.

Our Second Encounter

We had been walking for more than four hours and were going up a little hill from the top of which Juan wanted to check our location when we saw a jeep coming in our direction. It appeared so suddenly that we did not have time to hide ourselves. We stood still, looking at the jeep, which stopped about sixty feet from us. Three people got out and pointed their rifles at us. Our reaction was to get down on the ground; then they began to shoot. After the first shots it was obvious that they did not want to kill us but they kept on shooting and all the while we could hear them laughing and shouting. One of the bullets must have hit very close to me because I felt little pieces of dirt hitting my head.

They stopped shooting and came to us, laughing and insulting us in English. One of them told Juan something like, "Get up, you greaser, you are not dead."

We stood up and one of them asked me in very broken Spanish if I knew what "No Trespassing" meant; I said I did not. Then he said in English something like "You damn Mexicans don't know anything about law . . . you only know how to steal, huh?"

Then another said in an angry tone, "You better tell all the 'wets' to stop coming through this ranch." He added in broken Spanish that the next time they would shoot at us to kill.

Then a third one went to the jeep and talked to somebody by radio, stating that they had caught two "wets" and they were going to turn us in to the Border Patrol. Meanwhile the other two tied our hands behind our backs and told us to get in the jeep.

On the way to the checking point of the Border Patrol, they were making jokes about how scared we looked, and one of them asked the driver what would have happened if, *by accident*, they killed us. The driver said that an accident is an accident and nobody would say anything if you killed somebody who has trespassed on your private property, particularly if he is an outlaw, as in the case of all "wets." Before we reached the Border Patrol they untied our hands. The driver told one of the Patrol officers that they worked on a ranch and had found us "very probably" looking for a cow to kill. He added, "Last week we found a cow being killed by them . . . . You know how they are," he said. "They come starving from Mexico and we are the ones who pay for it."

The officer asked him how many wetbacks were working on the ranch. The one who was driving the jeep answered, "Gee, I don't know. How can you tell who is 'wet' and who isn't. We tell the people we hire that we don't want 'wets,' but it's impossible to know who is lying and who isn't."

The officer asked me if they had done anything to us. I showed my wrists, which were red from having been tied behind my back. The Patrolman looked accusingly at the driver of the jeep, who said, "He was trying to escape."

The Patrolman asked Juan to show his wrists, which were also red, and turning to the driver asked, "Was he trying to escape also?"

I was encouraged by what seemed to be a non-supporting reaction from the Border Patrol officer to what the jeep driver had said. I confirmed this suspicion when we were taken inside the station wagon, where the Border Patrol had a mobile office equipped with air conditioning, radio, and office equipment. They had asked Juan how we were caught and he just said, "Shooting at us with their rifles." While the officials were preparing the papers and forms for interrogating us they were making comments in English—assuming, I suppose, that we didn't understand it—such as, "The problem with those guys is that they watch T.V. too much. They don't know who is 'wet' unless they are hunting them." One of the officers suggested that they report the treatment we received from the ranch guards. The other officer said, "You won't get anything done by that; you know who owns that ranch."

Their comments about the ranch guards made me believe that Juan and

I had improved our situation by being in the hands of the Border Patrol.

Although being apprehended was an alternative plan that I had anticipated, once actually detained I felt depressed and frustrated. Juan had shown me a special kind of solidarity that at that moment was present in my mind, together with all of the reasons why he had to cross the border, repeatedly, as a wetback; besides, my role as participant observer did not make me any less humiliated at being surrounded by symbols of authority whose meaning seemed to suggest that we were criminals.

I was first to be interrogated. One of the officials asked me to take out everything from my pockets and my bag. The map I was carrying drew their attention and I was asked where and how I had gotten it. I gave them the same story I had given Juan, that a cousin of mine had taken the map with him to Mexico City, where he gave it to me. Then they asked me questions such as: What is your name? Where do you come from? How old are you? Marital status? Place of birth and date? How many times have you come to the U.S.? How many times have you been caught by Immigration officials? Where did you cross? When and at what time? How many persons crossed with you? Where were you going? What kind of job were you looking for? Who were you going to meet in San Antonio? What is your address in Mexico?

While I was being interrogated by one official the other was watching the cars, which have to make a stop in front of the Border Patrol station wagon and wait until they are motioned through. Sometimes the official got out of the station wagon and went to check the passenger's documents. I noticed they were particularly careful in the control of buses, less careful with trucks, and even less careful with passenger cars. In the half hour I was there they stopped four cars. In every case, the cars stopped were occupied by passengers who were apparently Mexicans or of Mexican ancestry and in all four cases the cars were older models.

Once my interrogation was over the official transmitted all the information by radio. Then he took his turn at watching the cars while the other interrogated Juan and transmitted his information also. They were called twice for reports on cars suspected of being used by smugglers and to inform them that I had no past record, but that Juan was an "old friend of ours," who should be taken to McAllen. From there he would be taken by plane to El Paso. I knew that probably meant that Juan was on his way to meet José in the federal prison of "La Tuna" near El Paso. That was the end of my journey with Juan. His companionship had left an indelible imprint on my mind.

Jail and Detention

What follows from here on was a different kind of depressing experience. I was taken to a jail in Falfurrias, Texas, where I spent almost two days in solitary confinement. Being alone I had some time to reflect on the meaning of what I was doing. It became clear to me how different the meaning of the same situation might be for the persons involved in the "wetback game." There is hardly another situation where symbols of subjection are more evident than inside a jail. Here is where the label of "outsider" that society reserves to some deviants is physically felt upon the so-labeled. Yet, the wetback seems not to consider himself a criminal. I was able to confirm this impression later on in the detention center located near Port Isabel, Texas, where I was taken from the Falfurrias jail. The wetback seems to think of jail as part of his destiny of being poor. One is in jail not because one is immoral or a "bad guy" but because one is poor.

When I was taken from the jail to Port Isabel, we made a stop in the holding station at McAllen to change buses and to be checked again by an official. While this processing was taking place we were in a small room waiting for our name to be called. I felt two eyes staring at me and soon recognized the face. It was the official who saw me at the bus station in Edinburg while he was apprehending another. I tried to look unperturbed, but I saw him asking for my record, pointing at me. He took a look at my report and then he called me and said, "You are not a first-timer. You had a *tarjeta* (Form I-186)* and showed it to me. Now, where is that card?" I told him that he was making a mistake, maybe because he had seen me at the bus terminal but that he never stopped me or asked if I had proper papers. He then seemed to doubt but did not relinquish his impression totally. He asked another official to make a "double check" of my record.

Around 9:00 P.M. we arrived at Los Fresnos, near Port Isabel, Texas. This is where the Border Patrol academy and the detention center are. I had visited the institution twice previously in order to conduct interviews with immigration officials and wetbacks, but this time I was being *taken* inside. I feared someone might recognize me, or even worse, consider my face familiar and conclude from that that I was not a first-timer. Fortunately nothing of this sort happened.

---

*Form I-186 is the visitor's card which permits entrance into the U.S. for seventy-two hours.

After a light meal in the dining hall we were classified either as Deportees (repeaters) or as "V.R." (Voluntary Return); I was classified in the latter category. They took a fingerprint of our right index finger, which was the first and only personal datum they kept that might lead to my actual identification.

Two officials made a careful check of our personal belongings and asked us to take off all our clothes and shoes for the same purpose. Then all the money and personal belongings were taken away from us, and we received a receipt. I will jump ahead a little to say that there were no complaints on this matter when we got our things back, at least not in the group of 40 with whom I was sent back to Mexico two days later.

The population of the detention center was approximately 250 when I was there. Twenty of the 250 were not Mexicans. They were also being detained for having entered the United States illegally. Fifteen were Chileans, one Spanish, one Lebanese, two from Central America, and one from Jamaica. This group was called by both the officials and the rest of the detainees as *los extranjeros* (the foreigners). Obviously all detainees are actually foreigners but because of the overwhelming ratio of Mexicans that distinction made by the Mexican detainees was also adopted by the officials. The foreigners were the ones called first for meals, which they took separate from the rest. It surprised me to hear from a detainee working in the kitchen that "the foreigners" received more and better food than the rest of the detainees. The explanation for this was that several months ago they had protested the quality and quantity of the food. They have to spend more time in custody because of the red tape involved in their deportation. The case of the Mexicans has been made by far more expeditious. The foreigner might spend several months in the institution, whereas the Mexican may spend from three days to two weeks, depending upon the circumstances. Since his stay in the center is brief, the Mexican detainee is apparently less resentful of the bad quality of food and he also has less time to take any type of organized action while in custody.

Observations Among Fellow Detainees

I concentrated all my attention on gathering information during my stay in the center. Of all the places where I have tried to collect information on the wetback phenomenon, the detention center has been the most profitable for seeing all kinds of details and aspects related to the wetback's life, and here one learns most about how it feels to be a wetback and why they act the way they do. This is so for several reasons: First, the number of wetbacks gives a wide variety of personal experience. Second, here one wetback speaks to another openly and candidly about his personal experiences because he does not fear further consequences, since he is already detained and on his way back to Mexico. Third, there is so much opportunity for getting together in small groups and talking about whatever one wants. And fourth, the shared ethnic and social background and the fact of being detained itself are conducive to socializing. Since I was taken for a wetback by those around me, I was able to ask questions freely regarding our research interests. My inquiry concentrated on aspects of our research where information was scarce or not clear. The following points were the most relevant to our study.

1. Six detainees said they found corpses on their way north from the border. Particularly interesting was the account of two of them who were caught while finishing the "Christian burial" of a body which appeared to have been dead only a few days. One person told me that his life was saved by three others who found him unconscious as a consequence of not having eaten for three days. Not only did he receive food from them but he was actually carried by them for two days until he recovered strength enough to continue walking by himself. Another three spoke of having found a body whose description and location coincided with one of the bodies which Juan had talked about. Another told me that on two different occasions he found human skeletons in the desert north of El Paso, Texas. Another spoke of different experiences with rattlesnakes. Some of their stories were very funny, others dramatic. One group encountered twenty rattlesnakes in two days. Two detainees who were caught while being smuggled in a car told me that they had chosen to come "via smuggler" because they would never again try to cross on foot. One of them said, "There are so many snakes that it is crazy to come on foot."

2. In spite of the mechanization of agricultural activities that has been going on in the lower Rio Grande valley, there is still a great demand for labor, which attracts many wetbacks.

3. Out of the group of approximately 100 that arrived with me, only four did not bring any money from Mexico. Approximately half of the group said they found jobs before being apprehended. Of the other half, or those who were apprehended without having found a job, thirty said they spent all the money they brought from Mexico by the time they were caught. This seems to indicate that for approximately half of that group who brought money from Mexico, becoming a wetback made them poorer than they were before. If this is true, one could hypothesize that

this is a significant drain on the Mexican economy. The term "significant drain" becomes meaningful when it is considered that 201,636 were apprehended in 1969.

4. With two exceptions all of those who came from the Central Plateau states in Mexico said they chose the Tamaulipas-Texas border to cross because it is the cheapest way to the U.S. from central Mexico.

5. In terms of place of residence in Mexico, the most numerous group was very clearly the one from San Luis Potosí. This fact made me decide to stay in San Luis Potosí for ten days after being expelled from the U.S.

6. From a systematic inquiry with my fellow detainees I deduced the following pattern of behavior: If the wetback is apprehended for the first time it is almost certain that he will cross the border illegally again; if he is apprehended for the second time he will cross illegally again but he will try to cross at a different place on the border. If he is apprehended for the third time he has learned that it is very likely that he will go to court and get a sentence, which is usually suspended. After this it is probable that he will not cross the border illegally again until the term of his suspended sentence has passed, since he knows that he might have to spend a few months in jail if he is apprehended while his sentence is pending. Once the time of the suspended sentence has passed, he may try crossing illegally again; however, this possibility seems to be diminished by the fact that he knows he might not be granted another suspended sentence.

This seems to indicate that there is a limit to the number of times that a person will take the risk of crossing illegally. Juan and José were exceptions, perhaps because of the fact that they live a few yards from the Rio Grande.

7. There seemed to be a consensus* about the following "principle": The greater the amount of money the intended wetback has, the lesser the possibilities of his being apprehended. With enough money he can either pay a smuggler, buy documents in the black market, wait in a Mexican border town until he can obtain a crossing card from the U.S. Immigration authorities (this card, I-186, will allow him to cross legally but not to work in the U.S), or get his passport and U.S. tourist visa with which he can enter the U.S. at any point. The tourist visa will have the same restrictions as the Form I-186, the difference being that with the latter he can only go no further than twenty-five miles north of the

---

*Consensus was indicated both in spontaneous comments and in answer to questions. For a discussion on participant observation see Howard S. Becker, "Problems of Inference and Proof in Participant Observation," *American Sociological Review* 23 (1958): 652–60.

border and can stay no longer than two days, whereas with the tourist visa he can go to Chicago or Detroit, for example.

8. I spoke with eight detainees who complained that they were not paid by their employer, but instead were turned in to the Border Patrol in order to avoid the payment. Three of those eight told me that an official had called their employers and they had come to the center to pay the wages due. One of the other five told me that their pictures had been taken for identification and that the same official had promised to do his best to get their money, in which case he would send it to them in Mexico. There seemed to be a general opinion that the officers of the detention center try to help those who did not receive their wages.

On the third day of my stay at the center I was taken with a group of forty to Matamoros, Mexico. We were then switched to a Mexican bus line and were told that no one could get off until we arrived at the city of San Luis Potosí. That was a nine-hour non-stop drive. Once in San Luis Potosí I went to the northeast part of the state, where I stayed for ten days gathering information on how a man decides to become a wetback and on how the stability of the family and the community is affected by this outward migration.

In contacts with wetbacks I had many occasions to witness events and circumstances in which ingenuity, human solidarity, and a sense of loyalty to friends were movingly demonstrated. That was the most rewarding part of my experiences. On the other hand, being exposed to the "meaning configurations"* of the wetback life stream increased my awareness that the individual and society should have a greater sense of responsibility for the perpetuation of a social system that has created, or allowed, or maintained the role of the wetback, who is placed in a position where he endangers his physical well-being, his human dignity, and even his life for a pittance.

---

*Alfred Schutz, *The Phenomenology of the Social World,* trans. by George Walsh and Frederick Lehenert (Evanston, Ill.: Northwestern University Press, 1967), p. 76.

25

"Plight of the Mexican Wetback"

Joe C. Ortega

They live in constant fear. The sight of a police or government car sends them scurrying into hiding. They do not venture far or into unknown places. They do not send their children to school. Entire families live in one-room homes with no plumbing facilities. They are paid substandard wages. Slick merchants prey on them, taking whatever money they have for overpriced, gaudy, cheap merchandise. Government agencies refuse to help them. Courts are available only to send them to jail. Due process is unknown to them. Yet they live in the land of milk and honey, the most prosperous, sophisticated, and civilized nation in the world.

They are the estimated one million "wetbacks" living in the United States. They live in fear, without rights of any kind, because they are in this country illegally, and they accept the risks and suffering of illegal entrants because of the basic human desire to work and to be able to feed themselves and their families. They come here illegally because their only alternative is to stay in their native Mexico and live in extreme poverty with little hope of improvement.

The term wetback, or *mojado,* is applied to those who enter the United States without legal permission. It comes from the fact that many came to the United States simply by wading across the Rio Grande, the river that forms the boundary between Texas and Mexico. It is generally applied to all Mexicans who are here illegally, whether they waded across, jumped across the fence at the Arizona or California border (these are also known as *alambristas*—wire jumpers), were brought in, packed as many as eight in the trunk of a passenger car, walked across with fraudulent documents or came in legally as temporary visitors but stayed after expiration of their permits. The term is generally not considered derogatory by the group.

That there are large numbers of them is beyond question. In 1969, 201,000 wetbacks were apprehended and sent back to Mexico by the

---

Joe C. Ortega, "Plight of the Mexican Wetback," *American Bar Association Journal* 58 (March 1972): 251–54. Reprinted by permission of the *American Bar Association Journal.*

United States Immigration and Naturalization Service. It is estimated that the number apprehended represents as little as one tenth of the total. In Los Angeles alone, in a 1969 drive, more than 4,000 of them a month were apprehended.

That they live in fear and that they are denied basic human rights also seems beyond question. Recently two of them were killed by a volley of police bullets fired into a crowded room where seven of them were living. The police officers were looking for a murder suspect, and, according to the police, as quoted in the *Los Angeles Times,* the wetbacks acted like fugitives and were shot. Ironically, the police chief stated, "These men had nothing to fear from Los Angeles Police officers . . . because we are not in the business of enforcing immigration laws. Unfortunately, these men did not know this, so they behaved in this fashion [like fugitives]." The border patrol and immigration officials are instructed not to shoot (although they are armed) at illegal entrants, even if they are attempting to escape. However, the wetback knows that his people are shot at and, in some instances, are killed.

But even if they are not shot at, wetbacks live in constant fear of apprehension, which will usually mean immediate deportation. The family is broken up, wages due are not paid, and possessions are lost. Sometimes a mother who has small children is deported without any opportunity to make arrangements to have the children cared for. In a 1970 case reported by the *Los Angeles Times,* a mother who had been here several years and had children born in the United States was apprehended, and deportation proceedings were started against her. Newspaper reporters asked the district director of the INS, "What will happen to the small children?" He replied, "We have no jurisdiction over them." The INS was concerned solely with getting rid of the mother—the children were no concern of theirs.

"Voluntary" Departure Is Questionable

Immediate deportation is carried out by the device known as "voluntary departure". The "voluntariness" of the departure is questionable. The suspect is told of his right to counsel and to an administrative hearing. He is then told that if he waives these rights, he will be shipped back to Mexico without any stigma and that he will be able to reenter the country legally. On the other hand, he is told that if he demands a formal deportation hearing, he will be kept in jail until the hearing, will be found deportable, and will never be able to enter the United States again. The immigration officers assume a paternalistic, benevolent attitude toward the suspect, leading him to believe that he has committed a serious crime, but that because they are good guys they will do nothing more than give him free transportation back. They intimate dire consequences if he does not cooperate.

The friendly persuasion works. In 1968, for example, 179,952 aliens were sent out of the country "voluntarily", while only 9,130 were deported. It has been suggested that the system could not work if all aliens were given formal hearings with full due progress guarantees. The numbers would overwhelm the system. In actual practice the wetback is denied all due process rights in deportation.

The system is not unlike our juvenile court proceedings prior to the Supreme Court's ruling in *Application of Gault*, 387 U.S. 1 (1967), in which the "highest motives and most enlightened impulses" led to a denial of due process. The denial of a hearing, of an opportunity to obtain counsel, and of a right to bail causes these aliens severe hardships and, at times, loss of possible legal remedies. The fact that there may be some legal reasons why he should not be deported cannot be raised by one who within twenty-four hours of his apprehension is on a bus back to Mexico. And he cannot possibly know of the existence of these rights and remedies in a "game" that most lawyers find extremely complex and bedeviling. When he is advised of his "rights", he is not told of all the possible legal remedies available. Instead, he is advised, in his own interest, to waive all his rights.

Employers who make a practice of hiring Mexican aliens are aware of these "voluntary" departures and many times count on them to save payroll. When his employees are apprehended, the employer usually denies he owes any back wages and pockets what the employee earned up to that time. He knows full well that the alien employee will be on his way to Mexico in a matter of hours and that he will have a hard time pursuing a claim for wages from there.

Many Take Advantage of Wetbacks' Vulnerability

The illegal status of employees also gives the employer other advantages. If any of them complains about low pay or substandard working conditions, the employer merely tips the Immigration Service, which will remove the complaining employee. There are always plenty of others willing to take the job. In fact, this rapid turnover is another source of income for the most unscrupulous of employers, who obtain their wetback help through employment agencies that specialize in Mexican nationals. The employment agencies charge the wetback as much as $300 to place him in a job. Employers who have a rapid turnover and provide many jobs for the agencies get a substantial kickback from them. Again, because the victim of these rackets is immediately shipped hundreds of miles into Mexico, law enforcement officers feel powerless to prevent these practices. Their vulnerability to immediate deportation allows others to take advantage of them.

A landlord can rent hovels that violate all local health and safety laws and can demand not only high rent but complete subservience from his wetback tenants. If they complain, a telephone "tip" to the Immigration and Naturalization Service removes the complainant. Many who take advantage of the wetbacks' vulnerability insist that they are doing them a great service by even dealing with them and that therefore they are justified in tipping off the INS. One jeweler in Los Angeles stated that he was justified in overcharging his wetback customers because, since they were wrongfully taking advantage of the economic benefits of this country, merchants were justified in taking advantage of them. He sold them $30 watches for $300.

Immediate departure causes other hardships. Some who are undergoing medical treatment cannot stay for completion of that treatment unless they can prove they are too sick to travel (a woman nine months' pregnant is not considered too sick to travel) or unless they can prove they cannot get medical treatment in Mexico.

Many illegal aliens purchase clothing and furniture on the "layaway plan", the credit system of the extremely poor. They put $10 down and pay $10 a week until the full purchase price is paid. Then the merchandise is given to them. A deported alien leaves behind all his "laid away" purchases.

Aliens Do Not Have As Many Rights As Criminals

Court opinion and statutes provide some due process rights.[1] In deportation proceedings the hearings are considered administrative and civil, and aliens are not entitled to all rights of one charged with a crime. There is no right to bail, and the hearing officer can act as both judge and prosecutor. Ex parte statements, hearsay evidence or any written or oral statement previously made by the alien may be admitted by the hearing officer.[2] The right to counsel is usually meaningless because it must be provided at the alien's expense.[3] Since deportation is not a criminal proceeding, the rationale goes, the government is not obligated to provide counsel for indigents. How poor peasants whose sole reason for entering the United States is to work at $1.65 per hour can afford attorneys is not a concern of the rationale. But again, most Mexican aliens are shipped back long before they reach this stage in the proceedings.

The human need for food and other basic necessities is stronger than the fear of being shot at or whisked away. This need keeps thousands of wetbacks here. Those who remain face other deprivations of basic human rights in addition to the fear of apprehension.

Children of Wetbacks Are Denied Education

The children of these illegal entrants are deprived of an education by most school districts. The California legislature provided extra funds for school districts that admit children here illegally on the proviso that the district turn over the names of the children to the INS so they can be deported.[4] Despite that provision and despite the compulsory education laws, many school districts refuse to admit Mexican aliens without proof of their legal status. Printed forms of the Los Angeles City Unified School District, for example, advise prospective entrants that they will be admitted to school only if they have all the necessary documentation proving their legal status and if there is room available in the schools.

The curious argument for keeping these children out of school is that there are so many of them. The argument is curious because it is made by "educators" and because they are, in essence, saying, "We would admit you if there were only a few of you, but since there are 50,000 of you, we can't. It is less unconscionable to us to see 50,000 children without any education walking the streets of Los Angeles than if there were only a few." Their stated reason for not admitting them is that these children are a financial burden on the district. But all children are a burden on a district. The fact is that these children and their parents pay taxes and contribute to the economic well-being of the community the same as residents. The argument is the same that for years kept children of non-property owners out of school, but that argument, so we thought, was discredited over a century ago.

Other government agencies deny these residents basic social services. Unemployment compensation, for example, is generally not available to the Mexican who is in this country illegally, no matter how many years he has been working. Technically, a person who is not in the country legally cannot be considered "available for work". If the claimant is not available for work, he is not eligible for unemployment benefits.[5] Two men working side by side for several years doing the same work, paying the same taxes, and living in the same life style are treated very differently when there is a layoff. The worker who is here illegally has no recourse and no governmental agency to help him when his paycheck stops. He can stop feeding his family; the state has little interest in him.

When he is injured on the job he fares a little better, but not much. Workmen's compensation is available to all employees regardless of legal resident status. The compensation awarded them, however, is often smaller than that for comparable American workers. Again the theory is that someone here illegally could not possibly earn as much as someone "available for work".

Wetbacks face other severe deprivations of what most consider basic human rights. They face the same racial discrimination as many Negroes in finding jobs, housing, places to eat, and public accommodations, but the discrimination and racial antagonism toward them is made worse because of their illegal status and inability to speak English. A wetback dares not go to the Equal Employment Opportunity Commission or to a fair housing office to complain about discrimination. To do so would be to reveal his illegal status. If he does go to an agency that can help him, the language problem prevents him from fully explaining his case. Although some agencies have made an effort to have Spanish-speaking personnel, their numbers are infinitely small compared to the number of wetbacks and Mexican Americans in the community. For example, although Los Angeles has had Spanish-speaking persons since its founding, and although they number about one million in the area, only this year were Spanish-speaking operators assigned to the police and fire departments' emergency switchboards.

The courts have always used interpreters when a person cannot speak English. But in practice this does not always help the wetback. Generally the court assumes that the person before the court (usually a defendant) speaks English. The defendant is not asked if he understands the proceedings and is not told of his right to an interpreter. In minor matters, especially in the lower courts, if the defendant can answer "yes" and "no", he is considered literate in English, and the proceedings start against him.

Spanish-speaking attorneys who represent Mexicans have stated repeatedly that in their experience working through an interpreter is extremely frustrating because interpreters tend to paraphrase and to say only what they think is the gist of the phrase to be translated. In a recent case, an attorney asked for a Spanish as well as an English transcript to preserve what the witnesses were actually saying. In most cases, however, no effort of this type is made.

Most attorneys, along with the courts, consider the use of interpreters and translators too time consuming and tend not to use them unless absolutely necessary. Public defenders' offices which represent many Mexican-Americans have almost no Spanish-speaking attorneys, and interpreting for them is usually done by anyone available, often including other defendants, no matter how poor their Spanish or English.

Some legal aid and OEO-funded legal services offices that normally are eager to accept the poorest and most downtrodden client are hesitant about accepting cases on behalf of Mexican wetbacks. They feel they cannot seek a remedy for a client with "dirty hands", but the principal objection to handling cases for them is that the interests of American citizens of Mexican descent conflict with the interests of the wetback. They argue that they are striving to improve the lot of the Mexican-American and that as long as wetbacks continue to pour into the country, efforts for improved wages and working conditions for Mexican-Americans will not be successful. In fact, some OEO offices have brought pressure for stricter enforcement of immigration laws.

Mexico Can Offer Limited Assistance

For the most part, Mexican consulate offices make every effort to assist these people, but they are severely limited in many ways. In the first place, the sheer numbers overwhelm their staffs. Second, since their mission is to foster diplomatic and commercial relations between the two countries, they have to devote much time and effort to establishing good relations between Americans and Mexicans. Dealing with the problems of wetbacks does nothing to improve those relations. Last, the bureaucratic technicalities usual in government offices keep many wetbacks from seeking their aid. For example, in the killing of the wetbacks already mentioned, the Mexican consulate accurately and legally stated it could not act until it had documentary evidence that the deceased were Mexican citizens. A *mojado* enters without any papers, American or Mexican; he is, in fact, a man without legal status.

What About Universal and Supranational Rights?

The United Nations' Universal Declaration of Human Rights enumerates rights to which "all men and women" and "all human beings" are entitled. Since these rights are not limited to national citizens, presumably the wetback or any other person without a country could assert them. Moreover, the scope of the rights enumerated suggests that the sufferings and deprivations of the wetback are violative of that declaration. For example:

> . . . claims which all men and women may legitimately make, in their search, not only to fulfill themselves at their best but to be so placed in life that they are capable, at their best of becoming in the highest sense citizens of the various communities to which they belong and of the world community . . . .
>
> * * *
>
> All human beings are born free and equal, in dignity and rights. They are endowed with reason and conscience, and should act towards one another in a spirit of brotherhood. (Article 1)
>
> * * *
>
> Everyone has the right to life, liberty, and the security of person. (Article 3)
>
> * * *
>
> Everyone has the right to a standard of living adequate for the health and well-being of himself and of his family, including food, clothing, housing, and medical care and necessary social services, and the right to security in the event of unemployment, sickness, disability, widowhood, old age, or other lack of livelihood in circumstances beyond his control. (Article 25)

But whether that declaration could be used as a legal basis for the improvement of the lot of the Mexican illegal is questionable.[6] The declaration, however, does serve to remind us all that as human beings we cannot ignore the plight of a large group of persons in our midst merely because they lack legal status. It serves to remind us that the world community has a commitment to preserve basic human rights for all persons.

As long as there is a great difference between the wealth of the United States and the poverty of Mexico, basic human needs will compel wetbacks to continue crossing the border no matter how harshly immigration laws are enforced and no matter what suffering they have to endure. The problem will not go away and indeed may become worse. It is for this reason that governmental agencies and the legal profession must look at the wetback as a fellow human being, begin to give him some attention and provide him with some basic human rights.

NOTES

1. The phrase "person" in the Fifth Amendment to the United States Constitution has been held to include aliens. Galvan v. Press, 347 U.S. 522 (1954); The Japanese Immigrant Case, 189 U.S. 86 (1903); 8 U.S.C. § 1252b.

2. See generally 8 U.S.C. § 1252B; 8 C.F.R. § 242; GORDON AND ROSENFIELD, IMMIGRATION LAW AND PROCEDURE 5-33f.f. While there is no right to bail, it is available at the Attorney General's discretion, 8 U.S.C. § 1252 (a), and usually granted if applied for. A different and more sympathetic view of deportation procedures is found in GORDON, DUE PROCESS OF LAW IN IMMIGRATION PROCEEDINGS, 50 A.B.A.J. 34 (1964).

3. 8 U.S.C. § 1252 (b) (2).

4. Calif. Educ. Code § 6950, 6957. Section 6957 states, ". . . regulations shall require the county superintendent of schools to list the non-immigrant children and non-citizen children without immigration status [defined in 6950 as those without documentary evidence of immigration status] by name and address to the Board of Supervisors, . . . [who] shall forward a copy of such list to the appropriate regional office of the United States Immigration and Naturalization Service."

5. Calif. Unemployment Insurance Code § 1253.

6. The declaration is a resolution of the U.N. General Assembly which imposes no legal obligation, but which declares that the states voting for such a declaration recognize these rights for all people. See generally *International Recognition and Protection of Fundamental Human Rights*, 1964 DUKE L.J. 846 (Autumn 1964).

26

"Mexico's President Comments On Wetbacks In The United States"

Luis Echeverría

The emigration of Mexican workers to the United States is disturbing to our national conscience. We are mainly concerned with the unjust and sometimes inhuman treatment they receive. Past agreements on this matter failed to provide an adequate solution. The U.S. Government has assured us of its willingness to attend to this problem and, for our part, we have created an Inter-Ministerial Commission to examine it in all its aspects.

However, we are convinced that the basic solution is to be found within our own frontiers. By fostering our economic and social development, we will increase opportunities for adequately paid work. When setting forth this viewpoint during my visit to the United States, I insisted that we want to export merchandise, not social problems.

I was especially interested in visiting those parts of the United States where communities of Mexican descent are located. Because of our close ethnic and cultural ties, we feel compelling responsibilities towards them. Without transgressing the constitutional norms of either country, we feel obliged to provide them with the means whereby they can preserve their bonds with Mexico. The vigor with which these communities assert their historical roots and identity shows how solid are the values that Mexico has created, and fills us with legitimate pride.

From English-language version of President Luis Echeverría's second State of the Union Address delivered to Mexico's Congress on September 1, 1972, *Mexican Newsletter* no. 8 (September 1, 1972): no pagination.

27

"The Impossibility of Illegal Mexican Entry Into the United States"

Obed Lopez

MR. LOPEZ. My name is Obed Lopez. I am a Mexican national, Mexican citizen. I recently immigrated to the United States, since 1956, and I am with the Latin American Defense Organization, which is a community group, a civil rights group in the city of Chicago.

MR. RODINO. Proceed.

MR. LOPEZ. I have a very brief statement that I would simply like to read for the record.

I understand we have two basic questions we are concerned with, Mr. Chairman, we have requested an opportunity to present testimony before this committee and answer pertinent questions you might have, because we have a number of objections to your stated position on the question of illegal aliens and the alleged effect to the economy.

We want the record to reflect that the views of our civil rights group on this matter is that we can enlighten you and thus assist you in the formulation of appropriate and just legislation in times of crisis, both social and economic, and as a way of not dealing with the real basic issues, scapegoats are created to put the blame where it shouldn't be. Social and racial groups are singled out and made a target of the majority because of prejudice and ignorance.

It is not long ago that a minority was singled out, branded, and finally exterminated by a government that also claimed to be protecting the economy, the economic interests of the working people. This extermination began with seemingly innocent measures; harmless and innocent measures being suggested now to determine who is a citizen and who is an alien could easily become instruments of repression and discrimination. . . .

Statement of Obed Lopez, U.S., Congress, House, Subcommittee Number One of the Committee on the Judiciary, *Hearings on Illegal Aliens*, Part 3, Chicago, Illinois, 23 October 1971, 92d Cong., 1st Sess., 1971, pp. 901–3.

We take the position that Mexicans as part of the native population of America have an inherent right to inhabit this territory.

We propose that you recognize, in considering this legislation, the fact that Mexican land was taken by the use of armed force. You have ignored the basic rights of Mexicans to live in the land while you opened your gates to the flood of European immigration. As long as this continues, the problem of illegal entry will persist. . . .

. . . Really what I am saying is, people that live south of the Rio Bravo, and we were able before 1848 to move to the other side, whenever we wished, should have at this point the same right, because you know what has happened since the end of the Mexican War is that you let all kinds of people from the European countries come in and populate California and Texas, Colorado, New Mexico, and you are depriving people that were there before to come in to live in that territory. You know, that is the kind of historical perspective that we have and that I wanted to communicate to you so that you would see that we don't necessarily feel that you are doing us a favor by allowing a large quota of Mexicans to come into the United States.

28

"The False Paradise"

Hispanoamericano

The number of laborers [braceros] deported of late from the United States exceeds 5,500, the laborers having been sent by plane to Mexico City and transported to their respective places of origin, in areas as distant as Durango, San Luis Potosí, Guerrero, Michoacán, Oaxaca, and Chiapas, principally.

This deportation by air has been interpreted as a simple measure of political propaganda as well as an indication of the intent to alter unilaterally the migratory equilibrium of the continent. Until now it has been

---

"Mexico Outside of Mexico: The False Paradise," *Hispanoamericano*, (25 October 1976), pp. 6–9; trans. Wilbur Nachtigall. Reprinted by permission of *Hispanoamericano*.

noted that, as a general rule, businessmen emigrate from the North in search of new profits in the South, coinciding with the departure from the South of the destitute who are seeking to survive.

Essentially, the United States is generating a constant and growing invasion by technical, economic, cultural, religious, and military missions, hungering to establish new bases for an investment hegemony, both ideological and political. The counterinvasion from the South has already produced some 20,000,000 Spanish-speakers who are established or at the point of establishing themselves in said country [U.S.A.] with the objective of solving their problems of employment, economic solvency, educational opportunity, or democratic expression. Both currents of emigration frequently operate extralegally, consistent with their motivation by forces of attraction and repulsion that bring them into being.

It has been observed that the currents of emigration are impelled by necessity in the home country and attracted by opportunity in the foreign country. Thus, the United States constantly needs to extend its markets and move toward the opportunities that the South offers it in order to take advantage of them. At the same time, south of the Río Bravo the huge masses suffer acute economic and social deprivation; and the nearer they are to the Río Bravo, the more they are attracted by the opportunities that they perceive in the North American [U.S.A.] abundance. Many well-informed persons believe that they perceive in all of this a fate of geographic origin that obliges Mexico to be the major exporter of laborers to the "paradise of the emigrants" and one of the major importers of expensive capital and cheap tourism, cast in the dies and bearing the stamp of the United States.

The North American market and Mexican emigration have frequently and conveniently ignored not only the law, but also the boundary lines between the two countries. Railroads, mines, ranches, and basic industries of Uncle Sam have been established and have prospered by attracting and giving freedom of movement back and forth to the untiring and cheap swarthy laborer. In this way there has come into existence an unofficial geography where the distance between Guadalajara, Jalisco, and Canada represents a familiar corridor of two-way traffic for the uprooted Mexican with or without a visa.

Thus many of them have established themselves permanently in the United States, whereas others choose "to work there and live here" on the border; while still others have accommodated themselves to the "half-and-half going and returning" of the day laborer [bracero]. But it has been the 1,500,000 alleged illegal aliens who are blamed for the recent public tensions between Los Pinos and the White House. (The figure was given by Dr. Howard Golberg, based on the 1960 census concerning the Mexicans who have not died nor emigrated legally and who do not appear in the 1970 census.)

With respect to the official North American statistics, they indicate that 88 percent of the illegal aliens arrested said they were Mexicans. The statistics also show that every year between 300,000 and 500,000 persons are deported, principally from Texas and California, who declare that they are natives of Michoacán, Guanajuato, Jalisco, Nuevo León, San Luis Potosí, Puebla, Hidalgo, and Mexico City, many of them entering the United States by means of the sadly famous *Puente Negro* ["Black Bridge"].

The "Black Bridge" is a railroad border entrance without customs; its central gates are continually opened and closed in order to permit the entrance of illegal Mexican aliens, according to the market demand for cheap day laborers in El Paso, Texas, and surrounding areas.

The air deportation bomb exploded in Mexico when General Leonard Chapman, Commissioner of Immigration and Naturalization of the United States, announed unexpectedly that he possessed funds to return by air in two months 15,000 Mexicans without legal papers. And upon the arrival in Mexico of the first 150 deportees, the reaction was immediate on the part of Deputy Mariano Araiza, who explained to the press that the spectacular deportations of Mexicans have always coincided with the presidential elections in that country. Another legislator, Lázaro Rubio Félix, observed that Washington was trying to produce a crisis in Mexico, saturating it with unemployed illegal aliens, in order to subject the new Mexican government to the interests of North American financiers; but the declarations of the Mexican officials merely placed in perspective the legal aspects of what had taken place.

For his part, Lic. Pedro Ojeda Paullada, attorney general of the Republic, has said that the peremptory deportation, accomplished without following the established procedures, not only has violated the accords signed by the United States before the International Organization of Labor (O.I.T.), but also that it is unjust and immoral to periodically attract laborers only to expel them later without cause. And Lic. Mario Moya Palencia, Secretary of the Government, insisted that all massive deportation is illegal, given the fact that law establishes that deportation is an individual process that requires as a first step an investigation as to whether the arrested individual is a Mexican or not, something that has not been done.

In short, the United States, as any other country, has the right to deport illegal aliens who are arrested on its territory; but it also has the obligation of not becoming a producer of illegal aliens on Mexican soil, by legalizing the deportation to Mexico of Mexican laborers.

Nevertheless, there are indications that the attitude of the Mexican government may change if it is confirmed that the Supreme Court of the United States would establish the racist judgment that it is constitutional to arrest persons simply for believing them to be Mexicans. Such is the possibility presented by Dr. Jorge Bustamente, researcher from El Colegio de México.

When it is a matter of identifying the causes of illegal emigration to the United States, it is natural to discover that opinions differ according to the side of the border where they are expressed. Thus, for example, from the United States it is observed that 400,000 emigrants are absorbed annually, 70,000 of whom are Mexicans, which constitutes the highest national quota admitted, producing a snowball effect of aliens without legal documents. It is also alleged that the law itself encourages the entrance of laborers by providing that the yesterday's emigrant without legal documents can automatically become a legal resident and citizen.

To this it is appropriate to point out the corruption that is frequently said to exist in the Immigration and Naturalization Service of the United States. Perhaps the most celebrated case in recent years began in 1972, and was more recently classified as a "national scandal" by Attorney General William Saxbe in his report to President Gerald Ford. According to *The New York Times* of November 22, 1974, the FBI documented before a subcommittee of the Congress the fact that high and low-ranking officials of the Immigration and Naturalization Service appeared to be directly involved in business transactions of extortion, bribery, arms and narcotics contraband, white slavery, sexual assaults on Mexican illegals, illegal sales of migratory documents, and commercial alliances with suppliers of undocumented Mexican laborers. The corruption becomes evident in the activities of *coyotes* [labor contractors who hire scabs] and *enganchadores* [Mexican labor contractors who hire "braceros"], who understand and take full advantage of the complicated interrelated legal implications on both sides of the border. For example, the judicial authorities of Ciudad Juárez, Chihuahua, announced recently the arrest of a well-oiled international band, dedicated to the export of illegal laborers to the United States.

Further, in Mexico the mirage of the large salary differential [between Mexico and the United States] is an invitation to speculation. Any laborer in Chihuahua is aware of the fact that his minimum weekly wage is worth less than what he can earn in one day's work for the minimum wage in Texas. In spite of the effort of the government to equalize incomes, the last census records that 75 percent of Mexican laborers still earn less than 1,000 pesos [$80 U.S.]* monthly; and to this is added the astronomical figure of the underemployed and the unemployed in the Republic.

But it is the population explosion in Mexico, related to illegal emigration, that could provoke collective irrational reactions in the North American community. The inhabitants of a neighboring country, whose population is believed to be hungry and that is growing by 3.9 percent annually could seem to be threatening to an overfed nation, which maintains a 0.9 percent annual population increase. At this growth rate, the statisticians predict that by 1996 Mexico will have doubled its present population. And given the fact that the majority of laborers taken into custody in the United States have been farm workers, it is clear that another cause for the illegal emigration exists in the current situation of the Mexican farmer.

In the First Congress on Workers Without Legal Documents, which took place last May in Ciudad Juárez the possibility was discussed that there may indeed have appeared a new kind of property holder, of farmer, and of peon. The new property holder would be the multinational food corporation that indirectly monopolizes the largest and best extensions of land; the new farmer would be an absentee farm manager, who hires the new peon for no more than 15 pesos [$1.20 U.S.] a day, without any grant [of land]; and this new peon would have been converted into the seedbed that sprouts the illegal alien emigrant. To all of this one must add the low productivity of the huge corporation farms, which must be attributed to the lack of adequate wages and social services, as well as the lack of technical assistance, caused by the landowning bureaucracy.

If one were to sketch a statistical profile, there would appear, among other characteristics, the fact that the great majority of the "wetbacks" are country youth who persistently cross the northern border on foot and in small family or neighborhood groups. Comparatively speaking, nine of every ten Mexicans enter the United States in search of work, in contrast to six of every ten arrested illegal aliens of other nationalities. These Mexicans work an average of 8.6 hours more each week than the illegal aliens of other countries, and they are also the ones who send more money back to their homes, in spite of the fact that they have the lowest educational

---

*This conversion and the one following are based on the exchange rate of 12.50 pesos to the dollar prior to the devaluation in late 1976.

level. They are the ones who earn less and those who are arrested more frequently—eight times more often.

And since the Mexicans are those who become the least Americanized, they have, precisely because of this, less opportunity to rise socially; furthermore, they organize themselves poorly and never receive salary increases. Likewise, they are the ones who more often inform on other illegal aliens, and those who are constantly being informed upon by U.S. citizens of Mexican origin. In this respect, only Chicano organizations like CASA and the farm workers union of César Chávez have concerned themselves with the support, defense, and organization of these *despapelados* [i.e., those without legal documents].

On the other hand, it is fashionable in the United States to look upon the "wetbacks" as the primary cause of the current economic crisis. For example, the Assistant United States Attorney General Lawrence Silberman assured a subcommittee of the House of Representatives in February 1975 that said country sustains the burden of 4,000,000 to 12,000,000 workers without legal documents. "They are," he said, "the ones who steal the jobs of qualified workers and of the new legal immigrants; they are the ones who depress the salary scale of the working class, the ones who contribute to the deficit in the balance of payments by sending so much money out of the country, and who, in the final analysis, are responsible for the increase in taxes by taking away jobs from those who could be working but now live at the expense of the government."

Such apprehension likewise is voiced by the academic community through scholarly studies such as the one by Dr. J. E. Day, professor at the University of Texas-El Paso, who predicts that if energetic measures are not taken in this respect, the Mexican population explosion will produce such pressure by illegal aliens that it will bring about economic chaos, massive hunger, and the destruction of the North American civilization. And among the solutions that stand out is the "modest proposal" of Dr. William Paddock, who suggested last year the utilization of the United Nations to permit the starvation of the inhabitants of every country that does not submit itself to birth control.

Nevertheless, Jimmy Carter, Democratic candidate for the presidency of the United States, declared on August 5, 1976, that it is a myth that the illegal alien is a fiscal burden and a cause of unemployment in the United States. And according to official statistics he cited, 80 percent of the aliens without legal documents pay revenue on profits and pay social security taxes; only 0.5 percent receive public assistance, and 1.3 percent food subsidies. This is to say that they give more than they receive.

Furthermore, the prominent jurist Richard Knight has supported statistically the contention that the cause of the current crisis is the North American economy, which also occasions, simultaneously, the disastrous international situation, one of the repercussions being the invasion of the United States by illegal aliens, where they are alternately attracted and expelled according to the convenience of the imperialistic market.

Several of Knight's arguments in his presentation before the Committee on Immigrants Without Legal Status, are: that the unemployment, the recession, the increase in taxes, and the inflation from which the United States is currently suffering are not caused by the large number of illegal aliens, but rather by the fundamental weakness of the dollar, dependent upon the manufacture of arms and expansionism. "And from a foreign perspective," he adds, "it is the United States that generates the migration of illegal aliens when it supports and finances dictatorial governments that accept onerous 'assistance,' exporting [to the U.S.] cheap raw materials and subjecting their own people to misery, ignorance, and oppression."

According to observers, wealth that is administered equitably, by means of a new international economic order, would cease to generate the poverty that impels emigration and the opportunity that feverishly attracts it. The other alternative is to continue coexisting between two worlds in tension, whose greatest communication seems to consist in an exchange of destructive migratory invasions.

That is how it was understood recently by a Mexican illegal alien at Benito Juárez International Airport who showed his companions a translation of the invitation that is directed to the immigrant by the Statue of Liberty in New York harbor:

> Give me your tired, your poor,
> Your huddled masses yearning to breathe free,
> The wretched refuse . . .

And thus, no doubt, that anonymous shopkeeper in one of those many North American urban centers invaded by the Spanish language also understood it when he defiantly nailed that sign on his shop window: "English spoken here."

Agreements. The problem of the Mexican farm workers without legal documents in the United States affects the latter as much as it does Mexico. Hence, it is incumbent upon both countries to seek an effective and mutually satisfactory solution.

The Mexican government does not favor nor encourage the emigration of laborers; on the contrary, it has made and continues to make efforts to check the causes that originate the said migratory current toward the United States. The Secretary for Foreign Affairs of Mexico has said: "This economic-social and human problem cannot be resolved by means of repressive measures, given the fact that such measures do not produce satisfactory results; rather, they originate collateral consequences that are as harmful and pernicious (as the problem itself)."

As a result of the councils that were held in Washington, D.C. in June 1972, commissions were established in Mexico and in the United States, charged with the responsibility of studying in detail this problem. Later, from July 16 to 17, 1973, representatives of the two governments met again in Washington for a frank discussion and exchange of points of view.

Nevertheless, until now the only decision that prevails with respect [to the problem] is the judgment of the United States Supreme Court on November 25, 1974, which did not reinstate the so-called "Bracero Program," nor did it mean greater facility for persons who desire to work in that country.

"The decisions of the Court," states an official communiqué, "reaffirms the policy followed by the Immigration and Naturalization Service of the United States in the last forty years, in the sense that it permits foreigners who originate in Canada and Mexico—admitted into the United States as legal immigrants—to work in this country and reside in their respective countries of origin. This refers only to the foreigners that have received a resident visa and to whom has been given a card that identifies them as legal residents, called Form I-151 or Green Card."

And the communiqué ends laconically with these words: "The Law of Immigration of the United States will continue in effect and all persons who violate it, entering illegally the territory of the United States, will be returned to their countries of origin."

Incongruities of a System of Self Interest*

- The Department of Immigration and Naturalization of the United States, according to Ellwyn Stoddard, acts more as an economic arm than as an agent of the law. It is equally feared by the "illegals" and by the managers of the enterprises that derive their livelihood from the "illegals."
- Even though the labor laws of the United States nowadays protect the

*This appeared as a table on page 8 of the original article. EDS.

"illegal" laborers, there are other laws that persecute them if they work in the United States.

- It is against the law for an illegal alien to seek work, but it is perfectly legal for someone to employ him.
- The longer one lives illegally in the United States, the greater are the possibilities for one to acquire legal residence in the country.
- There are many "illegals" who because of having been in the country a long time have the right to acquire legal residence, but they do not carry through the [necessary legal] process because they can be arrested as "illegal aliens."
- The morality of the United States seems to be governed by a criterion that is at the same time provincial and providential: while it is interested only in what takes place within its own borders, it also feels its "manifest destiny" to impose itself as policeman and arbitrator of the continent.

Fluctuations in the Emigration to the United States*

Dr. Julian Samora, sociologist, and three colleagues formulated a table of the history of emigrations to the United States during one century, in relation to other emigrations and other relevant events. This is a summary of that table:

1850–1889 The European and Oriental emigrations place restrictions upon that from Mexico.

1900–1909 Emigration of Orientals is restricted and a moderate increase in Mexican emigration is registered.

1920–1929 The Mexican emigration reaches its maximum in 1924 upon the restriction of European and Oriental emigrations, but by 1929 it begins to diminish because of restrictions placed upon it.

1930–1939 This lapse begins with a large repatriation and ends with a growing increase in legal and illegal emigration.

1940–1947 The Second World War produces the Bracero Program and an increase in legal emigration.

1948–1951 The "illegals" become "braceros" and the departure of "braceros" increases, as does also the number of emigrants that pass as legal residents.

1952–1959 The Korean War. The emigration of "illegals" and of legal residents increases dramatically while the great campaign to deport the "braceros" is initiated.

*This appeared as a table on page 9 of the original article—EDS.

1960–1970 The "bracero" disappears. The legal and illegal emigration increases until July of 1968, when new restrictive legislation is enacted.

29

Proposals Concerning Illegal Mexican Labor

Jimmy Carter

Undocumented Aliens Message to the Congress. August 4, 1977

To the Congress of the United States:

I am proposing to Congress today a set of actions to help markedly reduce the increasing flow of undocumented aliens in this country and to regulate the presence of the millions of undocumented aliens already here.

These proposed actions are based on the results of a thorough Cabinet-level study and on the groundwork which has been laid, since the beginning of the decade, by Congressmen Rodino and Eilberg and Senators Eastland and Kennedy. These actions will:

- Make unlawful the hiring of undocumented aliens, with enforcement by the Justice Department against those employers who engage in a "pattern or practice" of such hiring. Penalties would be civil—injunctions and fines of $1000 per undocumented alien hired. Criminal penalties could be imposed by the courts against employers violating injunctions. Moreover, employers, and others, receiving compensation for knowingly assisting an undocumented alien obtain or retain a job would also be subject to criminal penalties.
- Increase significantly the enforcement of the Fair Labor Standards Act and the Federal Farm Labor Contractor Registration Act, targeted to areas where heavy undocumented alien hiring occurs.

Reprinted from *Weekly Compilation of Presidential Documents*, vol. 13, no. 32 (8 August 1977), pp. 1170–75.

• Adjust the immigration status of undocumented aliens who have resided in the U.S. continuously from before January 1, 1970 to the present and who apply with the Immigration and Naturalization Service (INS) for permanent resident alien status; create a new immigration category of temporary resident alien for undocumented aliens who have resided in the U.S. continuously prior to January 1, 1977; make no status change and enforce the immigration law against those undocumented aliens entering the U.S. after January 1, 1977.

• Substantially increase resources available to control the Southern border, and other entry points, in order to prevent illegal immigration.

• Promote continued cooperation with the governments which are major sources of undocumented aliens, in an effort to improve their economies and their controls over alien smuggling rings.

Each of these actions will play a distinct, but closely related, role in helping to solve one of our most complex domestic problems: In the last several years, millions of undocumented aliens have illegally immigrated to the United States. They have breached our nation's immigration laws, displaced many American citizens from jobs, and placed an increased financial burden on many states and local governments.

The set of actions I am proposing cannot solve this enormous problem overnight, but they will signal the beginning of an effective Federal response. My Administration is strongly committed to aggressive and comprehensive steps toward resolving this problem, and I am therefore proposing the following actions:

Employer Sanctions

The principal attraction of the United States for undocumented aliens is economic—the opportunity to obtain a job paying considerably more than any available in their own countries. If that opportunity is severely restricted, I am convinced that far fewer aliens will attempt illegal entry.

I am therefore proposing that Congress make unlawful the hiring by any employer of any undocumented alien. This employment bar would be implemented in the following way:

• Enforcement would be sought against those employers who engage in a "pattern or practice" of hiring undocumented aliens, with the Justice Department setting priorities for enforcement.

• Penalties for violation of the employment bar would be both injunctive relief and stiff civil fines—a maximum of $1,000 for each undocumented alien hired by an employer. A violation of a court injunction would subject an employer to a potential criminal contempt citation and imprisonment.

• An employer would be entitled to defend any charge of hiring an undocumented alien by proving that a prospective employee's documentation of legal residence, as designated by the Attorney General in regulations, was seen prior to employment.

• The Social Security card would be designated as one of the authorized identification documents; and we will accelerate the steps already being taken to make certain that such cards are issued, as the law now mandates, only to legal residents. Those steps include requiring personal interviews of card applicants and making the cards more difficult to forge. But no steps would be taken to make the Social Security card, or any other card, a national identification document.

• To further restrict job opportunities, criminal sanctions would be imposed on those persons who receive compensation for knowingly assisting an undocumented alien obtain or retain employment, or who knowingly contract with such persons for the employment of undocumented aliens. These sanctions are directed at the substantial number of individuals who broker jobs for undocumented aliens or act as agents for alien smugglers. It is *not* directed at those who inadvertently refer an undocumented alien to a job, such as an employment agency or a union hiring hall.

To make certain that all of these new sanctions are uniformly applied, they would pre-empt any existing state sanctions.

In addition to the creation of these new sanctions, efforts to increase enforcement of existing sanctions will be significantly increased. The Fair Labor Standards Act, which mandates payment of the minimum wage and provides other employee protections, would not only be strictly enforced, but its existing civil and criminal penalties would be sought much more frequently by the government. To date, the inability of the government to enforce fully this Act, due in part to a lack of resources, has resulted in the hiring of undocumented aliens at sub-minimum wages, thereby often displacing American workers. Two-hundred-sixty new inspectors will be hired and targeted to areas of heavy undocumented alien employment. Similarly, the Federal Farm Labor Contractor Registration Act, which prohibits the recruiting and hiring of undocumented aliens for farm work, would be tightly enforced. The Departments of Justice and Labor will work closely in exchanging information developed in their separate enforcement activities.

While I believe that both the new and existing employer sanctions, and their strict enforcement, are required to control the employment of undocumented aliens, the possibility that these sanctions might lead employers to discriminate against Mexican-American citizens and legal residents, as well as other ethnic Americans, would be intolerable. The proposed employer sanctions have been designed, with their general reliance on civil penalties and "pattern or practice" enforcement, to minimize any cause for discrimination. However, to prevent any discriminatory hiring, the federal civil rights agencies will be charged with making much greater efforts to ensure that existing anti-discrimination laws are fully enforced.

Border Enforcement

The proposed employer sanctions will not, by themselves, be enough to stop the entry of undocumented aliens. Measures must also be taken to significantly increase existing border enforcement efforts. While our borders cannot realistically be made impenetrable to illegal entry, greater enforcement efforts clearly are possible, consistent with preserving both the longest "open" borders in the world and our humanitarian traditions.

I am proposing to take the following increased enforcement measures, most of which will require Congressional approval for the necessary additional resources:

- Enforcement resources at the border will be increased substantially and will be reorganized to ensure greater effectiveness. The exact nature of the reorganization, as well as the amount of additional enforcement personnel, will be determined after the completion in September of our ongoing border enforcement studies. It is very likely, though, that a minimum of 2000 additional enforcement personnel will be placed on the Mexican border.
- INS will shift a significant number of enforcement personnel to border areas having the highest reported rates of undocumented alien entry.
- An anti-smuggling Task Force will be established in order to seek ways to reduce the number and effectiveness of the smuggling rings which, by obtaining forged documents and providing transportation, systematically smuggle a substantial percentage of the undocumented aliens entering the country. The U.S. Attorneys will be instructed to give high priority to prosecuting individuals involved in alien smuggling.
- The State Department will increase its visa issuance resources abroad to ensure that foreign citizens attempting to enter this country will be doing so within the requirements of the immigration laws.
- Passage will be sought of pending legislation to impose criminal sanc-

tions on those who knowingly use false information to obtain identifiers issued by our Government, or who knowingly use fraudulent Government documents to obtain legitimate Government documents.

- The State Department will consult with countries which are the sources of significant numbers of undocumented aliens about cooperative border enforcement and anti-smuggling efforts.

Cooperation With Source Countries

The proposed employer sanctions and border enforcement will clearly discourage a significant percentage of those who would otherwise attempt to enter or remain in the U.S. illegally. However, as long as jobs are available here but not easily available in countries which have been the source of most undocumented aliens, many citizens of those countries will ignore whatever barriers to entry and employment we erect. An effective policy to control illegal immigration must include the development of a strong economy in each source country.

Unfortunately, this objective may be difficult to achieve within the near future. The economies of most of the source countries are still not sufficiently developed to produce, even with significant U.S. aid, enough jobs over the short-term to match their rapidly growing workforce.

Over the longer term, however, I believe that marked improvements in source countries' economies are achievable by their own efforts with support from the United States. I welcome the economic development efforts now being made by the dynamic and competent leaders of Mexico. To further efforts such as those, the United States is committed to helping source countries obtain assistance appropriate to their own economic needs. I will explore with source countries means of providing such assistance. In some cases this will mean bilateral or multilateral economic assistance. In others, it will involve technical assistance, encouragement of private financing and enhanced trade, or population programs.

Adjustment of Status

The fact that there are millions of undocumented aliens already residing in this country presents one of the most difficult questions surrounding the aliens phenomenon. These aliens entered the U.S. illegally and have willfully remained here in violation of the immigration laws. On the other hand, many of them have been law-abiding residents who are looking for a new life and are productive members of their communities.

I have concluded that an adjustment of status is necessary to avoid having a permanent "underclass" of millions of persons who have not been and cannot practicably be deported, and who would continue living here in perpetual fear of immigration authorities, the local police, employers, and neighbors. Their entire existence would continue to be predicated on staying outside the reach of government authorities and the law's protections.

I therefore recommend the following adjustments of status:

First, I propose that permanent resident alien status be granted to all undocumented aliens who have resided continuously in the U.S. from before January 1, 1970, to the present. These aliens would have to apply for this status and provide normal documentary proof of continuous residency. If residency is maintained, U.S. citizenship could be sought five years after the granting of permanent status, as provided in existing immigration laws.

The permanent resident alien status would be granted through an update of the registry provisions of the Immigration and Nationality Act. The registry statute has been updated three times since 1929, with the last update in 1965, when permanent resident alien status was granted to those who had resided here prior to 1948.

Second, all undocumented aliens, including those (other than exchange and student visitors) with expired visas, who were residing in the United States on or before January 1, 1977, will be eligible for a temporary resident alien status for five years.

Those eligible would be granted the temporary status only after registering with INS; registration would be permitted solely during a one-year period. Aliens granted temporary status would be entitled to reside legally in the United States for a five-year period.

The purpose of granting a temporary status is to preserve a decision on the final status of these undocumented aliens, until much more precise information about their number, location, family size, and economic situation can be collected and reviewed. That information would be obtained through the registration process. A decision on their final status would be made sometime after the completion of the registration process and before the expiration of the five-year period.

Temporary resident aliens would not have the right to vote, to run for public office, or to serve on juries; nor would they be entitled to bring members of their families into the U.S. But they could leave and re-enter this country, and they could seek employment, under the same rules as permanent resident aliens.

Unlike permanent resident aliens, temporary resident aliens would be ineligible to receive such Federal social services as Medicaid, Food Stamps, Aid to Families with Dependent Children, and Supplemental Security Income. However, the allocation formulas for Revenue Sharing, which are based on population, would be adjusted to reflect the presence of temporary resident aliens. The adjustment would compensate states and local communities for the fact that some of these residents—undocumented aliens—are currently not included in the Census Bureau's population counts. That undercount deprives certain states and communities of Revenue Sharing funds which, if Census figures were completely accurate, would be received and used to defray certain expenses caused by the presence of undocumented aliens. Those receiving adjustments of status through the actions I am proposing would be included in the 1980 Census, so that the allocation charges would have to be made only through 1980.

Third, for those undocumented aliens who entered the United States after January 1, 1977, there would be *no* adjustment of status. The immigration laws would still be enforced against these undocumented aliens. Similarly, those undocumented aliens, who are eligible for adjustment of status, but do not apply, would continue to have the immigration laws enforced against them.

In addition, the INS would expedite its handling of the substantial backlog of adjustment of status applications from those aliens entitled to an adjustment under existing law.

Finally, those persons who would be eligible for an adjustment of status under these proposals must not be ineligible under other provisions of the immigration laws.

Temporary Foreign Workers

As part of these efforts to control the problem of undocumented aliens, I am asking the Secretary of Labor to conduct, in consultation with the Congress and other interested parties, a comprehensive review of the current temporary foreign worker (H–2) certification program. I believe it is possible to structure this program so that it responds to the legitimate needs of both employees, by protecting domestic employment opportunities, and of employers, by providing a needed workforce. However, I am not considering the reintroduntion of a bracero-type program for the importation of temporary workers.

Immigration Policy

Our present immigration statutes are in need of a comprehensive review. I am therefore directing the Secretary of State, the Attorney General, and the Secretary of Labor to begin a comprehensive interagency study of our existing immigration laws and policies.

In the interim, I am supporting pending legislation to increase the annual limitation on legal Mexican and Canadian immigration to a total of 50,000, allocated between them according to demand. This legislation will help provide an incentive to legal immigration.

I urge the Congress to consider promptly, and to pass, the legislation I will submit containing the proposals described in this Message.

Jimmy Carter

The White House,
August 4, 1977.

V

Mexican Commuters[1]

Substantial numbers of Mexican nationals continue to live in Mexico while commuting to jobs in the United States. Some cross the border daily whereas others work several days or even weeks between trips home. Although some of these workers enter the United States illegally, many of them work under the so-called commuter program which is quite legal.

Although the commuter system has supplied only a small amount of Mexican labor in comparison to the second bracero program, its impact on the border region has been substantial. In 1974, daily commuters numbered more than 40,000 while there were over 8,000 seasonal commuters. It has been estimated that some 250,000 persons in Mexico are directly dependent upon the earnings of commuters, which may approach $50 million annually. In some of Mexico's border towns and cities, these earnings comprise about 25 percent of the total income of the labor force.[2]

No statute in American law explicitly establishes the commuter system. It was legalized instead by administrative rulings of the Immigration and Naturalization Service (INS) dating from 1927. But it should not be thought that those rulings pioneered the *idea* of Mexican citizens commuting regularly to jobs in the United States; they merely legalized and institutionalized a practice which dates from the nineteenth century.

Since no statute explicitly authorized the program, immigration authorities reinterpreted the regular immigration laws to make it possible. Their rationale was that because the United States had long had especially close relationships with Mexico and Canada, their citizens could be exempted administratively from certain general requirements of the immigration laws even though Congress had not specifically provided for such exceptions.

The INS decided that the commuting system could be legalized by turning the commuters into "immigrants." The problem was that to be an immigrant to the United States, one had to reside in this country. The INS cleared that hurdle by ruling that, for Canadians and Mexicans, the residence requirement could be met simply by working in this country. The prospective commuters would simply apply for an immigrant visa just like anyone else, and upon gaining immigrant status, they would have all the rights of other immigrants. They could live in the United States if they wished to exercise that right or they could continue living in their home countries while commuting to jobs in this country.

Observers less sensitive than logicians have been troubled by the logic of the INS rationale. For example, Samora has referred to the equation of place of employment with residence as a "legal fiction."[3] The commuter program involves the paradox of "immigrants" who do not immigrate and the conversion of immigrant visas into what are in effect nothing more than work permits.

It has long been thought that the legality of the commuter program was questionable because it was not created by Congress and because the INS conversion of commuters into immigrants violated the spirit of the immigration laws that Congress had passed. Yet, in 1974, the United States Supreme Court upheld the program's legality. The Court's main theme was that Congress had had half a century to end the program had it felt that the INS had misinterpreted the laws.[4]

In recent years, pressure for ending the commuter program has intensified. The major argument against it is that it undermines American workers because commuters can afford to work for lower wages. Yet, its defenders have argued that to end the program would create enormous problems. For instance, if the workers could no longer commute to jobs in the United States, they would probably exercise the right to live here and that would mean additional pressures on such resources as housing and schools in the border region.

The selection by the United States Commission on Civil Rights provides an overview of the Mexican "commuter." It examines the historical foundations of the commuter program, then considers its legal basis with emphasis on relevant court cases. The article examines the impact of commuter traffic and concludes that it has had a serious adverse effect on American workers in certain border regions. Finally, it considers proposed solutions to the commuter problem along with possible weaknesses in those proposals.

The selection by Anna-Stina Ericson provides statistics on the wages and occupational distribution of commuters. It examines the impact those workers have on unemployment and the unionization of American workers. The article identifies pressures in Mexico that have given rise to the commuting practice. Like the previous selection, it considers proposals to solve the commuter problem and possible weaknesses in those proposed solutions.

NOTES

1. On the commuter program, see: Richard A. Fineberg, "Green Card Workers in Farm Labor Disputes: A Study of Post-Bracero Mexican National Farm Workers in the San Joaquin Valley, 1968" (Ph.D. dissertation, University of California at Los Angeles, 1970); Roger A. LaBrucherie, "Aliens in the Fields: The Green Card Commuter Under the Immigration and Naturalization Laws," *Stanford Law Review* 21 (1969): 1750–76; David S. North, *The Border Crossers: People Who Live in Mexico and Work in the United States* (Washington: Trans-Century Co., 1970).
2. *Saxbe* v. *Bustos* 95 S.Ct. 281.
3. Julian Samora, *Los Mojados: The Wetback Story* (Notre Dame: University of Notre Dame Press, 1971), p. 22.
4. *Saxbe* v. *Bustos* 95 S.Ct. 272.

30

"The Commuter on the United States-Mexico Border"

United States Commission on Civil Rights

Introduction

One of the most commonly voiced concerns of the Mexican American community in the border area is with the commuter, the Mexican alien who resides in Mexico and commutes to work across the border in the United States,[1] forcing domestic workers to compete for wages with

---

United States Commission on Civil Rights, "The Commuter on the United States-Mexico Border," undated staff report. Reprinted from *Hearings of the Senate Subcommittee on Migratory Labor of the Committee on Labor and Public Welfare*, 91st Congress, 1st and 2d Sessions, Part 5-B, *Migrant and Seasonal Farmworker Powerlessness*. Reprinted by permission of the United States Commission on Civil Rights.

workers living in a much lower cost economy. Commuters represent a supply of workers in excess of the demand who depress the wage rate, displace the domestic worker, and lower his living standard. The commuter poses an even greater threat to the economic well being of the domestic worker when he serves as a strike-breaker, as he has done in Starr County, Texas and Delano, California, thus stifling the organizing and collective bargaining efforts of the American laborer.[2]

As viewed in the 1968 Report of the Senate Migratory Labor Subcommittee, *The Migratory Farm Labor Problem in the United States,* "(t)he problems created by the commuter are manifest":

> The Mexican aliens, as a group, are a readily available, low-wage work force which undermines the standards American workers generally enjoy throughout the rest of the country. More importantly, the normal play of free enterprise principles is subverted and prevented from operating to develop standards along the border comensurate with the American standard. So long as Mexican aliens are allowed indiscriminately to work in the American economy, and take their wages back to the low-cost Mexican economy, the growth of the American standards will continue to be stultified.[3]

What is a Commuter?

The term "commuter" is taken by most residents of the border area to refer to all persons who travel to their work on the American side of the border from their place of actual residence in Mexico, whether they commute daily or on a less frequent basis. Several classes of persons commute to work across the border, including American citizens living in Mexico and Mexican citizens with temporary visas (commonly referred to as "white carders"). The latter group acquires employment here in violation of their limited status. In its strict legal sense (and as it will be used here) the term "commuter" is limited to immigrants lawfully admitted for permanent residence and gainfully employed here, but who retain actual residence in Mexico (sometimes referred to as "green carders", although, in fact, all immigrants, whether or not "commuters" are issued "green cards").

There is wide disagreement about the actual extent of the commuter traffic. The Immigration and Naturalization Service conducted a survey on January 11 and 17, 1966, finding a total of 43,687 commuters. The United

Farm Workers Organizing Committee, AFL-CIO, on the other hand, has estimated the number to be closer to 150,000. While the former estimate includes only daily commuters working along the border, the latter includes aliens remaining here for periods of weeks or months, usually working in areas farther north.

The commuter should not be confused with the nonimmigrant Mexican contract laborer previously brought in for seasonal employment under Public Law 78 (known as the "bracero" program) and recently brought in under section 101 (a) (15) (H) of the Immigration and Nationality Act of 1952. The bracero program was originally established during World War II to augment the American labor shortage. Thereafter, Congress continually extended it (even when there was domestic unemployment) under pressure from an agri-business which had to come to assume a vested interest in this cheap labor supply.

In 1964, after the national conscience took stock of the rising rate of agricultural unemployment, the increasing of discrepancy between farm labor wage rates and those for comparable work, and the worsening conditions in migrant labor camps, Public Law 78 was terminated.[4] The effect of this termination was softened by the admission of a decreasing number of contract laborers under the above mentioned provisions of the Immigration and Nationality Act. During the last year of the bracero program 177,736 Mexican laborers were admitted; in 1965, under the new procedure, the number was reduced to 20,286. In 1966 the number decreased to 8,647 and in 1967 to 7,703. The year 1968 was the first year in which there was no admission of contract laborers and marks the final phasing-out of the contract labor program.

Like all persons immigrating to the United States, the commuter must apply for and obtain the status of a permanent resident alien and receive an alien registration card (Form 1-151, commonly referred to as a "green card") as evidence of his lawful admission. Under section 212 (a) (14) of the Act, in order to qualify for employment in the United States, the applicant must secure certification from the Secretary of Labor to the effect that:

> there are not sufficient workers in the United States who are able, willing, qualified and available at the time of application for a visa and admission to the United States and at the place to which the alien is destined to perform such skilled or unskilled labor, and the employment of such aliens will not adversely affect the wages and working conditions of the workers in the United States similarly employed.[5]

Under the present Immigration and Naturalization Service (hereinafter "Service") interpretation and enforcement of this section, compliance with this provision need only be made at the time of the commuter's original entry. Once his status is secured he may enter and leave the country at will, working wherever he pleases, regardless of the effect he might have on domestic working conditions.[6]

A 1967 amendment to the regulations[7] bars the employment of green card holders (commuters and residents) at locations where a labor dispute has been certified by the Secretary of Labor. On July 10 and 27, 1967, some 16 work stoppages were certified in Rio Grande Valley of Texas, El Paso, Texas and in Southern California, with the effect of preventing commuters from accepting employment at the struck concerns. Even commuters who have secured their immigrant status are covered by the section. A major exception exists, however, with regard to workers already employed at the struck concern at the time of certification. This exception renders the regulation somewhat ineffective in preventing commuters from working as strikebreakers since an employer usually has ample time after a labor dispute occurs to hire needed alien employees before the dispute is certified. This problem could be met if the regulation were modified so as to exclude all green carders not employed at the time that the dispute began.

Once admitted, a commuter is entitled to most of the rights and privileges of an ordinary citizen except the right to vote and hold public office. Unlike most of the more than 650,000 Mexican aliens currently possessing green cards, commuters are not seeking eventual citizenship. Instead they look upon their green cards as nothing more than work permits. In fact, by law commuters cannot claim naturalization benefits; it has been held that actual domicile here is a prerequisite to naturalized citizenship.[8]

Legal Background of and Legal Challenges to the Commuter System

The commuter system has deep roots. People have commuted to work across the United States-Mexico border since the border's inception. Up until the 1920s this traffic was unrestricted. In 1924 a quota system was established which, while not restricting Mexicans directly, required Mexican immigrants to present immigrant visas for entry.[9] An exception to the Act's definition of the term "immigrant" ("any alien departing from any place outside the United States destined for the United States"[10]) was made for "an alien visiting the United States temporarily as a tourist or temporarily for business or pleasure".[11] At first commuters were considered as being here "temporarily for business" and deemed not to be immigrants and, hence, were allowed to continue their employment pattern unrestricted. In 1927 immigration authorities reversed this position and classified commuters as immigrants.[12]

Two commuters contested this new classification and the Supreme Court, finding that one of the "great purposes" of immigration legislation "was to protect American labor against the influx of foreign labor", held unanimously that the term "business" was not meant to include everyday employment. The commuter was not to be exempt from the immigrant status.[13]

The Immigration authorities, however, saw their duty as the protection of diplomatic relations between the United States and Mexico rather than the protection of American labor. In a paper by the Immigration and Naturalization Service prepared for the Select Commission on Western Hemisphere Immigration, the Service stated:

> In studying the problem (status of the commuter) at that time, the immigration authorities concluded that Congress had not intended to interfere with the established pattern of regular border crossings by workers from Mexico or Canada who commuted to jobs in the United States. While such aliens could obtain immigrant visas without difficulty, they would be faced with an impossible task if they were required to obtain a new visa for each daily reentry. Consequently, the immigration authorities devised a border crossing identification card which could be used by aliens who frequently cross the international boundary. The issuance and use of such border crossing cards received express sanction by the Congress in the Alien Registration Act of 1940.
>
> Thus a commuter was able to procure an immigrant visa and subsequent lawful admission as an immigrant. Thereafter he would obtain a border crossing identification card, and with that card he could enter each day to go to his job as returning to his immigrant status in the United States. This arrangement was in harmony with the established good-neighbor policy with Mexico and Canada, facilitated travel across the Mexican and Canadian borders, and avoided serious dislocations in the border areas.[14]

Actually, the commuter system is without express statutory basis. In fact the term "commuter" is not to be found in the Act. Its special character has been described by the Board of Immigration Appeals in the following way:

> The commuter situation manifestly does not fit into any precise category found in the immigration statutes. The status is an artificial one, predicated upon good international relations maintained and cherished between friendly neighbors.[15]

In Gordon & Rosenfield, *Immigration Law and Procedure*, (1959) this description is found:

> Where this employment (of Canadians and Mexicans) is permanent in character administrative ingenuity has devised a "commuter" status, which enables the Canadian or Mexican to obtain lawful admission for permanent residence in order that he may be able to pursue his employment here, and his right to enter each day is attested by his alien registration receipt card. *Of course, this device is an amiable fiction*. . . .[16] (Emphasis added.)

Due to the absence of statutory foundation, immigration authorities have attempted to justify the commuter program's existence by its longstanding history, the fact that the program has long been well known to Congress and the fact that it was discussed and impliedly endorsed by the Senate Judiciary Committee study preceding the passage of the Act of 1952. "Nothing in the Immigration and Nationality Act of its legislative antecedents indicated that the Congress was dissatisfied with the commuter program or desired to change it in any way".[17] The continuation of the commuter program after the 1952 Act was endorsed by the Board of Immigration Appeals in the *Matter of H. O.* 5 I. & N., Dec. 716, 1954.

It also has been argued that the structure of the statutory and regulatory provisions facilitating re-entry supports the commuter program. Section 211(b) of the Act provides that

> . . . under such conditions as may be by regulations prescribed, returning resident immigrants, defined in section 101 (a) (27) (B) . . . may be readmitted to the United States by the Attorney General in his discretion without being required to obtain a passport, immigration visa, reentry permit or other documents.

A "returning resident immigrant" is defined by the statutory definition alluded to as "an immigrant, lawfully admitted for permanent residence, who is returning from a temporary visit abroad." In turn, section 101 (a) (20) defines the term "lawfully admitted for permanent residence" as

". . . the status of having been lawfully accorded the privilege of residing permanently in the United States as an immigrant in accordance with the immigration laws, such status not having changed". As pointed out by L. Paul Winings, past General Counsel for the Immigration and Naturalization Service, in defining the term "lawfully admitted for permanent residence", the Act

> . . . does not say one who has been admitted for permanent residence and has established such residence in the United States. What it says is that it is the status of having been accorded the privilege of permanent residence. In other words, I have paid my way into the ballpark; if I want to go out temporarily, I can come back in.[18]

The regulation promulgated pursuant to section 211(b), however, does not provide for the re-entry of persons "lawfully admitted for permanent residence" as that term is defined by the Act. Instead it says:

> In lieu of an immigrant visa, an immigrant alien *returning to an unrelinquished lawful permanent residence* in the United States after a temporary absence abroad not exceeding 1 year may present Form I-151, Alien Registration Receipt Card, duly issued to him . . .[19] (Emphasis added.)

Although the immigration authorities take the position that this section was not meant to be exclusive, a strong argument can be made that by its wording it in fact excludes commuters. As one commentator has noted, a commuter "is not returning to an unrelinquished, lawful, permanent residence after a temporary absence not exceeding one year because his residence is not in the United States and as a rule he has maintained . . . residence in a foreign country for a period exceeding one year."[20]

In *Amalgamated Meat Cutters v. Rogers,*[21] a case involving the Service's interpretation and enforcement of aforementioned section 212(a) (14) of the Act (precluding admission of aliens for skilled or unskilled labor when the Secretary of Labor certifies that such admission would adversely affect American labor), doubt was cast upon the Service's position. That case involved a strike situation where a certification had been made. In response, the Service instructed the authorities at the relevant points of entry that during the effectiveness of the certification no aliens applying for admission and destined for employment at the struck operation, "except returning lawfully domiciled resident aliens", should be admitted.

The Service took the position that commuters are "aliens lawfully admitted for permanent residence". The Court disagreed—"It is clear that Mexican commuters do not reside in the United States, and that it therefore is not possible for them to be aliens lawfully admitted for permanent residence." Any other construction, the Court felt, would " . . . make shambles of a provision which . . ." was designed to ". . . assure strong safeguards for American labor".[22] The suit had become moot by the time that final judgment was entered, and hence was not appealed by the Service. "However, the administrative authorities do not believe (the decision) is correct and do not follow it".[23]

The rationale in the *Amalgamated Meat Cutters* decision is equally relevant to the validity of the whole commuter system and, logically, should compel a conclusion contrary to that taken by the Service. The Court by way of *obiter dictum,* however, expressly limited its holding in this respect:

> This should not mean, however, that Mexicans or Canadians cannot commute to work in the United States. The defendants can utilize the documentary requirements and administrative procedures they think best under the applicable law for aliens who work in this country and live in Mexico or Canada. If the defendants are satisfied that an alien can enter the United States to work here, they could then permit the alien to commute. But when the Secretary of Labor has issued a certification under §212(a) (14) pertaining to particular employment, such as an alien would be excludable. It is not sufficient to resort to an "amiable fiction" to justify a wholesale evasion of the Secretary's certification—Mexican commuters destined for the employment covered by the certification must be excluded just as any other Mexican non-resident alien.[24]

The commuter program was squarely attacked in a 1964 case, *Texas State AFL-CIO v. Kennedy,*[25] where workers from the Texas border area, alleging economic detriment, sued the immigration authorities for injunctive relief against continuation of the commuter system. The Court avoided reaching the merits by dismissing the action on the grounds that the plaintiffs lacked standing to sue. Since 1964 the law of standing has changed radically,[26] and a similar suit has recently been brought by California Rural Legal Assistance in behalf of California farm workers displaced by commuters taking temporary employment in California and freely returning to Mexico for a period of weeks or months.[27] The complaint seeks an order requiring immigration officials to deny admission to "returning resident immigrants" who fail to demonstrate a bona fide permanent residence in the United States (e.g., commuters). "In determining the question of bona fide permanent residence . . .", the plaintiffs suggest the following indicia might be considered:

1. Possession of a U.S. Selective Service classification card in the alien's name, reflecting a United States address.

2. Possession of state and federal income tax returns in the alien's name, showing residence in the United States.

3. A driver's license in the alien's name issued by a State of the United States, reflecting a United States residence.

4. A vehicle registration in the alien's name reflecting a United States residence.

5. If the alien is married, the fact that both wife and children reside in the United States.

6. Evidence that his children attend school in the United States, or that a child was born in the United States.

7. Evidence of active membership in clubs, associations or unions organized or incorporated in the United States.

8. Convincing evidence of permanent employment in the United States.

9. Rent receipts, other than from a labor camp, hotel or motel, tending to evidence permanent residence in the United States.

10. Place of employment, occupation and length of employment.[28]

Although the Service deems the commuter status to be consistent with the letter and intent of the Immigration and Nationality Act of 1952, it has been held that a commuter cannot even become a citizen (the assumed purpose for immigration under the Act) because, by definition, his assimilated status does not conform to the standard of residency (actual domicile in the United States) required by the Act for naturalization.[29]

Similarly, although a commuter must notify his Selective Service board of his current address,[30] he is not actually subject to be drafted since he is not a resident of the United States under current Selective Service regulations[31] because he did not reside in the United States for the required three month period.

Commuters also are treated differently from other "immigrants" with regard to Federal income tax status. An alien who has established residence in the United States is liable for Federal income tax on his entire income, from sources both within and without the United States. Whether an alien is a resident depends on the facts and circumstances of each case. The type of visa issued is only one of the elements considered. In response to an inquiry on this matter from the House Judiciary Committee, the Internal Revenue Service had this to say about commuters:

> It appears from the information submitted that the aliens about whom you are inquiring have never established a residence in the United States, but have obtained permanent visas merely to facilitate their entry into and departure from this country. Under such circumstances, the status of these individuals is that of nonresident alien.[32]

Hence commuters, unlike other green card holders, are not subject to Federal income tax on income from sources outside this country.

The Impact of Commuter Traffic

Much of the border area has relatively large labor surpluses, partly because of the large number of low skilled U.S. citizens and resident aliens residing in the area.[33] Commuters, however, make up a significant part of the work force in many of the border communities. Although accurate statistics are not kept by the Immigration and Naturalization authorities, sample counts of the number of commuters crossing the border are taken from time to time. One such count, taken on January 11, 1966, showed that 42,641 commuters, of which 17,653 were employed in agriculture, entered the United States. The impact of these commuters on the labor market has been enormous. It has been estimated that over 17% of the labor market in El Paso, Texas, are commuters. Further estimates have shown that 5% of the San Diego, California, labor market and 23% of the Brownsville, Texas, labor market are commuters. Their presence can be directly related to high unemployment rates in these areas.[34]

Many people have commented on the impact of the commuter traffic in the border area. Senator Edward Kennedy of Massachusetts, speaking on a proposed amendment to Section 212 of Immigration and Nationality Act, said:

> In El Paso, where unemployment is currently some 35 percent greater than the State average, the estimated number of commuters in 1966 was more than double the number of unemployed. In El Centro, California, where the unemployment rate is currently 13.1 percent, the estimated number of commuters in 1966 was nearly double the number of unemployed.[35]

A report by the Social Action Commission of the Catholic Diocese of El

Paso indicated that one of the reasons for the low wages in El Paso is because " . . . the Mexican American must compete with some 25,000 workers from Mexico . . . legal alien commuters, U.S. citizens, and illegal entrants . . . who daily cross the bridge from Juarez to work in El Paso. Generally speaking, the workers from Mexico find no inconvenience in working for the barest of wages in El Paso."[36]

The employment of commuters in areas of high unemployment is a characteristic of the communities along the border area. Data published by the Texas Employment Commission in 1966, shows that the unemployment rate in the border towns on that date was substantially greater than in the interior cities. (See Table I.) Laredo had the highest rate—9.6%. The average rate for the four border areas (Brownsville-

TABLE I

Unemployment Rates in 22 Texas Cities
1966

City	Rate	Rank
4 Border Cities	6.6	—
Brownsville-Harlingen-San Benito	6.5	21
El Paso	4.4	17
Laredo	9.6	22
McAllen-Pharr-Edinburg	5.8	20
18 Interior Cities	3.4	—
Abilene	3.6	11
Amarillo	2.9	4
Austin	2.6	3
Beaumont-Port Arthur-Orange	4.0	15
Corpus Christi	3.7	12
Dallas	2.5	2
Fort Worth	2.9	4
Galveston-Texas City	4.7	19
Houston	2.4	1
Longview-Kilgore-Gladewater	3.3	8
Lubbock	3.8	13
Midland-Odessa	3.4	9
San Angelo	3.4	9
San Antonio	4.3	16
Texarkana	3.8	13
Tyler	3.3	7
Waco	4.4	17
Wichita Falls	3.0	6

SOURCE: *The Texas Labor Market*, Texas Employment Commission.

Harlingen-San Benito; El Paso; Laredo; and McAllen-Pharr-Edinburg) was 6.6%, compared with the 3.4 percent rate for the other 18 interior areas for which data was given.[37]

In a special survey held in Laredo by the Department of Labor during the summer of 1961, when the unemployment rate was 11.3%, the Department reported that a large number of unemployed American workers had the same occupational skills as the employed alien commuters. While two garment manufacturers employed 88 commuters as sewing machine operators, the Texas Employment Commission office had on file applications from 156 unemployed U.S. workers qualified for that position.[38] The survey showed that commuters were not limited to the garment industry, but were employed in hotels, restaurants, the retail trades and service establishments. The survey included a sample of firms employing 3,000 workers.

> (T)hese firms employed 438 Mexican aliens identifiable as commuters. In addition, the survey team suspected that other alien employees of these firms were commuters, although they had given U.S. addresses to their employers.[39]

The survey also included data on 19 occupational areas:

> (T)he firms employing only domestic workers paid higher rates for 15 occupations; in one occupation the rates paid were the same; and for three occupations the firms employing alien commuters paid higher rates. There were also instances where the same firm paid its alien commuters less than it paid U.S. workers for the same work. The average of the wage rates for these 19 occupation areas paid by the firms employing only U.S. workers was 38 percent higher than the average rates paid by the firms employing alien commuters.[40] (See Table II.)

United States Commission on Civil Rights field investigations in Laredo showed similar discrepancies in the trucking industry. For instance it was reported that Brown Express Lines, which hires few commuters, pays drivers $3.39 an hour; Alamo Express Lines, employing proportionately more commuters, pays $1.85 an hour.[41]

The pattern of commuter involvement in the Laredo labor market is found elsewhere with comparable effects. As in Laredo, a survey was conducted by the Department of Labor in El Paso, Texas, during the summer of 1961. About 1,000 commuters were employed in the 75 firms surveyed. It was noted, however, that " . . . these figures might be

Occupational Wage Structure
Laredo, Texas, June, 1961

Industry & Occupation	Average wage rate: Firms employing only domestic workers	Average wage rate: Firms employing domestic & alien commuter workers
Hotels & motels		
Cook	$58 per week	$34 per week
Maid	20 per week	17 per week
Hall boy	25 per week	20 per week
Waiter	15 per week, plus tips	18 per week, plus tips
Busboy	25 per week, plus tips	13 per week
Bartender	58 per week	46 per week
Bellboy	15 per week, plus tips	16 per week, plus tips
Drugstores & related firms		
Cashier	$27 per week	$12 per week
Stock clerk	52 per week	40 per week
Fountain girl	16 per week	23 per week, + $3 meal allowance
Drug clerk	77 per week	55 per week
Grocery & related firms		
Cashier	$24 per week	$24 per week
Stock boy	35 per week	20 per week
Produceman	45 per week	35 per week
Butcher	65 per week	52 per week
Warehouseman	37 per week	31 per week
Misc. retail firms		
Porter	$53 per week	$35 per week
Warehouseman	73 per week	21 per week
Stockman	53 per week	45 per week

Technical Note: Data were collected in the survey concerning the different rates paid each occupation in each firm. For some occupations monthly rates were reported; these were converted to weekly rates by dividing the monthly rate by 4.33. The number of workers paid each rate was not reported in all cases, making it impossible to compute an average rate weighted by the number of workers paid each rate. The average rates shown in the table represent the average of the highest and lowest rates paid. These averages correspond quite accurately with the weighted averages computed for the few occupations where data were reported for each worker.

more because one firm indicated that it did not employ commuters but sent a bus to the border each day to pick up workers."[42] The average wage in manufacturing in El Paso is extremely low. That city ranked lowest of the eight major Texas areas for which the Texas Employment Commission supplied data. (see Table III.)

TABLE III.
Average Hourly Earnings in Manufacturing Industries of Eight Major Texas Cities 1966

	Average Hourly Earnings		
Cities	All Manufacturing	Durable Goods	Nondurable Goods
	$2.57	$2.62	$2.52
El Paso	1.90	2.46	1.72
Austin	1.98	1.71	2.26
Beaumont	3.35	3.03	3.48
Corpus Christi	2.96	2.57	3.26
Dallas	2.37	2.52	2.10
Fort Worth	2.81	2.97	2.39
Houston	3.00	2.87	3.16
San Antonio	1.98	1.92	2.02

SOURCE: *The Texas Labor Market,* Texas Employment Commission.

In El Paso, nondurable goods employment is heavily concentrated in garment manufacturing—almost 75% of all nondurable goods workers are in this industry. The wage rate in garment manufacturing is little more than the minimum required by the Fair Labor Standards Act. Large numbers of commuters (mainly women) are employed in this occupation. Many people believe that the presence here of the garment industry, a recent phenomenon, is due to the large supply of labor and low wages—both conditions owing, in part, to the commuter program.[43] The El Paso survey concluded by showing that out of 11 construction firms 5 employed commuters; out of 4 retail dry goods firms, 3 employed commuters; out of 4 wholesale and warehouse firms, 3 employed commuters. In all these cases the firms employing commuters paid the lowest wages.[44]

The impact of the commuter is particularly acute in agriculture where mechanization is rapidly reducing job opportunities. Due to the high concentration of farms along the border and the fact that commuters often work in the lowest skilled, lowest paid jobs, farm workers, who are already underpaid, are the first to suffer competition from the commuter. Furthermore, the use of commuters as strike breakers . . . is especially damaging to this group's organizational struggles.

The wages paid farm workers in the border area are substantially lower than in interior regions. In the Rio Grande Valley, where 37% of the alien commuters worked on farm jobs, the 1966 wage rate was $.75 per hour, 31% less than the $1.10 average in the rest of the state.[45] Similarly, California farm rates are the lowest in the border areas where the bulk of the farm labor force is composed of commuters. The commuter's impact is also reflected in the agricultural unemployment rate. For example, "commuters constitute about 85% of the farmwork force in California's Imperial Valley, where unemployment in 1966 was 10% of the labor force, twice the average for the entire state."[46]

Employment of Illegal Entrants and White Carders

It is important to note the role of illegal entrants and white carders . . . in the employment picture in the border area. During 1967 the Border Patrol apprehended 86,845 deportable Mexicans working illegally, many in the border area. Of this number 27,830 were working in agriculture, 5,906 in trades, crafts and industry, and 53,109 in other occupations.[47]

The border crossing statistics kept are inadequate to accurately gauge the extent of white card employment. There are approximately 1,250,000 current white card holders, and about 450,000 new white cards are issued annually. In 1968 there were 25,000 white carders who were deported, most of these for illegal employment.[48] But it is felt by many residents of the border area that deportation figures do not fairly represent the number of white carders actually employed.[49] This is because many white card workers are employed in occupations with low visibility and even with the best efforts of immigration authorities, they cannot be easily discovered. Many white card holders use their 72 hour passes to engage in menial work as domestic maids, dishwashers, hotel and motel workers, and construction workers. Others work in such semi-skilled jobs as masonry and carpentry.[50]

One reason for this wholesale employment of white carders is the lack of legislation effectively preventing employers from knowingly hiring these workers. As it now stands, the law contains provisions expressly facilitating such employment. Section 274(4) of the Act, prohibiting the harboring and concealing of aliens, contains the following proviso:

> . . . for the purposes of this section, employment *including the usual and normal practices incident to employment* shall not be deemed to constitute harboring.[51] (Emphasis added.)

The need for legislation correcting this situation is manifest.

Use of Commuters as Strike-Breakers

Organized labor has been deeply concerned with the use of commuters as "strike-breakers, when workers were engaged in the process of trying to negotiate conditions covering their wages".[52] The recent strike in Starr County, Texas, presented an example of the use of commuters during labor disputes. In a hearing held by the Senate Subcommittee on Migratory Farm Workers Organizing Committee of the AFL-CIO, [a union leader] had this to say about one of the farms which his organization picketed:

Mr. Padilla: La Casita Farms, which we are on strike with. And this is a bona fide certified strike, issued by the State of Texas, the Texas Employment Commission. I witnessed that they load the bus full of Mexican nationals, and escort them right into the fields, and now they tell us that we don't have a right to picket, to talk to them.

Mr. Yarborough: You mean that La Casita Farms took their transportation to the bridge and picked these workers up with the green cards and brought them straight up to their farms, and put them on the farms?

Mr. Padilla: That is correct, sir.[53]

Domingo Arrendondo, Strike Chairman, United Farm Workers Organizing Committee, AFL-CIO, said with regard to the Starr County strike:

> (T)he problem about these green carders is that they come to work from Mexico every day. They will come in the morning and they will go back at night. Now that the minimum wage came up, or a little bit right after the strike started, they raised the price on these workers from 85 cents or 80 cents to $1 an hour and to $1.50. That was just a symbol to break the strike movement, to keep these people from joining the strike for better wages, or for a contract, or

> a union contract. We went and talked to these people at the bridge, international bridge. We told them to cooperate with us for better wages and working conditions, but they will always say that if their friend had already signed that they would sign, that they would sign but they would probably get laid off their jobs. So, really we couldn't get no where convincing them that a union is something that a worker needs. (Sic)[54]

A result of the misuse of green card workers as strikebreakers was the aforementioned 1967 amendment to the INS regulation, barring employment of green card holders at locations where a labor dispute has been certified by the Secretary of Labor.[55]

Relationship of Commuter Traffic to Migration

As a result of its impact on wages, unemployment and working conditions, the commuter traffic contributes to the annual massive migration of Mexican Americans from the border area. The Social Action Department of the Texas Catholic Conference estimates that because of the lack of opportunities, in South Texas, 88,700 farm workers must migrate to other areas of the country every year in order to find employment. These are people who live in the border areas and would otherwise seek employment there, but for the saturation of the labor market by the commuters. The Committee had this to say:

> Unfortunately, because of the vast supply of green carders . . . the domestic workers are unable to compete with the depressed wages that result from the availability of cheap labor to the growers. This accounts for the fact that almost one-half of the Texas migrant workers come from the four counties of the Lower Rio Grande Valley.[56]

Proposed Solutions to the Commuter Problem

Various recommendations have been made to alleviate conditions caused by the commuter program. Henry Munoz, Jr., speaking for the Texas AFL-CIO, urged that the Department of Labor issue a regulation for a minimum wage law of $1.25 to be applicable to green-card holders and commuters.[57]

In a letter from Chairman Richard M. Scammon and Stanley H. Ruttenberg, of the Select Commission on Western Hemisphere Immigration, the following recommendations to the President regarding commuters were made:

> As of a certain date, all visas issued for immigration into the United States [should] be firmly understood to include a clear commitment by those immigrating to establish and maintain their bona fide residence within the United States.
>
> A new form of border crossing authorization be established, this authorization being designed for use by non-citizens who do not intend to become immigrants in the ordinary sense of the word, but who do wish to work in the United States and continue to reside in their own "contiguous territory" country.
>
> Within a grace period, action should be taken to terminate the commuter status of present "green cards" holders.[58]

On December 14, 1967, Senator Edward Kennedy, a member of the Senate Subcommittee on Migratory Labor, introduced a bill in Congress to amend Section 212 of the Immigration and Nationality Act. As the Senator explained, the amendment would not eliminate the commuter system, but refine its current operation. The bill in essence provides ". . . that each commuter alien must be regularly certified every 6 months by the Department of Labor that his presence in the United States to seek or continue employment does not adversely affect the wages and working conditions of American workers similarly employed. The bill provides for the revocation of a commuter alien's labor clearance if he violates administrative regulations, such as a ban on strike breaking, prescribed by the Department of Labor and the Immigration Service to carry out the purpose of this bill".[59]

This bill has received strong opposition from Chamber of Commerce groups, farm grower organizations, and retailers. The Laredo Chamber of Commerce has gone on record as being opposed to any change in the commuter system.[60] This opposition is based on economic reasons. Laredo, last year, had retail sales of over 90 million dollars, much of this being to commuters. Business interests feel that if anything happens to change the status of commuters their towns will become "ghost towns". Organized growers are afraid that they will be cut off from a valuable supply of labor. Willis Deines, attorney for the Texas Citrus and Vegetable Growers, indicated why his group is in opposition to the Kennedy Bill: ". . . It is axiomatic that if our growers do not have a source of labor that can be depended upon to do their farming operations, particularly in the harvest of perishables, then of course we would not have an industry."[61]

Businessmen in the Valley area have indicated a fear that any effort to terminate the commuter program will result in a retaliatory refusal by Mexico to allow its citizens to carry on their extensive trade in American border towns. The suggestion by Antonio Carrillo Flores, Foreign Secretary of Mexico, that Mexican commuters have "acquired rights", lends authority to this suspicion.[62]

The American government also has officially voiced its concern with diplomatic relations in approaching the commuter problem. In the aforementioned case of *Texas State AFL-CIO v. Robert Kennedy, et al.*, where the legality of the commuter program was put into issue, Secretary of State Dean Rusk submitted an affidavit opposing interference with the commuter program on the grounds that it would " . . . do harm to good neighbor relations in the area".[63] He stated further:

> (I)f as a result of a substantial reduction in the commuter traffic across the border between Mexico and the United States, a significant number of Mexican nationals would be deprived of their earning power, the trade between the two countries along the border would be substantially reduced. We would expect that this would have an immediate depressing effect on the economy of the region on both sides of the border. Moreover, the loss of gainful employment and dollar earnings by 30,000 to 50,000 Mexican nationals, estimated at over $50 million annually, might compel the government of Mexico to consider compensating steps, which would do further damage to the economic life of the region.

The Mexican American in the border area is thus charged with the responsibility of protecting our diplomatic relations. The economic burdens involved in this charge, he may justifiably feel, should be borne by the Nation as a whole, not thrust upon a minority of its citizens.

NOTES

1. There is also, but to a smaller extent, commuter traffic across the American-Canadian border. Canadian commuters do not depress local economic conditions, as do Mexican commuters, because they live in a substantially identical cost-of-living economy, work in highly unionized occupations, and are highly unionized themselves. Being well assimilated into the labor force, they offer no undue competition to American labor.
2. See p. 232 infra.
3. Senate Migratory Labor Subcommittee, The Migratory Farm Labor Problem in the United States, S. Doc. No. 1006, 90th Cong., 2d Sess. 45 (1968).

4. REPORT FROM THE SECRETARY OF LABOR, YEAR OF TRANSITION—SEASONAL FARM LABOR 2 (1965).

5. Immigration and Nationality Act, §212 (a) (14), 8 U.S.C. §1182.

6. See discussion of Amalgamated Meat Cutters case p. 223 infra.

7. Title 8, §211 (b).

8. Petition of Wright, 42 F. Supp. 306 (1941); *In re* Barron, 26 F.2d 106 (1928); Petition of Correa, 79 F. Supp. 265 (1948).

9. Immigration Act of 1924, Ch. 90, 43 Stat. §153.

10. *Id.* §3.

11. *Id.* §3 (2).

12. General Order 86 of Apr. 1, 1927.

13. Karnuth v. United States *ex rel.* Albro, 279 U.S. 229, 243, 244, (1929).

14. REPORT OF THE SELECT COMMISSION ON WESTERN HEMISPHERE IMMIGRATION COMMUTERS, HISTORICAL BACKGROUND, LEGAL CHALLENGES, AND ISSUES 101 (1968).

15. Matter of M.D.S., 7 Immigration and Naturalization Dec. 209 (1958).

16. GORDON AND ROSENFIELD, IMMIGRATION LAW AND PROCEDURE 127 (1959).

17. See n. 15 supra, at 102.

18. HOUSE JUDICIARY COMMITTEE, STUDY OF POPULATION AND IMMIGRATION, ADMINISTRATIVE PRESENTATIONS (III), ADMISSION OF ALIENS INTO THE UNITED STATES FOR TEMPORARY EMPLOYMENT AND "COMMUTER WORKERS" 167 (1963).

19. 8 CER. 211.1 (6).

20. NEWMAN, THE LEGALITY OF THE "COMMUTERS" OR "GREEN CARD HOLDERS" WORKING IN THE UNITED STATES,IN CABINET COMMITTEE HEARINGS ON MEXICAN AMERICAN AFFAIRS 63 (1968).

21. 186 F. Supp. 114 (D.C. D. C.) (1960).

22. *Id.* at 119.

23. IMMIGRATION AND NATIONALITY ACT, WITH AMENDMENTS AND NOTES ON RELATED LAWS 231 (5th ed. 1966).

24. See n. 21 supra, at 119.

25. 330 F.2d 217 (C.A. D.C. 1964).

26. See Flast v. Cohen, 392 U.S. 83 (1968), overruling the 45-year old barrier to standing, Frothingham v. Mellon, 262 U.S. 447 (1923), and repudiating its doctrine of judicial restraint in this area.

27. Gooch, et al. v. Clark, et al., Civil No. 49500 (N. D. Cal., 1968).

28. Brief for Plaintiff at 10, Gooch, et al. v. Clarke et al., n. 28, supra.

29. See n. 9, supra.

30. See §35 of the Alien Registration Act of 1940, as amended, and regulations issued thereunder.

31. 32 C.F.R. 611.13(a) (6), 611.13(b) (7), (1944).

32. See n. 19 supra, at 170.

33. REPORT OF THE SELECT COMMISSION ON WESTERN HEMISPHERE IMMIGRATION, THE "COMMUTER PROBLEM" AND LOW WAGES AND UNEMPLOYMENT IN AMERICAN CITIES ON THE MEXICAN BORDER 116 (1968).

34. MOORE, MEXICAN-AMERICANS: PROBLEMS AND PROSPECTS 12 (1967).

35. 133 Cong. Rec. 205 §14 (daily ed. Dec. 14, 1967).

36. Catholic Conference Office of Immigration (Oct. 11, 1968). Organized labor also has shown concern. The following resolution was passed by the Texas AFL-CIO in Jan. 1968:

> . . . (T)housands of commuter aliens who cross the border daily to work, cause the unemployment of American citizens and create unfair competition in the labor market by working for sub-standard wages and then returning to Mexico at night where their living costs are much lower.

37. These unemployment rates, supplied by the Texas Employment Commission, are

somewhat conservative since they are based upon the number of persons registered with the T.E.C. offices. Many farm workers secure employment through the crew leader and never register with the T.E.C.

38. See n. 34 at 120.
39. *Id.* at 120.
40. *Id.* at 121.
41. Interview with Mr. David Jacobs, AFL-CIO, in Laredo, Texas, Sept. 10, 1968.
42. See n. 34 at 121.
43. *Id.* at 120.
44. *Id.* at 122.
45. *Id.* at 119.
46. See n. 3 at 45.
47. *Immigration and Naturalization Annual Report* 93 (1967).
48. Interview with Mr. Donald Coppock, Deputy Associate Commissioner for Domestic Control, Immigration and Naturalization Service, in Wash., D.C., October 15, 1968.
49. Interview with Mr. Henry Munoz, Jr., Texas AFL-CIO, in Austin, Texas, Sept. 10, 1968. The Service's recognition of the illegal employment of white carders was evidenced by a recent announcement of proposed regulation changes. Under current regulations white carders are issued undated cards and are expected to return within 72 hours and travel no farther than 150 miles from the border. "Government officials say the lack of dates on the present crossing cards makes it almost impossible to enforce regulations."

The proposed changes would limit the travel on undated cards to within 25 miles of the border. For those wishing to travel further a supplemental card that is dated will be issued allowing a 15-day visit. Of course these new limitations will not affect the employment pattern of white carders along the border area. See San Antonio Express, p. 1 (Nov. 29, 1968).

50. *Id.*
51. *See* Immigration and Nationality Act, n. 5, supra.
52. HEARINGS ON §8, 195, 197, 198 BEFORE THE SUBCOMM. ON MIGRATORY LABOR OF THE SENATE COMM. ON LABOR AND PUBLIC WELFARE, 90th Cong., 1st Sess. pt. 1, at 170 (1967).
53. *Id.* at 334.
54. *Id.* at 363.
55. See n. 7.
56. See n. 52 at 61.
57. MUNOZ, VIEW OF ORGANIZED LABOR 3.
58. Letter from Richard M. Scammon and Stanley H. Ruttenberg to President Johnson, July 22, 1968.
59. 113 Cong. Rec. 205 (December 14, 1967). The amendment read as follows:

S. 2790

> *Be it enacted by the Senate and House of Representatives of the United States of America in Congress* assembled, that section 212 of the Immigration and Naturalization Act is amended by adding at the end thereof a new subsection as follows:
>
> "(j) Any alien lawfully admitted for permanent residence whose principal, actual dwelling place is in a foreign country contiquous to the United States and is returning from a temporary stay in such foreign country to seek or continue employment in the United States shall be admitted into the United States only if the Secretary of Labor has determined and certified to the Attorney General within six months prior to the date of admission that the employment of such alien will not adversely affect the wages and working conditions of workers in the United States similarly employed, and if such certification has not been revoked on any ground. The provisions of this subsection shall be applicable to any aliens lawfully admitted for permanent residence, whether or not such aliens were so admitted prior to or on or after the date of enactment of this subsection."

60. See *Laredo Times,* p. 4 (Mar. 1, 1968).
61. *Id.*
62. See *Laredo Times,* p. 4 (Feb. 4, 1968).
63. Brief for Defendant, Texas State AFL-CIO v. Robert F. Kennedy, et al., Civil No. 3468-61, n. 25, supra.

31

"The Impact of Commuters on the Mexican-American Border Area"

Anna-Stina Ericson

Approximately 70,000 persons cross the Mexican border daily to work in the United States. Of these, 20,000 are U.S. citizens living in Mexico; about 50,000 are Mexican immigrants who have valid U.S. immigration documents but who, for various reasons, continue to live in Mexico while they work in the United States. The majority of those who cross the border work in nine U.S. border cities, where, in some cases, they make up a significant part of the local labor force. These commuters contribute to the labor surplus situation prevailing on the U.S. side of the border, which has a depressing effect on wages and on trade union organizing campaigns.

Various proposals have been made in Congress and elsewhere to alleviate the economic and social hardships commuters are said to cause in U.S. border towns. But the present commuter system also has defenders who point out that retail and wholesale trade in towns on the U.S. side of the border is dependent upon the purchases of Mexican workers who earn U.S. wages. There is a great deal of interchange between the U.S. and Mexican border cities in all aspects of trade, commerce, and tourism. The cities are engaged in many joint undertakings, mutually beneficial to the social and cultural development of the people as well as to their economic

---

Anna-Stina Ericson, "The Impact of Commuters on the Mexican-American Border Area," *Monthly Labor Review* (August 1970): 18–27. Reprinted by permission of the Bureau of Labor Statistics, *Monthly Labor Review*.

and social development. This article examines the impact of commuters on commerce, employment, wages, and trade union organization, and possible remedies to counteract problems created by the commuter system.

The Commuter

The Immigration and Naturalization Service refers to commuters as those aliens who lawfully have the privilege of residing in the United States but who choose to reside in foreign contiguous territory and commute to their jobs in the United States.[1] The practice of commuting internationally grew up because many towns along the Canadian and Mexican borders are really single communities separated by the international boundaries. The immigration laws of the 1920s, which were designed in large part to protect American labor standards, gave Mexicans and Canadians who worked in the United States admission as nonresident aliens coming to the United States for purposes of "business" or "pleasure," within the meaning of the immigration law. In April 1927, immigration authorities changed position and declared that aliens coming to work in the United States would be classified as immigrants and would have to acquire commuter status. This interpretation of the immigration law was upheld by the Supreme Court in 1929.

The first step in acquiring commuter status is to achieve lawful admission to the United States as an immigrant.[2] Since 1965, the immigrant applicant has also had to obtain a labor certification unless he is the parent, spouse, or child of a U.S. citizen or resident alien.[3] The immigrant's certification specifies that there is a shortage of workers in his particular occupation in the United States and that his employment will not adversely affect wages and working conditions of U.S. residents.

Upon admission to the United States, the commuter is registered as an immigrant and is given an Alien Registration Receipt Card (Form I–151), known as a "green card" from its former color. This card certifies his immigrant status and permits his reentry into the United States following temporary absences of less than one year. An alien is entitled to commuter status only if he has a job in this country and can lose this status if he is unemployed in the United States for more than six months.

In the past, the Immigration and Naturalization Service took periodic one-day counts of alien commuters and has kept a continuous unduplicated count since a survey it conducted in November-December 1967. At that time, all "green cards," as they were presented at the border ports of entry, were picked up for verification and were grommetted to identify commuter status. In November-December 1967, 40,176 alien Mexican commuters were registered. By the end of December 1969, their number had grown to 49,770, as shown in table 1.

In addition to immigrants who commute to jobs in the United States from their Mexican residence, about 20,000 U.S. citizens also commute from Mexico to U.S. jobs. Most of these citizens were born of Mexican or Mexican-American parents and probably never lived in the United States or lived there only briefly.

Border area residents also classify as commuters those nonimmigrant visitors who possess nonimmigrant visas or border crossing cards and work illegally in the United States. The largest number of these commuters have 72-hour border crossing cards, valid for purposes of business or pleasure within a 25-mile area from the border. These cards do not authorize their holders to live or work in the United States, but many do.

The numbers who work without proper authorization are difficult to determine. In fiscal year 1969 over 200,000 Mexicans were apprehended for being in this country illegally. Of this number, roughly one-fourth had been in the United States from one month to a year, long enough to have been employed. The largest group (80 percent) of deportable Mexican aliens apprehended had entered without inspection. The next largest group (14 percent) were those holding visitor border crossing cards. Obviously, not all people who have border crossing cards work in the United States, but a sufficient number do to cause U.S. border residents to consider the practice widespread.

Employment and Earnings

Employment in the border area is heavily concentrated in low-wage, low-skill industries: Agriculture, services, wholesale and retail trade, government, and light manufacturing. The San Diego area differs from the general pattern because there is more heavy manufacturing and higher wage industries.

There is limited information available about the jobs held by legal commuters, the "green carders." What is available was collected by the Immigration and Naturalization Service at the time of the 1967 survey of commuters. Commuters are found in the same types of occupations in which resident workers are found. Studies reveal that commuters generally receive the same wages resident workers receive when working in the same enterprise.

TABLE 1.
Number of Green Card Commuters from Mexico and of Americans Unemployed

Port of entry, by State and county	December 1969		November-December 1967	
	Mexican commuters[1]	American unemployed	Mexican commuters	American unemployed
Total border ports of entry	49,770		40,176	
California	20,753		15,284	
San Ysidro (San Diego)	11,697	18,300	7,535	17,300
Tecate (San Diego)	63		56	
Andrade (Imperial)	14	3,389	3	4,900
Calexico (Imperial)	8,979		7,690	
Arizona	5,647		5,148	([4])
San Luis (Yuma)	3,616	[2]869	3,553	1,500
Nogales (Santa Cruz)	1,388	175	1,118	275
Naco (Cochise)	113	577	94	800
Douglas (Cochise)	522		380	
Other	8		3	
New Mexico	31		30	
Columbus (Luna)	31	([3])	30	[5]287
Texas	23,339		19,714	
El Paso (El Paso)	13,493	3,325	11,760	4,200
Fabens (El Paso)	321		279	
Del Rio (Val Verde)	200	774	317	500
Eagle Pass (Maverick)	2,089	1,215	1,635	1,200
Laredo (Webb)	3,456	3,325	2,669	3,300
Roma (Starr)	106		73	
Hidalgo (Hidalgo)	1,061	3,960	937	4,200
Progresso (Hidalgo)	82		50	
Brownsville (Cameron)	2,430	2,770	1,917	2,000
Other	101		77	

[1]Cumulative unduplicated count since November-December 1967. Commuters cross into the United States at least twice a week.
[2]October 1969.
[3]Not available.
[4]These figures are 1967 annual averages.
[5]March 1968.
SOURCE: Immigration and Naturalization Service, U.S. Department of Justice, and Manpower Administration, U.S. Department of Labor.

Occupational Distribution

Forty percent of the commuters in November-December 1967 said they did farm work, 9 percent were general laborers, 8 percent were in clerical and sales occupations, 7 percent were maids in private households, 6 percent were in construction, and 5.6 percent were in hotel and restaurant occupations. Other significant occupational groupings were the following: Metalworkers, 4 percent; sewing machine operators, 4 percent; and truckdrivers, 2.7 percent.

Farm work was particularly important among commuters entering in California and Arizona. It accounted for 60 percent or more of all commuters in those States.[4] Calexico in Imperial County, Calif., and San Luis in Yuma County, Ariz., received the bulk of Mexican commuter farm workers; over 80 percent of all commuters entering these ports were farm workers. In Texas, only 18 percent of the commuters listed farm work as their occupation. The important Texas ports of entry for farm workers were Eagle Pass in Maverick County and Hidalgo in Hidalgo County (the port of entry for McAllen) in the Lower Rio Grande Valley. Commuters entering over Texas ports of entry were more likely to be general laborers, clerical and salesworkers, domestic servants, construction workers, metalworkers, or hotel and restaurant workers.

Commuters are found working with resident workers and competing with them for available jobs. Resident workers may occasionally find themselves at a disadvantage in the job market because some employers favor commuter workers. A study of the El Paso garment industry revealed that some employers prefer commuters because they believe they are superior workers, are more cooperative, less throublesome, and more reliable because "they have to work."[5]

Earnings

In the border cities, wage rates are lower than in the rest of the border States and lower than national averages for similar industries or occupations. Statutory minimum wages, where they apply, tend to be the prevailing wages, and there are numerous examples of prevailing wages below the statutory minimum where the legal minimum wage does not apply. A minority of workers are paid at wage rates above the minimum.

In January 1968 the Department of Labor made a survey of wages paid to commuters and U.S. residents in the same occupations in Laredo, Tex.[6] Data were obtained from 95 establishments for 1,075 residents and 608 commuters in 48 broad occupational groupings. The establishments surveyed employed at least 5 commuters at the time of the Immigration and Naturalization Service survey in November and December 1967.[7]

Twenty-five occupations, in which 5 commuters or more were employed, accounted for 84 percent of the residents and 94 percent of the commuters in the sample. The occupations in which the commuters were concentrated paralleled those reported in the Immigration and Naturalization Service survey, except that the Department of Labor study covered establishments only, excluding farm workers and domestics. Average hourly earnings for the 25 surveyed occupations ranged from $0.81 for busboys and $0.86 for service station attendants to $2.10 for customs appraisers. Commuters and resident workers in the same establishment received identical wages in each occupational classification.

The federal minimum wage in effect at the time ($1.40 an hour) was the rate most commonly paid to the commuters; 48 percent of the commuters surveyed received precisely that amount, and 28 percent received less. The ready supply of workers (both residents and alien commuters) kept the prevailing wage at the Federal minimum where it applied and below that level for the number who worked in occupations not covered.

Since this study was completed, a study was conducted to determine the impact of the commuter on the El Paso apparel industry in 1968–69.[8] It found that wages in the apparel industry in El Paso "were low compared to wages in the same industry for other States and regions in the United States and, in addition, when compared with the same industry in other cities in Texas." Most of the workers surveyed received the minimum wage or just slightly more. The study concluded that the Federal minimum wage for the industry was actually the maximum because of the large number of workers willing to work at this wage. Those workers included commuters, Mexican nationals with temporary visitor permits, "wetbacks," and the unemployed and underemployed residents of El Paso—all of whom have a depressing effect on wages in El Paso. Some employers do not differentiate between these categories of persons but consider them all from the same labor pool.

Besides being an area where the prevailing wages are at or below the Federal minimum wage, the border also has a relatively high incidence of Federal wage-hour violations. Almost one-fourth of the workers living in the border states who were paid less than the statutory minimum wage in 1969 lived in the border counties. A third of all workers in the border states who suffered equal pay and McNamara-O'Hara Service Contract Act violations lived in the border counties. These are high levels of violations, particularly since the border counties do not represent a high proportion of employment covered in those states.

Unemployment

Unemployment rates along the U.S. side of the border, except in two or three cities, are far higher than the average unemployment rates for the border states and are among the highest in the country. (See table 2.) Nevertheless, a comparison of the number of the unemployed with the number of commuters, as shown in table 1, suggests that at least in some

TABLE 2.
Border Area Labor Force and Unemployment Rates, 1968 and 1969

State and labor market area (county in parentheses)	Current labor force	Unemployment: 1969 annual average (percent)	Unemployment: 1968 annual average (percent)
Arizona	671,000	2.9	3.7
Yuma (Yuma)	[1]27,200	([2])	4.0
Tucson (Pima)	117,000	3.1	4.0
Nogales (Santa Cruz)	5,650	4.7	[3]5.7
Southern Arizona (Cochise)	20,625	3.2	3.4
California	8,496,000	4.0	4.5
San Diego (San Diego)	455,600	3.8	3.9
Imperial (Imperial)	35,400	8.6	8.1
Texas	4,650,000	2.7	2.7
Brackettville (Kinney)	1,100	6.7	9.5
Brownsville-Harlingen-San Benito (Cameron)	48,310	6.2	5.8
Carrizo Springs (Dimmit)	3,200	9.2	8.9
Crystal City (Zavala)	5,900	11.2	10.8
Del Rio (Val Verde)	9,670	7.5	6.8
Eagle Pass (Maverick)	7,940	11.9	9.1
El Paso (El Paso)	123,250	3.7	4.0
Laredo (Webb)	30,825	8.5	9.0
McAllen (Hidalgo)	63,280	5.9	5.8
Rio Grande City (Starr)	4,700	12.6	11.5
Uvalde (Uvalde)	6,200	6.6	6.4
Zapata (Zapata)	1,900	11.7	10.7

[1]Data for labor force in October 1969. Data for all other labor market areas are for December 1969.
[2]Not available.
[3]6.6 percent after removing Mexican commuter workers from the labor force figure.

of the border cities there would be a labor shortage without the commuters. Other estimates of the local manpower situation quickly dismiss this suggestion. These estimates, prepared by area CAMPS committees,[9] reveal that unemployment figures published by the local employment services understate actual conditions. Job opportunities are so limited in some cities that large numbers of potential workers do not actively seek work and are not counted as unemployed. In most of the cities, large numbers of employed workers work fulltime at jobs that pay less than poverty-level wages, or they work only part time because they are unable to get full-time employment. These workers are classified as underemployed.

Combining the estimated unemployed and underemployed reveals a very different picture of the economic conditions of workers in the U.S. border cities from that shown by published unemployment data. In the cities for which such calculations could be made, estimates of unemployment and underemployment range from about 8 percent to almost 50 percent of the labor force. (See table 3.) The presence of large numbers of Mexican commuters in these labor markets is an obvious disadvantage to resident workers.

Pressure of Mexican Unemployment

Unemployment is also a serious problem along the Mexican side of the border. For years, commuters have crossed into the United States to work, but since the end of the bracero program in 1964, they have been more visible and have increasingly entered agricultural occupations. Because of the bracero program, large numbers of Mexicans migrated to the border area in hopes of getting jobs in the United States. As a result, the populations of the Mexican border towns have increased dramatically, faster than it has been possible to create jobs, and the pressure to work on the U.S. side of the border has increased greatly.

At the same time that the bracero program ended and restrictions were placed by the U.S. government on temporary agricultural workers from Mexico, the duty-free allowance that Americans were permitted to bring back into the United States after a trip abroad was reduced from $500 to $100. The liquor allowance was simultaneously cut from a gallon to a quart. These events had an immediate negative impact on several of the Mexican border cities, since bracero remittances and tourist purchases, including the sales of liquor, were the mainstays of their economies.

Until Mexico launched its border industrialization program in late 1966, the Mexican government had done little to help create jobs in its border area.[10] By the end of January 1970, over 17,000 persons were employed in the industries created under this program, and an unknown number of workers were employed in ancillary jobs. This program stimulates additional northward migration of Mexicans eager to work in the new plants.

TABLE 3.
Estimated Unemployment and Underemployment in Selected Border Labor Market Areas, 1969, and Published Labor Market Statistics

Labor market area (County in parentheses)	Labor force 1969[1] average	Published unemployment 1969[1]		Estimated unemployment[2]	Estimated underemployment[2]	Combined underemployed and unemployed	
		Number	Rate			Number	Rate
San Diego (San Diego)	436,400	16,600	3.8	16,600	26,300	42,900	9.8
Imperial (Imperial)	32,600	2,600	8.0	[3]7,824	[4]	7,824	24.0
Nogales (Santa Cruz)	5,650	322	5.7	[4]	[4]	476	8.4
El Paso (El Paso)	122,000	4,390	3.6	14,375	45,000	59,375	48.7
Laredo (Webb)	29,700	2,520	8.5	3,115	4,152	7,267	24.4
McAllen (Hidalgo)	62,900	3,700	5.9	4,320	17,000	21,320	33.9
Brownsville (Cameron)	48,800	3,040	6.2	2,940	12,965	15,905	32.6

[1]Based on reports from State Employment Security Agencies.

[2]Based on the Comprehensive Manpower Plans, Fiscal Year 1970, prepared by the local Area Manpower Coordinating Committees, and published in the Arizona, California, and Texas Cooperative Manpower Plans for Fiscal Year 1970.

[3]Estimated on the basis of the proportion of Mexican Americans in the labor force and Mexican American unemployment rates (both given in the CAMPS plan) and assuming that Mexican Americans make up 50 percent of the area's unemployed.

[4]Not available.

NOTE: Where the information on underemployment differentiated between disadvantaged and nondisadvantaged, the figures for the disadvantaged underemployed only were used. The figures on those not in the labor force but who local manpower planning officials thought could or should be in the labor force are not included, if it was possible to identify them.

In an effort to determine the magnitude of unemployment and underemployment, the Mexican National Minimum Wage Commission, under the auspices of the U.S.-Mexico Commission for Border Development and Friendship, conducted a survey of unemployment and underemployment in six border cities in 1969. This survey inquired about the characteristics of the people surveyed and the number who commute to work in the United States. Without the U.S. jobs, the Mexican figures on unemployment and underemployment would be significantly higher. Officials interviewed during the surveys said that a cause contributing to the high rates of unemployment on the Mexican side of the border is the continuing migration of workers from the interior regions of Mexico who hope to find jobs on the U.S. side of the border. Table 4 summarizes the findings of the Mexican survey.

In the six border cities, from 119,587 to 130,587 workers were unemployed and underemployed in 1969—roughly one-fifth of the combined labor force of 611,100 of these cities. Close to 10 percent of this group of workers were looking for work for the first time. Forty to 45 percent of the workers reported that they were holding or had held jobs in the United States. Of those who had worked in the United States, the largest number worked as farm laborers. The next largest groups worked as factory workers, domestics, office workers, and gardeners, in that order. Of those who worked in Mexico, the unemployed and underemployed were most often farm laborers or bricklayers. Significant numbers were mechanics, chauffeurs, carpenters, and painters.

TABLE 4.

Summary Findings of Survey of Unemployment and Underemployment in 6 Border Cities, 1969

			Unemployed and underemployed		Number reported working in the United States	
Municipio	Population (late 1968–early 1969)	Labor force	Number	Percent of labor force	Number	Percent of labor force
Tijuana	450,000	157,000	31,000	19.7	9,000	5.7
Mexicali	564,700	181,381	[1]33,587	[1]18.5	10,000	6.0
Nogales	60,000	19,000	8,000	42.1	[2]3,500–4,500	6.7–7.9
Cuidad Juarez	480,000–500,000	150,000	30,000–40,000	20.0–26.7	[3]18,000–22,500	12.0–15.0
Nuevo Laredo	135,000	43,600	10,000	22.9	4,500	9.2
Matamoros	185,000	60,125	7,000–8,000	11.6–13.3	2,800	4.7

[1]If the total number of persons looking for work for the first time (an estimated 10,000) is included, as they are in the other municipios, the number of unemployed increases to 39,355. The higher figure produces an unemployment rate of 21.7 percent.

[2]An estimated 3,000 additional persons were reported as having applied for papers to work in the United States and were awaiting a reply.

[3]An estimated 19,000 additional persons were reported as having applied for papers to work in the United States, but the survey indicated that it takes from six months to a year before their papers are acted upon.

SOURCE: Based on data published in "Revista Mexicana del Trabajo," Secretaría del Trabajo y Previsión Social, September 1969.

Over a third of the workers surveyed fell into the 25 years or younger age group (the proportion was as high as 75 percent in Matamoros), and close to half of them were single. Between 30 and 52 percent were natives of the area. In Ciudad Juárez only 15 percent were natives, and in Tijuana none of those surveyed were natives of the area. These figures confirm the strong attraction the border area has for Mexicans elsewhere in the country and indicate no lessening in the pressures of continuing population growth and migration.

Trade Union Organization

Organized labor in the United States is concerned that the presence of Mexican commuters, particularly in the grape fields of California, is a deterrent to the organization of farm workers and to the right of organized workers to strike. At its 1969 convention, the AFL-CIO passed two resolutions about Mexican border crossers. Resolution 208, which identifies the commuter with "strikebreaking and unfair competition with workers seeking their rights to organize on the farms and in the factories of the U.S.," calls for Congressional action to control the "widespread use of Mexican commuters which undermines American wage and labor standards, narrows employment opportunities for American workers, and provides a constant threat of strikebreaking." In its resolution supporting the farm workers' organizing efforts (Resolution 233), the AFL-CIO describes how the growers employ green card commuters as strikebreakers, reiterates its support to bring farm workers under the protection of the National Labor Relations Act, and urges "improvements in the Government's immigration policies."

The use of green card commuters as strikebreakers was barred in June 1967, by a Federal regulation which precludes the use of the green card by an alien who has left this country and seeks to reenter to accept or continue employment at a place where the Secretary of Labor has determined that a labor dispute exists. In practice, this regulation has been difficult to enforce because green card commuters may decide to become residents of the United States during a labor dispute in order to keep their jobs.

The United Farm Workers Organizing Committee (UFWOC) claims that the Immigration and Naturalization Service has yet to use the regulation for its expressed purpose and that commuters have had little difficulty crossing the border to work in strikebreaking situations. A UFWOC organizer in Delano, Calif., testifying before the Subcommittee on Migratory Labor of the Senate Committee on Labor and Public Welfare in May 1969, reported that the fear of losing their jobs to commuter workers stops many resident agricultural workers from striking.

Several legislative proposals responsive to trade union concern have been introduced in the Congress in recent years. These include an amendment to the National Labor Relations Act to make it an unfair labor practice for employers to hire aliens illegally in the United States or for employers to hire commuters to replace regular employees during a labor dispute. Some of the proposals would extend coverage of the National Labor Relations Act to the agriculture industry.

Proposals for Change in the Commuter System

There is a lack of consensus among border area residents about commuters. In its 1968 report, the Good Neighbor Commission in Texas, an organization which has statutory responsibility for the State of Texas to survey the conditions and problems of migrant labor, stated that the positions of persons for and against the commuter system are "adamant almost to the point of being unnegotiable and without compromise."[11]

There is concern, however, about the effects on the U.S. border cities of changing the longstanding practice of commuting. Any curtailment of the commuter system would probably result in the large-scale movement of commuters and their families to the United States. The housing supply for low- and moderate-income families is already in short supply, and a sudden or even fairly gradual influx of the commuters would seriously exacerbate this situation.

The large-scale movement of Mexican commuters and their families to the United States could also have serious short-term consequences for resident workers. The change in status from commuter to resident would do nothing to alleviate the labor surplus situation already existing in more border cities. During periods of recession, there would be increased competition for jobs, since the commuters then would not have the option of returning to Mexico to live while retaining their immigrant status.

In spite of these and other misgivings about the consequences of changing the commuting system, the concern of the labor movement for the organizing efforts of border area workers and the newly aroused concern of the Mexican-American community with poverty and their lack of economic opportunities are gathering support for a change in the commuter system.

Eliminating the Commuter System

Some opponents of the commuter system would like to see all commuters prohibited. But eliminating the commuter system immediately seems to be a harsh alternative. Since the system of commuting has been sanctioned administratively by the United States for over 40 years, the commuters have obtained their immigrant status on the good faith assurance that the United States would not change an administrative practice of such long standing. An abrupt change could create serious personal hardships for the commuters and would probably cause diplomatic difficulties with both Canada and Mexico. Closing the border to commuters could also result in a great increase in illegal entrants. Terminating the commuter system over a period of time might prevent some of the difficulties mentioned. At least it would make it possible for the U.S. communities to start constructing housing and schools to meet anticipated needs and for the commuters to plan how to move their families to this country.

If the government were to adopt this alternative, it could eliminate commuter status as of a certain date. Only those aliens already having "green cards" would be permitted to continue to cross the border to jobs in the United States. The question then becomes how long they would be permitted to continue commuting. If they were permitted to continue indefinitely, there would be minimal hardship on Mexican commuters' families. Families would not have to be uprooted, and the commuter practice would disappear through attrition, since no new commuter cards would be issued, not even to family members.

Alternatively, the present commuters could be given a time period, say a period of two to five years, in which to make the transition from Mexican residents to bona fide U.S. residents or lose their immigrant status. Under this alternative, special arrangements would probably have to be made to give the immediate families of present commuters unique consideration in regard to the Western Hemisphere annual immigration ceiling of 120,000. The family members could be admitted on a one-time-only basis without regard to this ceiling during the transition period, or additional numbers could be added to the ceiling to take care of those already on the waiting list. A bill (S. 3545) introduced by Senator Edmund S. Muskie on March 4, 1970, would accommodate the family members by the addition of numbers to the Western Hemisphere immigration ceiling for a two-year period following the effective date of the bill.

A recent survey of commuters[12] reveals that between 80 and 90 percent of all commuters would want to move to the United States if commuting were no longer permitted. An influx of between 40,000 and 45,000 commuters and their families could create a massive shortage of housing, education, and other public services. If that number of commuters decided to take up permanent residence in the United States and were able to bring their families with them, a Mexican population of between 200,000 and 300,000 people could be expected to move to the United States in a relatively brief span of time. Probably a small proportion of these families would try to move to areas away from the border, but a majority could be expected to reside in the U.S. border towns.

Absorbing such large numbers of Mexicans would be an intolerable financial burden for the border communities. Income generated by the new residents through the payment of rents or mortgage loans, payments for utilities, and local taxes would be more than offset by the cost of providing low-income housing, schools, sanitation, and other services. At least in the early years, federal and state aid would undoubtedly be needed. Administration of such a program might be similar to that provided in federally impacted areas, or to that provided to Cuban refugees since the revolution which brought Fidel Castro into power.[13]

Strenuous efforts at all levels of government and by private organizations would have to be made to attract new industries to the U.S. border towns so that the change in the commuter system would not result in added burdens of underemployment and unemployment. Large scale training and education programs coupled to credit availability, tax relief, and other programs would make these incentives even more attractive. Consideration might also be given to mobility and relocation assistance to help both local residents and immigrants who are not able to find employment or who want to locate elsewhere. If the numbers who locate away from the border area are sufficiently large and if they tend to concentrate in specific locations, these localities might also need financial assistance.

Labor Certification

Much of the controversy centering around the commuter system stems from the effect that commuters have on wages and employment levels in the border communities. Because large numbers of commuters, indeed the bulk of them according to Immigration and Naturalization Service officials, are not required to get labor certification because of their relationship to a citizen or an immigrant, current labor certification procedures have little impact on the regulation of commuter traffic. If the decision is made to permit the continuation of commuting, or to continue it only for those Mexicans who are commuters as of a certain date, consideration should be given to changing the labor certification requirements. At the present time, immigrants to this country need to be certified only once, at the time of application, and then only if the immigrant applicant is a parent, spouse, or child of a U.S. citizen or resident alien.[14] To be effective in controlling the numbers of commuters from Mexico (and Canada), the certification by the Secretary of Labor would have to apply to all commuters, or be required at periodic intervals.

Under the present Immigration and Nationality Act, labor certifications are made either through the use of lists of occupations (schedules), which permit the processing of applications without individual review by the Department of Labor, or by individual case review. These methods are responsive to economic and manpower conditions and expedite the processing of cases. The wage level used is that prevailing for the occupation. The legislative proposals currently before Congress would not change the present method of certification; they would merely require it periodically.

If, in addition, the exceptions to the labor certification requirement were tightened and an adverse effect wage were added to the certification language, the procedure of labor certification might be more effective in limiting the numbers of commuters from Mexico. For example, the exception from labor certification applying to Western Hemisphere immigrants could be amended to prevent the automatic exception of the parents of children under a certain age. (Many Mexican children are U.S. citizens by virtue of having been born in a U.S. border city hospital but have never lived in this country.) Also, an adverse effect wage requirement could be added which would require commuters to be paid at a somewhat higher rate than the prevailing wage. This might have the advantage of preventing wage competition by Mexicans and pushing local prevailing wages upward. Administration of an adverse effect wage that is higher than the prevailing wage could be very cumbersome unless a system of wage information, similar to the occupation schedules, could be developed.

If a change in the system is made, it would be useful to provide safeguards in the new system to prevent commuters from losing their immigrant status immediately if their jobs would not qualify for recertification and to prevent unscrupulous employers from abusing the commuters. The safeguard would allow for a specified interval during which the commuter could seek another job or move to the United States.

Work Permit

An alternative to the commuter system would be to institute a new nonimmigrant border crossing card—the nonresident work permit. This alternative would permit workers living in Canada or Mexico to work in the United States at jobs where qualified U.S. residents were not available. The work permit could be issued for a specified period of time and would be renewable if the condition under which it was originally granted continued to exist. A periodic review to make such a determination would be required. Care should be taken that this system not be used to exploit the foreign worker and that more than a pro forma certification of lack of availability of resident workers is made before issuing the work permit.

Other Alternatives

Commutation Tax

Commuters are frequently cited as a financial drain on the muncipal services of U.S. border cities because they pay no property or school taxes, yet use many local services. It has been suggested[15] that a weekly commutation tax, collected from the employers, would help pay for these services. A tax of $1 a week per commuter would provide $2.5 million annually (50 weeks times 50,000 commuters), which could be divided among the local, county, state, and federal governments. While such a tax might not be a serious financial liability for employers, it might be enough of an administrative problem that it would encourage employers to hire U.S. residents instead of Mexican commuters. Such a tax could also be paid by the commuters themselves as a payroll deduction. This would put the tax burden on the commuters who are already earning only a minimum salary in most cases; but, since living costs on the Mexican side of the border are lower than on the U.S. side, this tax might be tolerable.

Commuter Ticket

Large numbers of people in the United States commute daily on the railroads from their residences in the suburbs to their jobs in the cities. A similar system could be developed for border commuters. Cards or tickets could be issued subject to labor certification rather than a fee. A fee could also be charged, that would in effect be a commuter tax added to the commuter ticket. In any event, the card or ticket would be punched or picked up automatically each time the commuter crosses into the States, and an accurate record would simultaneously be made of the number crossing on any one day.

Local Initiative

There are steps which the border area people themselves can take to reduce the abuses of the commuter practice and to provide greater opportunities for U.S. residents. Chambers of commerce, industrial development groups, state employment offices, women's organizations, and other business and service groups could begin a major campaign to give job preference to U.S. residents. Some employers in border cities already do this. Since many commuters have U.S. addresses, such a campaign would force employers and workers alike to prove that a worker's U.S. address is a bona fide residence which he inhabits.

Local businessmen, instead of advertising the special advantages of establishing plants in the Mexican border area, might advertise the benefits of a U.S. border location and aggressively seek the means of raising local revenues to provide favorable plant sites, good transportation to and from major markets, and other facilities.

Workers in the border area could strive to make their state employment security agencies provide manpower services in a more effective manner. They could do this individually or work through their own Mexican American organizations or their unions. Union organization in most of the border area is very weak, because of obstacles put up by employers and state laws and because of the surplus of labor in the border area. However, the major unions have few organizing campaigns in the border area outside of southern California.

Conclusions

In various studies, the following adverse effects of the commuter system have been identified:

- Wages are lower along the border because of the impact of the commuter.

- Unemployment is higher in areas where commuters are present.
- The incidence of violations of the wage and hour law is greater in the border area.
- Collective bargaining in the border areas is hampered by the availability of commuter workers.

There are difficulties, however, in changing the present system which has had legal validity for so many years. Mexican nonresident aliens, as well as many U.S. border residents, consider it a right. The economies and the social and political climate of the border communities have been shaped by the availability of a large pool of low-skill and relatively low-wage Mexican labor.

A number of alternative solutions to the commuter system have been suggested. A major consideration in choosing any alternative or combination of alternatives is that an abrupt end to the practice of commuting would result in hardships for both the commuters and their families and for the U.S. border cities in which they work. The studies that have been made conclude that, if forced to choose between taking up permanent residence in the United States or surrendering their "green cards," an overwhelming proportion—as high as 80 or 90 percent— of the commuters would move to the U.S. side of the border. They would become residents of communities which may already be in some economic distress and are ill-equipped to handle unanticipated massive demands for services. If the commuters and their families are to be relocated without seriously disrupting these border communities, provision must be made to ensure the availability of basic services such as housing, education, medical care, and family assistance and to expand employment opportunities.

NOTES

1. There are also Canadian commuters, but because of more similar wage and other labor standards between Canada and the United States, the employment of Canadian workers does not have the depressing economic effect that the employment of Mexican workers has.

2. Until July 1, 1968, when an annual ceiling of 120,000 was imposed there was no numerical limitation on immigration from independent Western Hemisphere countries and the Canal Zone.

3. Immigration and Naturalization Service officials have stated that this exclusion means that the "bulk" of immigrants from Mexico do not need labor certification.

4. At the time this survey was conducted, seasonal agricultural employment was at or near its peak in the border areas. Among the commuters who listed farm work as their occupation were 7,743 who had been doing migratory farm work in the United States but were then back in the border area and commuting from Mexico. Had they not been identified as commuters at that time, it is likely that they would now be counted as seasonal

workers, that is, Mexicans with immigrant visas who enter the United States and follow the crops, returning to Mexico to live at the end of the season. Since August 1968 the Immigration and Naturalization Service has listed these aliens as seasonal workers, and by December 1969 had identified 4,628 of them in an unduplicated, noncumulative count.

5. Brian Scott Rungeling, "Impact of Mexican Alien Commuters on the Apparel Industry of El Paso (A Case Study)" (Ph. D. dissertation, University of Kentucky, 1969), p. 74.

6. Stanley M. Knebel, "Restrictive Immigration Standards: Probable Impact on Mexican Alien Commuter," *Farm Labor Developments* (U.S. Department of Labor), November 1968.

7. A subsample of eight gasoline service stations employing less than five commuters was also included.

8. Rungeling, "Apparel Industry," chapters IV and V.

9. Committees of the Cooperative Area Manpower Planning System (CAMPS). Composed of officials working with manpower and related matters, these committees are organized at local, state, regional, and national levels, the initial local plans being acted on and consolidated at successively higher levels.

10. See Anna-Stina Ericson, "An Analysis of Mexico's Border Industrialization Program," *Monthly Labor Review*, May 1970, pp. 33–40.

11. "Alien Labor, Commuters and Immigration Reform," in *Texas Migrant Labor, The 1968 Migration* (Texas Good Neighbor Commission, 1969), p. 5.

12. David S. North, "The Border Crossers, People Who Live in Mexico and Work in the United States," September 1, 1969, draft of a study financed under a Manpower Administration Research Contract, p. 225.

13. The number of Cuban refugees who have been registered in the Cuban Refugee Program (which is entirely voluntary) since it began in January 1959 was 366,902 as of March 20, 1970. Of these, 242,606 have been resettled in over 3,000 communities in 50 states. (Department of Health, Education, and Welfare, Office of the Cuban Refugee Program.)

14. This exception applies to all Western Hemisphere applicants. The exception is slightly different for Eastern Hemisphere applicants.

15. North, "The Border Crossers" p. 254.

VI

Mexico's Border Industrialization Program[1]

The final section of this book deals with a form of Mexican labor which does not actually enter the United States. These workers are employed in Mexico's Border Industrialization Program, and the factories in which they work are known as *maquiladoras*. They are included in this book because this program was deliberately designed by the Mexican government as a functional substitute for the bracero program which ended in 1964. And like the bracero system, the Border Industrialization Program supplies Mexican labor for American employers. The difference is that in the former case Mexican labor came to the United States whereas under the new program, American firms go to Mexico and use the labor there.

Although Mexican officials had never been completely satisfied with the bracero program, many of them viewed its termination with apprehension. That they did so is not surprising because for over two decades it had provided jobs for massive numbers of Mexican nationals. Many people saw it as a sort of safety valve for Mexican society, plagued as it was with widespread unemployment and underemployment. As the bracero program drew to a close, the key problem from Mexico's perspective was how it could create new jobs *within* Mexico as a means of offsetting the loss of bracero jobs.

Mexico's answer to this problem was the Border Industrialization Program, inaugurated in 1966. It was designed to attract foreign manufacturing operations, especially those involving assembly, to locate within Mexico. They were to participate under terms designed to protect both Mexican labor and Mexican manufacturers. At least 90 percent of the workers at each factory were to be Mexican and all goods produced were to be exported from Mexico. Although the program was flexible enough to permit participation by firms other than American, the overriding goal was to attract United States factories which would produce for the vast United States market.

This program has often been called the "twin plant" concept because it ordinarily involves close relationships between a major United States parent corporation and its branch assembly plant in Mexico. However, the Mexican operation is sometimes subcontracted to a separate company. Ordinarily "labor-intensive portions of an assembly operation would be done in the Mexican plant where wages are low, whereas the capital-intensive production and machinery, or portions for which special tariff advantages are not available, remained in the United States."[2] Typically components are shipped from the United States, assembled in Mexico, then returned to the United States for the finishing and shipping phase. Consequently, the success of the program has been heavily dependent upon the tariff provisions of both countries. So long as the finished products are exported, Mexico permits the raw materials and component parts to enter duty-free. And when the products re-enter the United States, this country's tariff is levied only against value added to them while they were in Mexico.

Initially, the program provided that the foreign corporations were to be located in that area of Mexico that extends twelve-and-a-half miles from the United States border. Two major considerations prompted this decision: the chronic unemployment of this rapidly growing region and its closeness to the United States market. Since then the provisions have been altered to allow the plants to locate also in other areas of Mexico. However, the border zone still contains most of the shops.

The number of American firms participating in the Border Industrialization Program has increased rapidly. From 72 in 1967, they had climbed to 665 in 1974. Goods assembled or processed cover a broad spectrum, ranging from electronics to clothing and toys. Some of the shops have as few as three workers while others are operated by such giants as Motorola, General Electric, and Hughes Aircraft each employing hundreds of Mexicans.

The program's obvious benefit to Mexico lies in its creation of desperately needed jobs. However, Mexican officials view it with some reservations. Ever since Mexico's revolution, the emphasis has been on Mexicanization of the economy, yet the Border Industrialization Program has brought new dependence upon foreign capital and foreign markets as well as vulnerability to changes in United States tariff provisions.

For American corporations, the attractiveness of the program lies primarily in the abundance of cheap Mexican labor. Many of them have claimed that they were priced out of the United States labor market by high wage demands combined with increasingly keen competition from products manufactured with cheap labor in Europe and Asia.

From the perspective of American labor unions, these firms have grossly exaggerated their inability to afford American labor. What they really want is a labor force without significant bargaining power, and, according to the unions, Mexico's desperate need for the jobs goes a long way toward assuring such a docile labor force.

The selection by David Lopez, an AFL-CIO field representative in Texas, is illustrative of this union perspective. In the Border Industrialization Program, he sees a continuation of the historic efforts of American employers to undermine American labor. And he sees the United States government as a crucial actor in this antilabor scheme. Lopez also develops the theme that the program involves extensive exploitation of increasingly bitter Mexican workers.

The next selection is an American State Department report on the Border Industrialization Program. It examines the legal basis of the program, the reasons for its growth, the nature and number of participating firms, sources of capital, the nature of the Mexican labor force used in the program, the program's effect on United States border cities, and prospects for the future.

The final selection, reprinted from an official Mexican publication, argues that the Border Industrialization Program benefits investors, Mexico, and the economies of countries in which participating firms have their home base. The article also explores the legal foundations of the program.

NOTES

1. On the Border Industrialization Program, see: Donald W. Baerresen, *The Border Industrialization Program of Mexico* (Lexington, Mass.: D.C. Heath & Co., 1971); North American Congress on Latin America, "Hit and Run: U.S. Runaway Shops on the Mexican Border," *NACLA's Latin America and Empire Report* 9 (July-August 1975): 1–30; Peter Van der Spek, "Mexico's Booming Border Zone: A Magnet for Labor Intensive American Plants," *Inter-American Economic Affairs* 29 (Summer 1975): 33–47; "Mexico Fears U.S. Border Industries Periled," *Los Angeles Times*, 6 November 1970, p. 1.

2. North American Congress on Latin America, "Hit and Run: U.S. Runaway Shops on the Mexican Border," p. 7.

32

"Low-Wage Lures South of the Border"

David T. Lopez

From the boundless beaches where the Rio Grande joins the Gulf of Mexico at the tip of Texas, our southern border runs up the river, then turns west under New Mexico, Arizona, and California, meeting the Pacific near San Diego.

The 1,800-mile-long border area between the United States and Mexico is one of sharp contrasts. There are lush orange groves and arid goat country, deep canyons and flatlands, teeming urban centers and desolate wastelands.

As far back as one cares to go, however, there has been one common denominator for the land and the people of the border: a chronic, pervasive poverty that has joined citizens of both the United States and Mexico in an endless communion of despair.

For generations, the root of the economic problem has been the worker who resides in Mexico, where the living is cheap, but who is allowed by a twisted immigration law to work in the United States.

The Mexican "commuter," as he is known, will work for as little as 35 or 50 cents an hour so he is eagerly sought out by employers while many United States residents are unemployed most of the year.

When a union on the border strikes there is an endless supply of "commuter" strikebreakers, delighted to work at the federal minimum wage.

The "commuter" system made a border city, Laredo, Texas, "the poorest city in the country," according to a national news magazine, and a border county, Starr County. Texas, scene of beatings of striking farm workers by Texas Rangers, the county with the lowest family income in the nation.

Insistent protests by organized labor at local, state, and national levels have limited the problem of what the Immigration Service calls the "nonresident alien." But token action was enough to move employers into coming up with an even more insidious and devastating program.

David T. Lopez, "Low-Wage Lures South of the Border," *AFL-CIO American Federationist* 76, no. 6 (1969): 1–7. Reprinted by permission of *AFL-CIO American Federationist*, the official monthly magazine of the AFL-CIO.

The new plan is known by many names: PRONAF (from the Spanish-language words for National Border Program), or the Border Industrialization Program, or—to the American unions which have seen hundreds of jobs rush across the border—"runaway plants."

Regardless of the name, the program was aptly described by Dr. Ramiro Casso of McAllen, Texas, a physician friendly to the farm workers, as "bringing the mountain to Mohammed."

"They figured they might not be able to keep bringing in cheap labor from Mexico to jobs in this country, so they are taking the jobs out of the country to the cheap labor in Mexico," Dr. Casso said.

In essence, the plan, supported by the governments of both countries, is for American businesses to set up along a zone 12.5 miles deep just across the border in Mexico. The attractions offered are special tax and tariff concessions by Mexico, similar tariff concessions by the United States, and labor at sweat-shop rates.

The cheap-wage attraction is loudly touted by chambers of commerce on both sides of the border.

J. Carl Meyer, executive secretary of the Development Authority for Tucson's Expansion (DATE), boasts, "The Mexican border station at Nogales marks the gateway to an inexhaustible 30-cent-an-hour labor supply." Nogales, on the border, is an hour's drive from Tucson in southern Arizona.

Why would Tucson be so anxious to lure plants to Mexico? The answer is what promoters of the runaway industries call the "twin-plant concept." Supposedly, this calls for the company to set up a plant on the United States side of the border to be the "twin" of the one in Mexico.

Actually, the "twins" on the U.S. side, if and when they are established, turn out at best to resemble poor cousins. They employ far fewer workers and are designed mainly to justify a special import tariff on the Mexican-manufactured goods, which supposedly are to be "finished" in this country.

An example of the concept is the "twins" of Transitron, an electronics component manufacturer, employing about 75 in Laredo and 1,500 in Nuevo Laredo, Mexico.

"Finishing" could mean little more than pasting on a label. Many plants on the U.S. side hire Mexican residents anyway. Attempts to organize are met by threats to move the rest of the operation to Mexico. And for every job supposedly established on the American side, at least 10 jobs are being set up in Mexico and often at the direct expense of American workers.

The United Rubber Workers represent employes of Mattel, the toy manufacturer, at two plants in the Los Angeles area. Since Mattel opened a toy plant in Mexicali in 1967, some 820 union workers at the City of Industry plant have lost their jobs, and the Hawthorne operation has been similarly affected.

The losses can be documented by shift and job classification, but a Mattel excutive denied to the *Los Angeles Times* that a single job has been lost. Other less restrained entrepreneurs talk about the program creating "new jobs" for the United States.

More revealing, however, are statements made by officers of a company that specializes in subcontracting electronic assembly work in Tijuana, Mexico, near San Diego.

Enrique Mier y Teran, manager of IMEC, S.A., the Mexican branch of International Manufacturing, Electronics and Consulting Corp., puts it plainly: "I believe tremendously that the future of Tijuana lies in selling its labor."

At the Beverly Hills offices of IMEC, a division of that Republic Corp. conglomerate, R. Lee Hill, operations manager, said: "We should ship $800,000 to $1,000,000 in labor (from Tijuana) in 1969."

Trinkets sold to tourists in border markets may bear an imprint, "Made in Mexico," but the products of the special industry program not only are not labeled, but often are even hard to trace. Portable television sets sold by Sears, Roebuck and Co., for example, are bought from Warwick Electronics Inc. of Chicago, which initially subcontracted the work to IMEC, S.A., in Tijuana.

Kayser-Roth has its Catalina-brand sportswear cut at two small plants in California and Arizona, but the sewing is done at a larger operation in Mexicali, Mexico.

District 12 President Bill Drohan of the IUE in Los Angeles said that among the firms represented in the expanding electronics complex in Tijuana are Litton Industries, Control Data Corp., and Fairchild Camera. Dozens of less well-known electronic firms are scattered throughout the border area.

Vice President Leonard Levy, director of the Amalgamated Clothing Workers West Coast Region, reports getting worried calls from his staff as more of the companies represented by the union establish Mexican operations.

"El Paso, where probably more work pants and sports slacks are manufactured than any other place in the country, stands to be hurt very badly," Levy said. "Just recently, Hicks-Ponder, which has three plants in Texas and Arizona, set up in Juárez (across from El Paso). And I just got a call from a representative in El Paso. He said a company where we are hoping to get an election soon is talking about going to Mexico."

Amalgamated has organized many of the Mexican residents commuting to U.S. jobs, helping them get fair wages. Recently, however, there have been so many "illegals" (in Texas known as "wetbacks" because they sometimes wade the Rio Grande) that there is conjecture about employer "deals" with immigration officers.

At the office of the International Ladies Garment Workers Union in Los Angeles, Vice President Sam Otto said that already there are about 30 American garment plants in Mexicali and about 20 in Tijuana.

"In Mexicali, where the border is a tall wire fence, the American and Mexican plants are almost side by side," Otto said. "Some cutting is done on this side, and sometimes when the water pressure in Mexico is not enough, they press the clothes on this side, but the rest of the work is done in Mexico."

"But you sure don't see many 'Made in Mexico' labels, and of course, not enough union labels," he added.

Among the actions called for by the AFL-CIO Executive Council in its February 1969 statement on U.S.-Mexican Border Problems was the adequate labeling of goods wholly or partially manufactured in the Mexico border plants.

The U.S. State Department tried to discourage opposition to the Mexican plan when it began in 1966 by assuring American labor that American plants would not be moved, that the idea was to move to Mexico plants which otherwise would have become established in other low-wage areas abroad, such as Hong Kong or Taiwan.

The line was echoed by the Mexican government. Mexican Minister of Industry and Commerce Octaviano Campos Salas, in a press conference August 6, 1968, told reporters: "The Mexican government does not encourage a massive exodus of American companies to the Mexican side of the border . . . especially when they operate normally and profitably in the United States."

Less than one year later, it is apparent that there is an increasing exodus of jobs and industries from the United States, perhaps without Mexican "encouragement," but certainly with the same considerable concession given to any others.

The Mattel experience of the United Rubber Workers, and the manifold problems of the Amalgamated Clothing Workers and the ILGWU, certainly are not isolated examples.

When Transitron opened its plant in Nuevo Laredo, Mexico, employing some 1,500 electronic assemblers, a similar operation of the same company in Kansas City, Mo., lost about 45 percent of its work force. When the plant in Mexico had a three-week work stoppage, employment and overtime shot up in Kansas City only to fall again at the end of the stoppage.

Standard Components Division of Standard Kollsman Industries, which opened a television tuner plant in Ciudad Acuña, across from Del Rio, Texas, has announced it may double production in 1970, with possible displacement of 800 workers in a similar plant of the company in Oshkosh, Wis.

IUE President Paul Jennings, who with AFL-CIO Vice Presidents Joseph D. Keenan, David Dubinsky, and Jacob Potofsky served as a special subcommittee of the AFL-CIO Executive Council studying the problem, said that 48,000 jobs in the manufacture of radio and television sets and components alone were lost from 1966 to 1968.

In Harlingen, Texas, close to the border, the Albertti Seafoods Co. won a decertification election against the Amalgamated Meat Cutters and Butcher Workmen, then moved most of its Texas plant into an expanded operation in Mexico.

Two other plants organized by the Butchers in the area, Booth Fisheries and United Foods, both processors of shrimp have decreased their operations tremendously, displacing more than 1,000 workers since similar processing plants opened just across the border.

Last year, a newsletter which analyses Latin American affairs in the United States said that Mexican economists are projecting an eventual employment of 300,000 workers by the border industries, with a production of one billion dollars of goods a year, multiplying tenfold the already serious effect of the program on American unions and the considerable impairment of the federal minimum wage law.

Two agents of IMEC are reported contacting electronic plants in Southern California. An American company which provides sewing machines for the Mexican garment plants reportedly has trucks soliciting manufacturers in Los Angeles to send their cut patterns to be sewn in Mexico.

Nowhere in the elaborate brochures and prospectuses prepared by DATE of Tucson, or the El Paso Chamber of Commerce, or Joe Richards and Associates of Laredo, is there any mention of the Mexican program being an alternative to plants in Europe or the Far East. Their approach is direct: "If you have a labor-intensive production, move to Mexico." The same pitch is carried in Wall Street Journal advertisements.

Joe Richards and Associates says in its brochure: "The only requirements for participation in Mexico's border industrialization program are that production be exported in its entirety and that Mexican labor be used." The firm offers assistance in securing permits, handling customs, furnishing legal and other professional services, compiling statistics, negotiating leases, and selling and financing the product "worldwide," according to the brochure.

Exactly which manufacturers are being lured to Mexico is virtually impossible to determine before the fact, and the established plants are as easy to inspect as the Chinese Communist atomic plants. Photographers hired in Laredo, El Paso, and San Diego all were unable to come up with pictures inside existing plants. They said they were denied permission to enter the plants and shooed away by guards.

United Press International, in a recent dispatch, noted, "The stampede of American firms for locations south of the border has been a quiet one. Most of them are so security conscious they won't even admit what they manufacture until they actually have signed the papers and agreed to build their plants in Mexico."

The government has joined the hide-and-seek game. A meeting in El Paso last April to tempt U.S. manufacturers to go into Mexico was sponsored by the U.S. Department of Commerce as an "Executive Conference on World Trade." Jennings, protesting to President Nixon, said in a telegram: "The Department of Commerce has no business serving as a front for international cheap labor manipulators." A similar conference was held in Brownsville in May, and more are scheduled.

The solicitousness of the government toward businessmen is not matched by its attitude toward labor. Henry Muñoz Jr., equal opportunities director of the Texas AFL-CIO, requested information on the borde program in February 1968, from Raymond Télles, until recently chairman of the U.S. Section of the U.S.-Mexico Commission for Border Development and Friendship.

When Muñoz got a reply, it was five months later, from the State Department. The letter said: "Unfortunately most of the information you requested is unavailable to us."

Andres Sandoval, a Texas AFL-CIO field representative, said that he asked Télles about the border industry program, and Télles replied: "What border are you speaking of?"

Speaking to a group of businessmen on the program, former U.S. Ambassador to Mexico Fulton J. Freeman said, "I have great confidence that this 1,800-mile boundary can continue to serve as an inspiring example of constructive and harmonious relations and of actions to the mutual benefit of two friendly neighboring nations."

The "inspiring example" may be as disastrous for Mexico as it is for the United States.

In Nuevo Laredo, a 19-year-old girl named Maria Luisa sees her new job with Transitron in terms of a chance to get out of Mexico. "Well, maybe now I have a better chance of going to the United States," she said. "Maybe I'll get a chance to learn something."

Last year, Maria Luisa was a live-in maid, earning the equivalent of $8 a week, her meals and Sunday off. She said she still works six days, long hours at more intensive work, and now takes home $14 a week. She went through the three-week stoppage because, among other things, workers were not getting the mandatory one-half hour off for lunch.

"They say we are going to get $26 a week when we finish our training, but who knows?" Maria Luisa said. "I have been working here more than seven months now. We all know the government, in order to bring these factories down, made a deal with the United States so that they don't have to pay us good money like they pay the American workers."

How much does she think U.S. workers get? "At least $60 or $75 a week," she said. "We ought to get the same for the same work. Well, maybe at least $50."

Through joint border committees, AFL-CIO unions along the border share information freely with their counterparts in the Mexican Confederation of Workers (CTM), and Maria Luisa's union representatives will have a chance to know exactly how much American workers are getting for the same jobs under an IUE contract.

In negotiations with other electronics manufacturers, however, CTM representatives recently report they were told by the employers that the government would not authorize any more than a 10 percent increase from the present earnings around the Mexican minimum wage because the workers were not classed as "professionals."

Ambassador Freeman listed as one of the alleged benefits of the industry program that residents of the Mexican side of the border spend 50 to 80 percent of their earnings in the United States.

IUE Representative Juan Mariscal, a native of Mexico, recently conducted an extensive survey, and his findings are much different. Housing, food, and services, including medical attention, are at least 50 percent cheaper on the Mexican side of the border, he said. Consumer goods like clothes and appliances are priced about the same.

If Freeman were correct, then, the Mexican workers earning about $25 a week or less, would spend most of that either for expensive consumer goods made in the U.S., or for items which they can get more cheaply in Mexico.

Asked if she shops in the United States, Maria Luisa replied angrily, "Are you crazy? You forget I get paid Mexican wages. Maybe I could buy some of the used clothing sold from boxes on the sidewalks, but the 'gringos' can keep that junk."

The only times she has been shopping in the United States, she said, have been when her cousin, a secretary in Mexico City, sends her some money to buy her some clothes or cosmetics not available in Mexico. "She always tells me to get something for myself," Maria Luisa said. "I get some hose, or maybe a sweater."

Ambassador Freeman's confusion is perhaps understandable. American shops on the border do sell a large quantity of consumer goods, particularly clothing and cosmetics, to Mexicans.

A simple check with store clerks, however, quickly shows that these are of the most expensive merchandise, almost always to businessmen, artists, or government officials from Mexico City or other principal cities of the Mexican interior. The buyers spend $300 or $400 cash at a time. They certainly could not be $25-a-week industrial workers.

Maria Luisa's responses were fairly representative of those given by other workers in Matamoros, Reynosa, Piedras Negras, Ciudad Acuña, Juárez, Nogales, Mexicali, and Tijuana, border cities across or near Brownsville, McAllen, Eagle Pass, Del Rio, and El Paso, Texas; Nogales, Arizona, and Calexico and San Diego, California. In sum, Maria Luisa does not feel particularly lucky in having found an industrial job.

"I don't like to be treated badly," she said. "The señora where I was a maid was very nice to me. At the job now I'm always nervous."

A manager of one of the Tijuana plants would be surprised to hear such comments. He considers that American business is a blessing to the Mexican workers. "You can always tell a new gal," he said. "The first couple of days they gobble up six or seven doughnuts at every break."

Maria Luisa said: "I work on these small things under a microscope, and they get very angry if we make any mistake or if we don't work fast enough. The foreman always is trying to date us, and if we say no, we have problems, or we can get fired."

Professor Pedro Pérez Ibarra, general secretary both of the Nuevo Laredo CTM and the electronic workers local, describes Maria Luisa's bosses as "slave drivers of the worst sort."

He said he believes the three-week stoppage at Transitron was only the beginning of their problems. "These companies feel that Mexico is just a field ripe for exploitation," he said. "We're going to show them that's not so."

American plants are being established in the Mexico border zone so quickly, and security is so tight, that up-to-date figures are hard to get. Most observers estimate that already there are 30,000 to 50,000 workers employed in the runaway plants, but the total easily could exceed twice that.

There is general agreement, however, that at least 75 percent of the employes are women. Mariscal says that has created another problem.

"They are destroying the Mexican family along the border," he said. "Up to just a few years ago, Mexican women did not work outside the home after they were married. Now you see many wives working while the husbands are unemployed."

"Mexicans are proud, and nothing hurts a man's pride more than to feel 'mantenido' (kept) by his woman," he said. "Some of the men can't cope with it. They take to drinking, or they cross the border illegally to try to find work. Many don't go back."

A number of economists have pointed out other adverse effects the program probably will have in Mexico. One article suggests that productivity is significantly lower in Mexican plants, and that even the great disparity in wages may not be sufficient to keep the plants in Mexico long.

The same article claims that many companies are moving to Mexico just to postpone major capital investments in modern equipment. When the companies finally are forced to make the investment, they probably will want to return to the better-trained American workers. A sudden withdrawal of such companies and the resulting unemployment would leave the area worse off than it was before the plants came in, according to the economists.

Several plants established in Tijuana have shut down, but information on the reasons is skimpy and conflicting at this time.

What is proving to be easily the most regrettable effect of the program on either side, however, is that the promise of new jobs acts like a magnet to attract thousands of families from the Mexican interior to the already overcrowded Mexican border cities.

Because of the "commuter" practice and the "bracero" agreement for Mexican farm labor (now terminated), Tijuana exploded in 30 years from 20,000 to 400,000 population. Unemployment now is estimated at close to 50 percent, and more people arrive daily.

Approaching Tijuana, or Juárez, which also has multiplied rapidly to its present 500,000 population, one is struck by the pathetic sight of countless slum dwellings precariously clinging to the hillsides.

Recent Mexican government figures indicate the country's population is rapidly urbanizing, but a full 25 percent still is "economically inactive." There are so many peasants migrating to Mexico City and the cities of the northern Mexico border that they have become a national institution with a popular nickname.

Partly because of the way they load all their belongings on their backs, and mostly because they have no idea where they will land once they leave their rural homes, these migrating peasants are known as "parachutists."

For a family of such "paracaidistas," Estéban Macías, 34, his wife and their seven children, their landing was in an unimaginably squalid slum overlooking El Paso across the border.

For almost three months, they lived in a cave, until they could gather enough scraps of wood, cardboard and flattened tin cans to make a shack which does not look like it could stand a healthy sneeze.

Macías was no stranger to poverty, but on the border the oppressive struggle for existence has left him drained and submissive, an old man before 40. "My life is gone, and I have nothing," he said. "Nothing for me. Nothing to leave my children."

The Macías family increasingly is dependent for support on Susano, at 15 the oldest son, who is a "commuter."

Officially, the U.S. government counts 12,000 "commuters" crossing from Ciudad Juárez to jobs in El Paso. The figure certainly is more likely twice that. Susano, who just a few months ago had never seen the United States is not counted as a "Mexican alien commuter," and neither are about 45 to 65 percent of the "commuters" who cross with documents purporting to prove they are American citizens.

Some of the "commuters" actually are citizens. Susano, not having been born in the United States, "rents" a birth certificate. For $2 paid in advance, he can use the certificate for one day to cross into the United States, where he can earn $6 to $8, if he finds work.

When there is no work, he's out $2, and if he doesn't like the deal, there are plenty others waiting to take his place.

"Sometimes I have to work for even $3 a day, just to pay for 'el pasaporte,' bridge toll or bus fare, and have something left over to feed my little brothers," Susano said.

If he doesn't maintain himself as a steady customer, someone about his age (and the age on the birth certificate) will be found and will be taught by rote the facts on the document which immigration officials, if they have the time, will ask: "Where were you born? On what date? What is your mother's name?"

If he loses his turn, Susano will have to take his chances with jobs on the Mexican side, where the going rate is about 75 cents a day and work is much harder to find.

The evidence of the abject poverty faced by the thousands who hoped to find a new and better life on the border is everywhere. In Tijuana, the lean-to's sit on the right-of-way between the highway to Mexicali and the fenced-off property. In Nuevo Laredo, they are but a minute from the million-dollar mansion of the Longoria family. In Matamoros and Ciudad Acuña, they trail along the river.

In Piedras Negras, a young "wetback" named Enrique described what desperation born of poverty can bring. Over coffee, obviously pained by the memory, he told this story:

"We were screaming, praying, crying. It was so hot I could feel sweat pouring down my body.

"I was suffocating, yet when I tried to breathe the stench made me dizzy and turned my stomach. I must have gone crazy for some time, because all I remember is that finally I was so tired I wouldn't move.

"I knew—we all knew—we were going to die."

Enrique was one of 47 Mexicans attempting to enter the United States illegally who were locked in a hot and unventilated van so long that all had to be hospitalized and three died.

He left his wife and five children 50 pesos, $4, for food and took the rest of their meager savings and some borrowed money to seek work in the United States. At Piedras Negras, he found a recruiter who signed him up for jobs of $2 and $3 an hour in Chicago, and offered to take him there for a fee.

In the early morning hours of September 30, 1968, Enrique and the 46 others, all from the northern Mexico countryside, huddled in the darkness near the river across from Eagle Pass. At about 2 A.M., they were led into the river and waded across, where $50 was collected from each. They then walked to a ravine near a deserted road where the man with the van picked them up around noon and collected another $50 before letting each one board.

The men were crowded into a space 7 by 16 feet, and when the door was closed the heat and lack of fresh air quickly became intolerable. They pounded on the sides and begged the driver to let them out. He replied the door had been padlocked and he did not have the key. The van was driven to San Antonio, more than 150 miles away, and there it was parked and abandoned.

Passersby heard noises from the van and called police, and the men were rescued many hours after their ordeal began. The three for whom rescue came too late received pauper's burials in San Antonio.

Enrique and the other survivors were returned to Mexico by the U.S. Immigration Service. But Enrique did not go home.

"I can't go back until I have the money to pay back what I owe and to give my wife for what she has suffered without me," he said.

That may take sometime. In Piedras Negras, working as a laborer in the day and cleaning up three bars and a restaurant at night he seldom makes as much as $12 a week. (Piedras Negras is about 75 miles from Marroteran, where 156 coal miners who were earning $6 to $17 a week recently were buried by an explosion.)

Enrique is looking for a good job, but he is not optimistic. "Every day more come. They get off the buses by the dozen. Or they say they come by train, or walking or asking for rides, anyway they can."

Why do they keep coming if there are no jobs? "They hear there's much money to be made in 'la frontera' (the border)," Enrique said. "They're fools like me. Some may be lucky, but most of them come to suffer."

"What's worse," he said, "some bring their families. Here you can't grow food. You don't have any land, or chickens, or goats for milk. For everything you have to pay.

"Those are the ones I pity. You see them get more and more desperate. Then they get drunk because some little one died, or because their daughter ran off and they think she's selling herself to the 'gringos.' At least my woman and my children, they're where they can get food, too little maybe, but still enough to live. God keep them."

Crossing from Mexicali into the U.S. at Calexico, one can't escape seeing a large sign in two languages informing "commuters" that their crossing cards, which "allow them to work in the United States" are not to be used to work at places where labor disputes have been certified by the Department of Labor. A list, the sign informs anyone interested, is available in the immigration office.

In preparation for their drive in the Coachella Valley of California, members of United Farm Workers Organizing Committee recently followed five busloads and assorted cars and pick-ups full of "commuter" farm workers going from Calexico the 90 or so miles to Coachella.

The buses stopped at many of the farms on the certified strike list, and the UFWOC members questioned the workers as they got off. They discovered that most of the "commuters" had to arise at 1 A.M. to catch the bus and had long trips home after they were returned to Calexico.

"I figured they were spending 16 hours for 8 hours pay," says the Rev. Jim Drake, an aide to UFWOC Director César Chávez. "That figures around 80 cents an hour."

"Most of them didn't know they were going to work at a struck place," Drake said. "But once they got there, they had the choice of staying in the bus for eight hours without pay, or getting commercial transportation back, or, of course, going to work. In other words, they had no choice."

In Texas, a January 1968 survey showed 80 percent of the "commuters" interviewed in Laredo were earning less than $1.60 an hour.

The presence of a seemingly limitless supply of "commuter" labor compounds the daily work of union representatives on the border.

David L. Jacobs, business agent of a Laborers local in Laredo, recalls a group of cafeteria workers striking for union recognition. "One of the pickets had a sign saying they were paid 25 cents an hour," Jacobs said. "The owner was very angry when he saw it. He said he actually was paying 32 cents."

The strike resulted in recognition and a contract calling for $1 an hour in the third year.

In El Paso, Hector R. García, president of the El Paso Central Labor Union, tells of a recent strike in which, after a 20-year bargaining history, the union had to remain out six months to keep arbitration in the agreement. García said the union struck with 250 of 256 production employees on a Thursday to see 300 strikebreakers hired by the following Monday at $1.60 an hour.

By letting selfish economic interests mold its policy toward Mexico, the United States has managed to bring about the worst imaginable situations on either side of the border.

On the United States side, there is talk of putting up picket lines at the international bridges to keep out the "commuters."

On the Mexican side, anti-American literature circulates freely and thousands of industrial workers, students, and teachers call themselves "communists" because they can't think of any other word which can adequately express their antipathy towards the United States. And one hears often repeated, not always with a smile, the plaintive lament of a former Mexican president, who said:

"Poor Mexico—so far from God—and so close to the United States."

33

"Report On Mexican Border Industry Program"

United States Department of State

Border Industry Programs

Summary

The Mexican border industry program which was established in 1965 and amplified in March, 1971, has experienced particularly rapid growth in recent months. Approximately 290 firms are presently engaged in assembly operations along the U.S. border with a total employment of about 31,000. Prospects are for continued growth during the near future with perhaps 330 firms employing almost 40,000 workers by the end of 1971. The [U.S.] Embassy estimates that total product value of these firms will reach $500 million in 1971.

The Mexican government has generated considerable publicity for the border industry program as a result of its push for exports and closer economic integration of the border area with the rest of Mexico. The authorized zone for such operations has been significantly expanded to include coastal areas, and indications are that further expansion to interior cities, on a case-by-case basis, is probable.

Although fairly extensive information concerning the program has been made available through public statements, selected studies, and promotional publications, most of it is limited in scope or significantly dated. Furthermore, a large number of essentially border industry firms have elected to operate under free zone rather than border industry provisions. This [report], therefore, has been prepared as a general analysis of the present status of the entire border industry program.

U.S. Department of State, "Border Industry Programs." Reprinted from U.S., Congress, House, 92d Cong., 1st sess., 3 November 1971, *Congressional Record* 117: 39454–56.

Legal Basis

When the bracero program which permitted temporary Mexican farm labor to enter the United States was terminated in 1965, the Mexican government was faced with an unemployment problem in northern border cities. In May, 1965, it announced a Border industrialization Program designed specifically to attract foreign manufacturing operations, particularly that involving assembly, in an effort to promote the economy of that area. The initial resolution permitted Mexican or foreign-owned (not limited to U.S.) firms to establish manufacturing operations in cities along the northern border. Such operations were confined to the customs zone of the city—effectively within 20 kilometers of the border—but not so specified. Raw materials and equipment could be imported in-bond and duty free, but all production was required to be exported.

A further resolution of March 17, 1971, extended the authorized zone to a specific 20-kilometer-wide strip along all borders and coasts, but did not change the substance of the other provisions. About 85 percent of the firms so established are U.S.-owned with the remainder Mexican owned, and all but four are located along the U.S. border. All production by firms registered under the program is exported to the U.S., although a small amount is subsequently re-exported to third countries.

The border industry program was developed solely by the Mexican government, and all participating firms are subject to relevant Mexican laws and regulations. The only U.S. government involvement in the program is through the application of appropriate U.S. import and export regulations. A large portion of the re-imports into the U.S. under this program are made under Sections 806.30 and 807.00 of the U.S. Tariff Code which provide that, under certain conditions, manufactured products of U.S. origin when re-imported into the U.S. are assessed import duties only on the value added through foreign processing. These provisions, of course, are of general application and not merely for re-imports from Mexico.

Border Industries Operating Under Special Circumstances

The Mexican government executive resolution of March 17, 1971, defines the border industry zone [as] a 20-kilometer-wide strip along all coasts and borders. Several cities along the western portion of the border (principally Tijuana, Mexicali, Nogales, and Agua Prieta) have for a number of years, however, been designated as free zones. Accordingly, firms establishing operations in such areas are not required to register with the Secretariat of Industry and Commerce as border industries in order to obtain duty-free importation privileges. Several firms were actually engaged in assembly operations in those areas before the establishment of the program, and a large number of firms (about 90) have chosen to operate under free zone as opposed to border industry regulations. Firms operating under free zone regulations, incidentally, can also sell their products in Mexico within the limits of the free zone. In practice, only a few firms producing finished products, such as radios, have actually taken advantage of this privilege.

Four firms in the interior have also been granted border industry status. Three of these are firms that found local markets insufficient to continue operation. Rather than lose the employment offered by these firms, the Mexican government has permitted them to use existing facilities for border industry-type assembly operations. Such firms are presently located in Guadalajara, San Luis Potosí, and Torreón. President Echeverría in a speech at Nuevo Laredo on May 6, 1971, also announced that border industry status was being granted to three small towns, Sabinas Hidalgo, Anáhuac Rodríguez, and Cerralvo, in the state of Nuevo León near the U.S. border but beyond the 20-kilometer limit. Most observers of the program are of the opinion that if a firm can offer sufficient economic advantage to Mexico, it will be permitted to establish a border industry plant almost anywhere in the country. Finance Minister Margain recently stated in Nogales and again in Mérida, Yucatán that more such firms should establish in the interior, not only to provide additional employment, but to avoid Mexican balance of payments loss through salary expenditures on the U.S. side of the border.

Many persons in commenting on border industry operations have identified the program with re-imports into the U.S. under Tariff Sections 806.30 and 807.00. A number of border industry plants, however, do not utilize these Sections. These firms either perform operations on which no duty is assessed (such as the Matamoros shrimp deveining industry, cleaning of scrap copper, and a number of classification operations involving commercial coupons, used clothing, and sausage casings), or operations in which transformation of the product results in full duty application (such as in railroad car disassembly, tire recapping, manufacture of most adornments, food products and furniture, and even some electronic products).

Accordingly, the Mexican government considers a "border industry" to be primarily one which a) temporarily imports most of its equipment and raw materials, and b) exports all of its production. In practice the following characteristics can also be added: c) it is either an assembly or limited processing operation, and d) is labor intensive. The Embassy has, therefore, included in its consideration of border industries those firms which meet the above characteristics but are not registered as such with the Secretariat of Industry and Commerce.

Growth

The recent growth in the number of border industry plants dates essentially from the release in October, 1970 of the U.S. Tariff Commission Report to the President on Sections 806.30 and 807.00. The Commission concluded that repeal of these two Sections "would probably result in only a modest number of jobs being returned to the U.S., which likely would be more than offset by the loss of jobs among workers now producing components for export and those who further process the imported products" and that based on 1969 data, "the net effect of repeal would be a $150-200 million deterioration in the U.S. balance of trade." Growth of the program was relatively slow under the course of the Tariff Commission study, but approximately 75 firms have begun operation since that time, and another 30-40 firms are actively considering establishment.

The Mexican government is also offering significantly more publicity to border industry operations than in the past. In March, Industry and Commerce Secretary Torres Manzo addressed a border industries seminar in Phoenix, Arizona, sponsored by the American Chamber of Commerce of Mexico. President Echeverría, accompanied by several cabinet members and numerous other high-ranking government and industry officials, recently presided at the inauguration of a new border industry plant during a visit to Nogales. The theme of the visit was economic development of the border area, and the president and other speakers dwelt at length on the importance of the program to border city economics.

Management consultant firms and both private and public industrial development groups along the border have also increased their promotional efforts as to some extent border cities compete for interested firms. Industrial parks have recently been established in several Mexican border cities and are planned for others. U.S. border city chambers of commerce have been particularly active in promoting the program on the grounds that new industries inevitably benefit both sides of the border. A number of firms also indicate that recently increased labor costs in the U.S. combined with stronger foreign competition and decreased demand have accelerated establishment of border operations.

Principal Characteristics

Given the limitation of Mexican government statistics resulting partly from free zone activity, the Embassy has attempted its own calculations concerning the extent of border industry operations (based on the definition of border industries indicated in Section 3). While these statistics are considered reasonably accurate, they are not—and can never be—entirely exact because of the constant change involved. A number of firms are in the process of establishment; several others are known to be on the verge of discontinuing operation. Estimates concerning employment, production, and balance of payments are based on limited data available from the Mexican and U.S. governments and from the industries involved.

A. Number and nature of firms

About 290 firms are presently engaged in border industry operation and approved applications for establishment have been granted another 35 firms, of which perhaps 20 will actually set up operations. The Embassy would expect that by the end of 1971 about 330 firms (including those in the free zones) will be in operation. Almost 70 percent of these firms are engaged in the assembly of either textiles or electric-electronic products. Recently established firms show a greater diversification, however, as other industries seek to reduce labor costs. New ventures include dismantling of scrap railroad cars, diverse food processing and packaging, and assembly of musical instruments, boats, and caskets. While electronics and textiles will probably remain the bulwark of the program, their relative predominance is expected to decrease somewhat.

B. Capital

Most of the firms are wholly-owned subsidiaries of U.S. companies. Many, however, have chosen names which do not identify the parent company, and a significant number have been set up under the mantle of already existing subsidiary companies in Mexico. Accordingly, no meaningful estimate of U.S. investment is available. A rapidly growing number of companies are being set up as subcontracting operations by either U.S. or Mexican businessmen. While major operations in the area will continue to be subsidiaries of U.S. companies, the number of subcontractors, especially Mexican-owned, is expected to grow. No third country has yet established a border industry plant, although several Japanese firms have expressed interest in west coast operations.

C. Employment

Approximately 31,000 persons are presently employed in border industry operations, and this total is expected to rise to 35,000-40,000 by the end of 1971. (Employment may show fairly significant fluctuations as a result of changes in demand in the United States, primarily in electronics.) An estimated 85 percent of the employees in border industry plants are female. The electric-electronic industry supplies over 50 percent of the total employment and textiles an additional 20 percent. The tedious assembly and sewing involved in these operations are areas in which women have long been considered to be optimum employees. A few firms have experimented with male employees in these fields and found them quite satisfactory, but others have been less successful. Many of the new industries entering the border program are heavier operations which require male workers. However, these firms usually do not employ large numbers, and the over-all proportion of female employees is expected to continue to be high. Most of the employees are paid the minimum wage which, including all fringe benefits, averages about $.55 per hour. Skilled technical workers receive a significantly higher salary, and many textile firms offer piece-work incentive systems beyond the minimum wage.

D. Trade Unions

Slightly over one-half of the border industry firms are unionized—with a notably higher percentage along the eastern, as opposed to western end of the border. With only a few exceptions, labor conflicts have not been a problem for border industries. In a few cases, plant managers indicate that unionization has facilitated operation. On the other hand, labor militancy has reportedly been a major factor in limiting border industry growth in some areas—notably Reynosa and Nuevo Laredo. Mexican labor leaders, while supporting growth of the program, have expressed concern over its stability. They suggest that the Mexican government should seek assurance from the U.S. Government that no unilateral action, i.e., repeal of Sections 806.30 and 807.00, will be taken which might result in precipitate terminations of the program.

Labor leaders have also requested some form of guaranty that a firm cannot withdraw overnight leaving unpaid salaries and termination benefits. (In some smaller plants with little capital equipment, this could easily be done and was one of the early problems of the program in the Tijuana area.) Border city officials have expressed similar concern and suggested that at some later date the Mexican government may require a bond to ensure adequate employee compensation.

E. Value Added and Foreign Exchange Flow

Total production of the border industries should reach approximately $500 million in 1971. Around $350 million of this production will re-enter the U.S. under Sections 806.30 and 807.00, with duty assessed on $125 million value added in Mexico.

Value added data, however, should not be confused with foreign exchange flow. For U.S. Customs purposes the percentage of U.S.-origin components in a reimported product under Sections 806.30 and 807.00 takes into consideration only those components which have maintained their identity.

The remainder is considered "value added" for duty purposes. Accordingly, value added in Mexico may include not only labor costs, fixed overhead, and any local raw materials, but also U.S.-origin components which have been transformed (lost their identity), U.S. products consumed in processing (such as hydrogen and liquid nitrogen), and a reasonable profit margin. (Value added calculations by the Mexican government, however, include only processing costs and locally produced inputs.) The gold wire soldered to an integrated circuit, for example, is fully dutiable under Section 807.00 even though of U.S. origin since it is no longer in the spool form in which it was exported. The profit margins included in duty calculations often do not actually exist since wholly-owned subsidiaries in many instances are inctuded in parent plant costing and either have no profit on their own account or remit such profits as do exist.

Other direct factors which must be taken into consideration in calculating actual foreign exchange flow resulting from border industry operations include some electricity and natural gas (most border cities are tied into both U.S. and Mexican distribution networks) and salaries spent on the U.S. side of the border. Most observers estimate that about 60 percent (although estimates range from a low of 30 percent to a high of 80 percent) of salaries paid to border plant employees returns to the U.S. in the form of retail purchases. Finally, while only a few of the U.S. firms engaged in border assembly indicate that such operations have permitted them to increase exports to third countries, a number state that they have been able to substitute U.S.-origin components for previously imported foreign components.

F. Effect on U.S. Border Cities

Discussion of the border industries in the United States has involved considerable disagreement over the possible creation of new jobs in U.S. border cities. Statistics indicate that approximately 3,000 new industrial positions directly related to Mexican border industries (as opposed to increased service and commercial employment) have resulted along the Texas border. No adequate data are available, however, as to whether these are totally new positions or merely transferred from another section of the U.S. Texas border city officials do indicate that the presence of border industries dampened the rise in unemployment in their areas during the recent U.S. economic slow-down.

While U.S. border cities have unquestionably benefitted from the border industry program both in new industrial employment and in increased commercial activity, the "twin plant" concept has not developed to the extent originally expected. This concept encouraged U.S. firms to establish counterpart operations on both sides of the border. The products would be initially processed in the U.S. plant, shipped to the Mexican plant for labor intensive assembly or finishing, and then returned for additional operations such as inspection, finishing, packaging, and distribution. A majority of the U.S. firms involved in border industries are located in the border states, but only a limited number have established a significant manufacturing operation in U.S. border cities themselves.

6. Outlook

Given the large possibilities for labor intensive assembly combined with advanced technology, the immediate outlook for the border industry program is for continued growth, probably at a rather high rate. Mexican government officials, however, have indicated that the program will not be permitted to expand indefinitely. President Echeverría in his recent visit to Nogales stated that the "Government must for the time being, temporarily, continue facilitating the operation of border industries" (emphasis added). At the same time Industry and Commerce Secretary Torres Manzo suggested that Mexican capital should begin to play a greater role in the program. Torres Manzo subsequently noted in Tijuana on May 26, 1971, that the border industry program is a "necessary evil" which provides employment and training to local workers until such time as they may be absorbed by Mexican industries. He also stated that eventually the free zones must also be abolished and integrated into the economy of the rest of the country. Accordingly, while border industry operations will continue to be welcome in Mexico in the immediate future, the long-term goal of the present administration is toward development of Mexican industry in the area including both basic industry utilizing local raw materials and Mexican control of assembly operations.

A number of circumstances already exist which could lead to restriction of the program. Publicity concerning employment offered by border industries has resulted in increased migration to border areas. Combined with already heavy migration resulting from relatively higher border wage levels and from aspirations to enter the U.S., an ever greater demand is being placed on social responsibilities of Mexican border cities. One border city official even voiced the philosophical question of whether, considering all aspects of the border industry program over a period of several years, urban problems might not show an increase. He specifically noted possible shortages in housing, water, electricity, and medical facilities. Others have voiced particular concern over the growing sociological problem created by women rather than men becoming the chief wage earners of households.

Another factor already creating some difficulty is the shortage of technical personnel in Mexico. While border industries usually train their basic assembly employees, most industries seek to employ technicians (electricians, machinists, etc.) with existing skills. Since the supply of such persons in the border areas is limited, some firms are reported to be now recruiting in Mexico City, Monterrey, and Guadalajara.

Finally, as interested public and private officials all along the border have pointed out, the program has a basic characteristic of instability. The heavy predominance of electronics and textiles makes operations quite sensitive to change in U.S. demand. Should the products of these industries encounter a prolonged slump in the U.S. market, operations of border firms would undoubtedly be substantially reduced.

34

"Assembly Plants in Mexico"

Mexican Newsletter

Regulation of item third, Article 321, of the Customs Code of the United Mexican States went into effect on March 17. It establishes new operational norms for northern border assembly plants and enlarges their scope of action to include coastal areas.

This is the first of a series of measures to redesign official policy regarding assembly plants with the object of expanding the scale of their operations in Mexico.

These plants assemble or process temporarily imported primary materials and intermediate goods. Finished goods are exported in their entirety.

The advantages of setting up assembly plants became evident when the agreement governing the entry of seasonal workers into the United States ceased to function. They were particularly interesting as new sources of employment in an area beset by unemployment and underemployment.

[In] 1966 the Ministry of Finance and the Ministry of Industry and Commerce drew up the Northern Border Industrialization Program by which ample facilities were granted for foreign capital investment in assembly plants.

The program was aimed principally at businesses not requiring heavy investments. As an inducement it abolished the domestic capital parti-

---

"Assembly Plants in Mexico," *Mexican Newsletter,* 30 May 1971, pp. 6–7.

cipation requirement and liberalized temporary import authorizations.

Assembly plants have proliferated. Twenty companies existed in late 1966, their joint output accounting for less than 1 percent of all U.S. processed-product imports. Mexican assembly production today supplies over 12 percent of this type of U.S. import and the country holds third place as exporter.

Some 215 plants operate in Mexico at present with a total investment of 22 million dollars, providing employment for 23,000 persons. They produce mainly wooden articles, paper articles, wearing apparel, chemical products, ceramics, metallic products, office equipment, electronic products, toys, and scientific instruments.

Assembly plants enjoy the benefits of special tariff schedules set up by countries of origin for re-import of assembled or processed goods, which levy duties only on the value added outside their frontiers.

Though the United States is the largest investor in this type of industry—at least as far as Mexico is concerned—, other countries operate similarly. Canada, Germany, Belgium, the Netherlands, Italy, Great Britain, Switzerland, and Japan have also entered the field. Their tariff systems in this regard resemble those of the United States.

Assembly plant operation in Mexico is advantageous to foreign industries. It means an appreciable cut in production costs, thus improving their competitive position in world markets.

Futhermore, Mexico's proximity facilitates access to the U.S. market, increasingly invaded by Japanese, German, and Italian goods, mainly, which are beginning to displace local products.

The benefits to be derived by foreign companies from investment in assembly plants are multiple. Labor costs, for one, are considerably lower. The minimum wage rate in Mexico's northern border zone is 48 cents an hour. Labor costs in Mexican ports are even lower.

The minimum hourly wage in Germany, on the other hand, is 1.30 dollars and 94 cents in Japan.

The assembly system also stimulates employment in the investor country where the lesser cost and price of processed articles created greater demand and, in consequence, increased local production of parts and other inputs.

Mexico's extensive border with the United States—the world's largest market—constitutes a significant economic advantage for investors. It means reduced shipping costs, time-saving rapidity of communications, and easier plant control and supervision.

Mexico, moreover, accepts and encourages the establishment of assembly plants, particularly along its coasts, and reckons with infrastructure works that provide companies with external economies.

The desirability of this type of investment is evident by the way U.S. businessmen have expanded operations. The United States in 1966 imported processed products for 950 million dollars. Its current yearly imports total 1.9 billion, a 100 percent rise in only four years.

Some 1,200 U.S. companies work through the assembly plant system. There is plenty of room for expansion in Mexico since, notwithstanding its proximity to the U.S. market and the many advantages it offers to investors, it supplies only 12 percent of all U.S. processed-product imports. It is evident that many potential areas remain to be exploited.

With the object of promoting the establishment of assembly plants in Mexico, a work program has been drawn up and already set in motion. Its primary target is to gather reliable information of interest to investors.

The program's major points are: to determine the volume of U.S. imports through the assembly plant system; to publicize the advantages to be obtained from this type of investment, particularly among U.S. companies most affected by foreign competition and in other developed countries; to coordinate Mexican government and private efforts in this area.

In its initial stage the promotion is aimed at U.S., German, Italian, and Japanese investors. Socioeconomic and geographic studies of different Mexican ports and cities are under way in order to be able to provide potential investors with basic information as soon as possible.

Comparative studies relative to shipping and cargo handling costs in Mexico will soon be initiated.

Selected Bibliography

American GI Forum of Texas and Texas State Federation of Labor. *What Price Wetbacks?* Austin, Texas: GI Forum of Texas, 1954.

Anderson, Henry P. *The Bracero Program in California, With Particular Reference to Health Status, Attitudes and Practices.* New York: Arno Press, 1976.

Baerresen, Donald W. *The Border Industrialization Program of Mexico.* Lexington, Mass.: D.C. Heath & Co. 1971.

Betten, Neil and Mohl, Raymond A. "From Discrimination to Repatriation: Mexican Life in Gary, Indiana, During the Great Depression." *Pacific Historical Review* 42 (1973): 370–88.

Bogardus, Emory S. "Mexican Repatriates." *Sociology and Social Research* 18 (November-December 1933): 169–76.

Bustamante, Jorge A. "The Historical Context of Undocumented Mexican Immigration to the United States." *Aztlán* 3 (1973): 257–81.

Coalson, George O. "Mexican Contract Labor in American Agriculture." *Southwestern Social Science Quarterly* 33 (1952): 228–38.

"Controversy Over Proposals to Reduce the Number of Illegal Aliens in the U.S.: Pro and Con." *Congressional Digest* (January 1975): entire issue.

"Controversy Over Proposed Amnesty for Illegal Aliens: Pro and Con." *Congressional Digest* (October 1977): entire issue.

Coombs, S. W. "Bracero's Journey." *Américas* 15 (December 1963): 7–11.

Copp, Nelson G. *Wetbacks and Braceros.* San Francisco: R and E Research Associates, 1971.

Corwin, Arthur F. "Mexican-American History: An Assessment." *Pacific Historical Review* 42 (1973): 269–308.

Craig, Richard B. *The Bracero Program: Interest Groups and Foreign Policy.* Austin: University of Texas Press, 1971.

Creagan, James F. "Public Law 78: A Tangle of Domestic and International Relations." *Journal of Inter-American Studies* 7 (1965): 541–56.

Dinwoodie, D. H. "Deportation: The Immigration Service and the Chicano Labor Movement in the 1930's." *New Mexico Historical Review* 52 (1977): 193–206.

Elac, John C. "The Employment of Mexican Workers in U.S. Agriculture, 1900–1960: A Binational Economic Analysis." Ph.D. dissertation, University of California at Los Angeles, 1961.

Fineberg, Richard A. "Green Card Workers in Farm Labor Disputes: A Study of Post-Bracero Mexican National Farm Workers in the San Joaquin Valley, 1968." Ph.D. dissertation, Claremont Graduate School, 1970.

Galarza, Ernesto. *Merchants of Labor: The Mexican Bracero Story.* (Santa Barbara: McNally and Loftin, 1964.

——— *Strangers in Our Fields.* Washington, D.C.: United States Section, Joint United States-Mexico Trade Union Committee, 1956.

———. "They Work for Pennies." *American Federationist* 59 (April 1952): 10–13, 29.

Gamio, Manuel. *The Mexican Immigrant.* New York: Arno Press, 1969.

Gilbert, James C. "A Field Study in Mexico of the Mexican Repatriation Movement." Master's thesis, University of Southern California, 1934.

Gilmore, N. Ray and Gilmore, Gladys W. "The Bracero in California." *Pacific Historical Review* 32 (1963): 265–82.

Graves, Ruth Parker. "A History of the Interrelationships Between Imported Mexican Labor, Domestic Migrants, and the Texas Agricultural Economy." Master's thesis, University of Texas at Austin, 1960.

Greene, Sheldon L., "Immigration Law and Rural Poverty—The Problems of the Illegal Immigrant," *Duke Law Journal* 3 (1969): 475–94.

Gwin, J. B. "Mexican Labor Problems." *Survey* 20 (1920): 273.

———. "The New Mexican Immigration." *Survey* 40 (August 3, 1918): 491–93.

Hadley, Eleanor M. "A Critical Analysis of the Wetback Problem." *Law and Contemporary Problems* 21 (1956): 334–57.

Haltigan, William J. "A Federal Court Looks at the Mexican Labor Problem." *Employment Security Review* 29 (May 1962): 19–21.

Hancock, Richard H. *The Role of the Bracero in the Economic and Cultural Dynamics of Mexico.* Stanford: Hispanic American Society of Stanford University, 1959.

Hawley, Ellis W. "The Politics of the Mexican Labor Issue." *Agricultural History* 40 (1966): 157–76.

Hoffman, Abraham. "Mexican Repatriation Statistics: Some Suggested Alternatives to Carey McWilliams." *Western Historical Quarterly* 3 (1972): 391–404.

———. "Stimulus to Repatriation: The 1931 Federal Deportation Drive and the Los Angeles Mexican Community," *Pacific Historical Review* 42 (1973): 205–19.

———. "The Trinidad Incident." *Journal of Mexican American History* 2 (1972): 143–51.

———. "An Unusual Monument: Paul S. Taylor's *Mexican Labor in the United States* Monograph Series." *Pacific Historical Review* 45 (1976): 255–70.

———. *Unwanted Mexican Americans in the Great Depression: Repatriation Pressures, 1929–1939.* Tucson: University of Arizona Press, 1974.

Humphrey, Norman D. "Mexican Repatriation from Michigan: Public Assistance in Historical Perspective." *Social Service Review* 15 (1941): 497–513.

Jones, Robert C. *Mexicans in the United States: A Bibliography.* Washington: Pan American Union, 1942.

Kibbe, Pauline R., "The American Standard—For All Americans." *Common Ground* 10 (Autumn 1949): 19–27.

Kirstein, Peter N. "American Railroads and the Bracero Program, 1943–1946." *Journal of Mexican American History* 5 (1975): 57–90.

———. "Anglo Over Bracero: A History of the Mexican Worker in the United States from Roosevelt to Nixon." Ph.D. dissertation, Saint Louis University, 1973.

Kiser, George C. "The Bracero Program: A Case Study of its Development, Termination, and Political Aftermath." Ph.D. dissertation, University of Massachusetts at Amherst, 1974.

———. "Mexican American Labor Before World War II." *Journal of Mexican American History* 2 (1972): 122–42.

———. and Silverman, David. "Mexican Repatriation During the Great Depression." *Journal of Mexican American History* 3 (1973): 139–64.

LaBrucherie, Roger A. "Aliens in the Fields: The Green Card Commuter Under the Immigration and Naturalization Laws." *Stanford Law Review* 21 (1969): 1750–76.

Lee, John Franklin. "Statutory Provisions for Admission of Mexican Agricultural Workers—An Exception to the Immigration and Nationality Act of 1952." *George Washington Law Review* 24 (1956): 464–77.

Leibson, Art. "The Wetback Invasion." *Common Ground* 10 (Autumn 1949): 11–19.
Levenstein, Harvey A. "The AFL and Mexican Immigration in the 1920's: An Experiment in Labor Diplomacy." *Hispanic American Historical Review* 48 (1968): 206–19.
Lipshultz, Robert J. *American Attitudes Toward Mexican Immigration, 1924*–1952. (San Francisco: R and E Research Associates, 1971.
Lyon, Richard Martin. "The Legal Status of American and Mexican Migratory Farm Labor: An Analysis of U.S. Farm Labor Legislation, Policy and Administration." Ph.D. dissertation, Cornell University, 1954.
McBride, John G. *Vanishing Bracero: Valley Revolution.* San Antonio: The Naylor Company, 1963.
McCain, Johnny Mac. "Contract Labor as a Factor in United States-Mexican Relations, 1942–1947." Ph.D. dissertation, University of Texas at Austin, 1970.
McLean, Robert N. "Goodbye, Vicente." *Survey* 66 (May 1, 1931): 182–83, 195–97.
———. "Tightening the Mexican Border," *Survey* 64 (April 1, 1930): 28–29, 54–56.
McWilliams, Carey. *Factories in the Field.* New York: Little, Brown, and Co., 1939.
———. *Ill Fares the Land.* Boston: Little, Brown and Co. 1944.
———. *North From Mexico.* New York: Greenwood Press, 1960.
Madrid-Barela, Arturo. "Alambristas, Braceros, Mojados, Norteños: Aliens in Aztlán, An Interpretative Essay." *Aztlán* 6 (1975): 27–42.
Martinez, John. *Mexican Emigration to the U.S., 1910*–1930. San Francisco: R and E Research Associates, 1971.
Mason, John Dancer. "The Aftermath of the Bracero: A Study of the Economic Impact on the Agricultural Hired Labor Market of Michigan From the Termination of Public Law 78." Ph.D. dissertation, Michigan State University, 1969.
Meador, Bruce Staffel. " 'Wetback' Labor in the Lower Rio Grande Valley." Master's thesis, University of Texas at Austin, 1951.
Norquest, Carol, *Rio Grande Wetbacks: Mexican Migrant Workers.* Albuquerque: University of New Mexico Press, 1972.
North American Congress on Latin America. "Hit and Run: U.S. Runaway Shops on the Mexican Border." *NACLA's Latin America & Empire Report* 9 (July-August 1975): 1–30.
North, David S., *The Border Crossers: People Who Live in Mexico and Work in the United States.* Washington, D.C.: Trans-Century Company, 1970.
North, David S. and Houston, Marian F. *The Characteristics and Role of Illegal Aliens in the U.S. Labor Market: An Exploratory Study.* Washington, D.C.: Linton and Co., 1976.
Pfeiffer, David G. "The Mexican Farm Labor Supply Program—Its Friends and Foes." Master's thesis, University of Texas at Austin, 1963.
Portes, Alejandro. "Labor Functions of Illegal Aliens." *Society* 14 (September-October 1977): 31–37.
———. "Return of the Wetback." *Society* 11 (March-April 1974): 40–46.
Reisler, Mark. "Always the Laborer, Never the Citizen: Anglo Perceptions of the Mexican Immigrant During the 1920's." *Pacific Historical Review* 45 (1976): 231–54.
———. *By the Sweat of Their Brow: Mexican Immigrant Labor in the United States, 1900*–1940. Westport, Conn.: Greenwood Press, 1976.
Romo, Ricardo. "Responses to Mexican Immigration, 1910–1930." *Aztlán* 6 (1975): 173–94.
Rooney, James F. "The Effect of Imported Mexican Labor in a California County." *American Journal of Economics and Sociology* 20 (1961): 513–21.
Rungeling, Brian Scott. "Impact of the Mexican Alien Commuter on the Apparel Industry of El Paso, Texas." Ph.D. dissertation, University of Kentucky, 1969.
Salandini, Paul. "The Short-Run Socio-Economic Effects of the Termination of Public Law 78 on the California Farm Labor Market for 1965–1967." Ph.D. dissertation, Catholic University of America, 1969.

Samora, Julian. *Los Mojados: The Wetback Story.* Notre Dame: University of Notre Dame Press, 1971.

Saunders, Lyle and Leonard, Olin E. *The Wetback in the Lower Rio Grande Valley of Texas.* Austin: University of Texas Press, 1951.

Scruggs, Otey M. "The Bracero Program Under the Farm Security Administration, 1942–1943." *Labor History* 3 (1962): 149–68.

———. "Evolution of the Mexican Farm Labor Agreement of 1942." *Agricultural History* 34 (1960): 140–49.

———. "The First Mexican Farm Labor Program." *Arizona and the West* 2 (1960): 319–26.

———. "Texas, Good Neighbor?" *Southwestern Social Science Quarterly* 43 (1962): 118–25.

———. "The United States, Mexico and the Wetbacks, 1942–1947," *Pacific Historical Review* 4 (1961): 149–64.

Servín, Manuel P. and Spude, Robert L. "Historical Conditions of Early Mexican Labor in the United States: Arizona—A Neglected Story." *Journal of Mexican American History* 5 (1975): 43–56.

Severo, Richard. "The Flight of the Wetbacks," *New York Times Magazine* 10 March 1974, pp. 17, 77–84.

Spradlin, T. Richard. "The Mexican Farm Labor Importation Program—Review and Reform (Parts I and II)." *George Washington Law Review* 30 (1961): 84–122; and 30 (1961): 311–27.

Stevenson, Emma Reh. "The Emigrant Comes Home." *Survey* 46 (1 May 1931): 175–77.

Stoddard, Ellwyn R. "A Conceptual Analysis of the 'Alien Invasion': Institutionalized Support of the Illegal Mexican Aliens in the United States." *International Migration Review* 10 (1976): 157–89.

———. "Illegal Mexican Labor in the Borderlands: Institutionalized Support of an Unlawful Practice." *Pacific Sociological Review* 19 (1976): 175–210.

Taylor, Jack. *God's Messengers to Mexico's Masses: A Study of the Religious Significance of the Braceros.* Eugene, Oregon: Institute of Church Growth, 1962.

Taylor, Paul S. *Mexican Labor in the United States,* 2 vols. New York: Arno Press, 1976.

———. "More Bars Against Mexicans," *Survey* 44 (1 April 1930): 26–28.

Tercero, Dorothy M. "Workers from Mexico." *Bulletin of the Pan American Union* 78 (1944): 500–506.

Tomasek, Robert D. "The Migrant Problem and Pressure Group Politics." *Journal of Politics* 23 (1961): 295–319.

Tomasek, Robert Dennis. "The Political and Economic Implications of Mexican Labor in the United States Under the Non Quota System, Contract Labor Program, and Wetback Movement." Ph.D. dissertation, University of Michigan, 1958.

U.S. Congress. Senate. Committee on Labor and Public Welfare. *Border Commuter Labor Problem. Hearings Before the Subcommittee on Migratory Labor, 91st Cong.* Washington, D.C.: Government Printing Office, 1970.

U.S. Congress. House. Committee on the Judiciary. *Illegal Aliens. Hearings Before Subcommittee No. 1, 92d Cong., 1st sess.* Washington, D.C.: Government Printing Office, 1971.

Van der Spek, Peter, "Mexico's Booming Border Zone: A Magnet for Labor Intensive American Plants." *Inter-American Economic Affairs* 29 (1975): 33–47.

Virgo, John Michael. "Economic Impacts of International Manpower Flows: A Consideration of the Bracero Program." Ph.D. dissertation, Claremont Graduate School, 1972.

Walker, Helen W. "Mexican Immigrants as Laborers." *Sociology and Social Research* 13 (1928): 55–62.

Waters, Leslie L. "Transient Mexican Agricultural Labor." *Southwestern Social Science Quarterly* 22 (1941): 49–66.

"Wetbacks: Can the States Act to Curb Illegal Entry?" *Stanford Law Review* 6 (1954): 287–322.

Wiest, Grace Leona. "Health Insurance for the Bracero: A Study of Its Development and Implementation Under Public Law 78." Ph.D. dissertation, Claremont Graduate School, 1966.

Wollenberg, Charles. "Working on El Traque: The Pacific Electric Strike of 1903." *Pacific Historical Review* 42 (1973): 358–69.

Index